Upcountry South Carolina
Goes to War

UPCOUNTRY SOUTH CAROLINA
GOES TO WAR

Letters of the
Anderson, Brockman, and Moore Families
1853–1865

EDITED BY *Tom Moore Craig*

INTRODUCTION BY
Melissa Walker and Tom Moore Craig

THE UNIVERSITY OF SOUTH CAROLINA PRESS

Published in Cooperation with the South Caroliniana Library
with the Assistance of the Caroline McKissick Dial Publication Fund

Published by the University of South Carolina Press
Columbia, South Carolina 29208

www.sc.edu/uscpress

Manufactured in the United States of America

18 17 16 15 14 13 12 11 10 09 10 9 8 7 6 5 4 3 2

Library of Congress Cataloging-in-Publication Data

Upcountry South Carolina goes to war : letters of the Anderson, Brockman, and Moore families, 1853–1865 / edited by Tom Moore Craig ; introduction by Melissa Walker and Tom Moore Craig.
p. cm.
"Published in Cooperation with the South Caroliniana Library with the Assistance of the Caroline McKissick Dial Publication Fund"—T.p. verso.
Includes bibliographical references and index.
ISBN 978-1-57003-798-6 (cloth : alk. paper)
1. Spartanburg County (S.C.)—History—19th century—Sources. 2. Spartanburg County (S.C.)—Social conditions—19th century—Sources. 3. South Carolina—History—Civil War, 1861–1865—Sources. 4. Rural families—South Carolina—Spartanburg County—Social conditions—19th century—Sources. 5. Country life—South Carolina—Spartanburg County—History—19th century—Sources. 6. Agriculture—South Carolina—Spartanburg County—History—19th century—Sources. 7. Anderson family—Correspondence. 8. Brockman family—Correspondence. 9. Moore family—Correspondence. I. Craig, Tom Moore. II. Walker, Melissa, 1962– III. South Caroliniana Library. IV. Caroline McKissick Dial Publication Fund.
F277.S7U63 2009
975.7'2903—dc22

2008042216

This book was printed on Glatfelter Natures, a recycled paper with 30 percent postconsumer waste content.

Dedicated to Harriet Means Moore Fielder (1877–1949),
who preserved and annotated many of these letters.

‡

Contents

Illustrations

ACKNOWLEDGMENTS

This book would not have been possible without the encouragement and assistance of Dr. Melissa Walker, an inspiring teacher and thorough researcher, who saw the promise of these letters and encouraged me to publish them. She critiqued the manuscript at every stage, giving me the confidence to continue.

My research was facilitated by Debra Hutchins and staff, Kennedy Room, Spartanburg (S.C.) County Library; the staff of the South Carolina Room, Hughes Library, Greenville County (S.C.) Library System; and Dr. Allen Stokes and the staff of the South Caroliniana Library, Columbia. Christopher S. Thompson provided many hours of technical support and designed the map of the families' territory.

I am indebted to Jeannette Anderson Winn for transcribing several significant Anderson letters in her possession and allowing me to use them, and to Jeannette and her sister Elaine Anderson Sarratt for their suggestions in my research of Brockman family history.

T. Alexander Evins shared his father's family papers, enabling me to learn more about Col. S. N. Evins, Nancy Montgomery Moore's second husband and the Moore boys' guardian.

In Marion, Alabama, I was assisted in researching the history of Charles Moore Jr., Governor A. B. Moore, and the family of Dr. Robert Foster by Mary Katharine Arbuthnot Avery (a Mary Foster Moore Barron descendant), Eleanor Drake, and Astrid Knudson, then the Perry County librarian.

My fellow great-grandson of Mary Elizabeth Anderson and Thomas John Moore, Paul Seabrook Ambrose, M.D., read and critiqued the entire manuscript and shared his mother's research with me. Paul had listened to the family stories when we were growing up more attentively than I had and helped me incorporate details that add interest to the work.

Edward Lee Anderson inspired me as a young man to care about family history, and his 1955 *History of the Anderson Family, 1706–1955* made my research much simpler.

My parents, Lena Heath Jones Craig and Thomas Moore Craig Sr., inculcated a love of history in their children and were early advocates of historic preservation in Spartanburg County. My sister and brother-in-law, Susan Heath Craig Murphy and John Ramsey Murphy, have been patient and supportive in all my endeavors over the years.

To my lifelong friend J. Bancroft Lesesne, M.D., here's the dissertation I promised you years ago.

And to my nephews John Ramsey Murphy Jr. and Thomas Craig Murphy, the next generation, this book is for you.

INTRODUCTION

Melissa Walker and Tom Moore Craig

In the rolling foothills of Spartanburg County, South Carolina, the Anderson and Moore families established themselves on the banks of the North and South Tyger rivers. They carved out new farms on former Cherokee hunting grounds near the present communities of Moore and Reidville. They had arrived in the Piedmont of South Carolina in the 1760s, having made their way earlier from northern Ireland to Philadelphia and to the Pennsylvania backcountry before beginning the long trek south down the Great Philadelphia Wagon Road.

Typical of the Scots-Irish settlers, Charles Moore (1727–1805) had come to America in the early 1750s, probably from county Antrim, northern Ireland. His wife was Mary Barry; it is not certain when they married. After a short time in Pennsylvania, he joined the migration south and lived in Old Anson County, North Carolina, where his signature has been found as a witness to deeds in 1752 and 1762. On May 30, 1763, he was granted 550 acres on the North Tyger River by King George III. The survey, completed in July, indicated that the parcel was surrounded on all sides by "vacant land." He and his wife, Mary, first took up residence under a lean-to shelter near the river while clearing land and constructing a house on higher ground nearby. This latter residence, made of hewn logs covered with clapboards, still stands and is known as Walnut Grove Plantation. It is restored and open to the public.

Charles and Mary had ten children, all surviving to adulthood. The oldest daughter, Margaret Catherine "Kate," born 1752, married Captain Andrew Barry and was a scout and spy for the patriots in the American Revolution. Their seventh child, Thomas (1759–1822), served seven terms in the U.S. Congress, 1801–13 and 1815–17. He was the general in charge of the defense of Charleston in the War of 1812. Charles and Mary's ninth child, Dr. Andrew Barry Moore (1771–1848), practiced medicine from his small office located on the family plantation for fifty years and is the father of three of the letter writers, Margaret Anna Moore Means, Andrew Charles Moore, and Thomas John Moore. The tenth

James Mason "Tyger Jim" Anderson and his wife, Mary "Polly" Miller Anderson.
From Edward Lee Anderson, *A History of the Anderson Family, 1706–1955*
(Columbia, S.C.: R. L. Bryan Company, 1955); used with permission

child, Charles Moore Jr. (1774–1836), went west to Alabama in 1826, settling in Marion, Perry County. His son Andrew Barry Moore was governor of Alabama, 1857–61, and is mentioned in his much younger first cousin Andrew Charles Moore's letters of May and June 1860. Charles Moore Jr.'s daughter Juliet married Dr. Robert Foster and was the mother of Mary Foster, to whom Andrew Charles Moore was married at the time of his death.

William Anderson (1706–ca. 1779) came to America in 1742 from county Antrim, northern Ireland. He lived in Pennsylvania before moving south to the Waxhaws settlement in South Carolina. He lived for a time in Charleston but took up a two-hundred-acre land grant in Laurens County, South Carolina, in 1763. He soon left that land to move farther west, eventually to the South Tyger River in Spartanburg County, near his son Major David Anderson. William Anderson was murdered near the end of the Revolution by a group of Indians and Tories and his house burned. Major David Anderson (1741–1827) was a land surveyor and distinguished patriot soldier.

James Mason Anderson (1784–1870) was the fourth child of Major David Anderson and Miriam Mayson. He lived on the South Tyger and was a successful farmer, miller, and wagoner, hauling goods as far north as Washington and Baltimore. He married Mary "Polly" Miller, and they had ten children. He promised each of his eight sons a gold watch and a sizable tract of land if they would "complete a liberal education and study a profession."

Letter writer Captain David Anderson (1811–1892) was James Anderson's oldest son. He married Harriet Maria Brockman from Pliny, just across the Enoree River in Greenville County, and brought her to live at Pleasant Falls, his plantation on the North Tyger River. Their older children, Mary Elizabeth and John Crawford, are major correspondents in this collection of letters, as are Harriet's much younger sisters, Ella and Hettie Brockman, who made their home with the Andersons.

For nine decades after their arrival, the Andersons and Moores improved their positions, moving from being cabin-dwelling pioneers eking out a subsistence living to enjoying comfortable lives as well-to-do planters, millers, and food brokers.

The Upcountry World of the Andersons and Moores

The Andersons and the Moores made their home in the southern part of Spartanburg County. Located in the upper Piedmont of South Carolina, southern Spartanburg County is a land of rolling hills and shallow rivers and creeks. The region's long growing seasons and the fertile bottomland along the streams attracted Scots-Irish settlers like the Andersons and Moores. The Scots-Irish were the majority of the earliest white inhabitants in the upcountry, but families of English, German, and French Huguenot extraction also settled there. Making their way down the Great Wagon Road from Pennsylvania, Virginia, and North Carolina in the mid–eighteenth century, the pioneer families created a yeoman culture rooted in Calvinist religious traditions. The earliest farming families sought to be as self-sufficient as possible, but from the beginning they sold surplus production both locally and in distant Charleston markets. Some established sawmills, gristmills, and ironworks to serve their neighbors.[1]

By the 1850s the South Carolina upcountry was a region of well-established farms. Local farmers raised corn, wheat, and oats in the rich alluvial soil of the bottomlands. Most raised hogs for their own use. Many joined the Andersons and Moores in growing cotton on the red clay hills; a few also produced small quantities of tobacco. According to the U.S. Census, in 1860 half of the county's

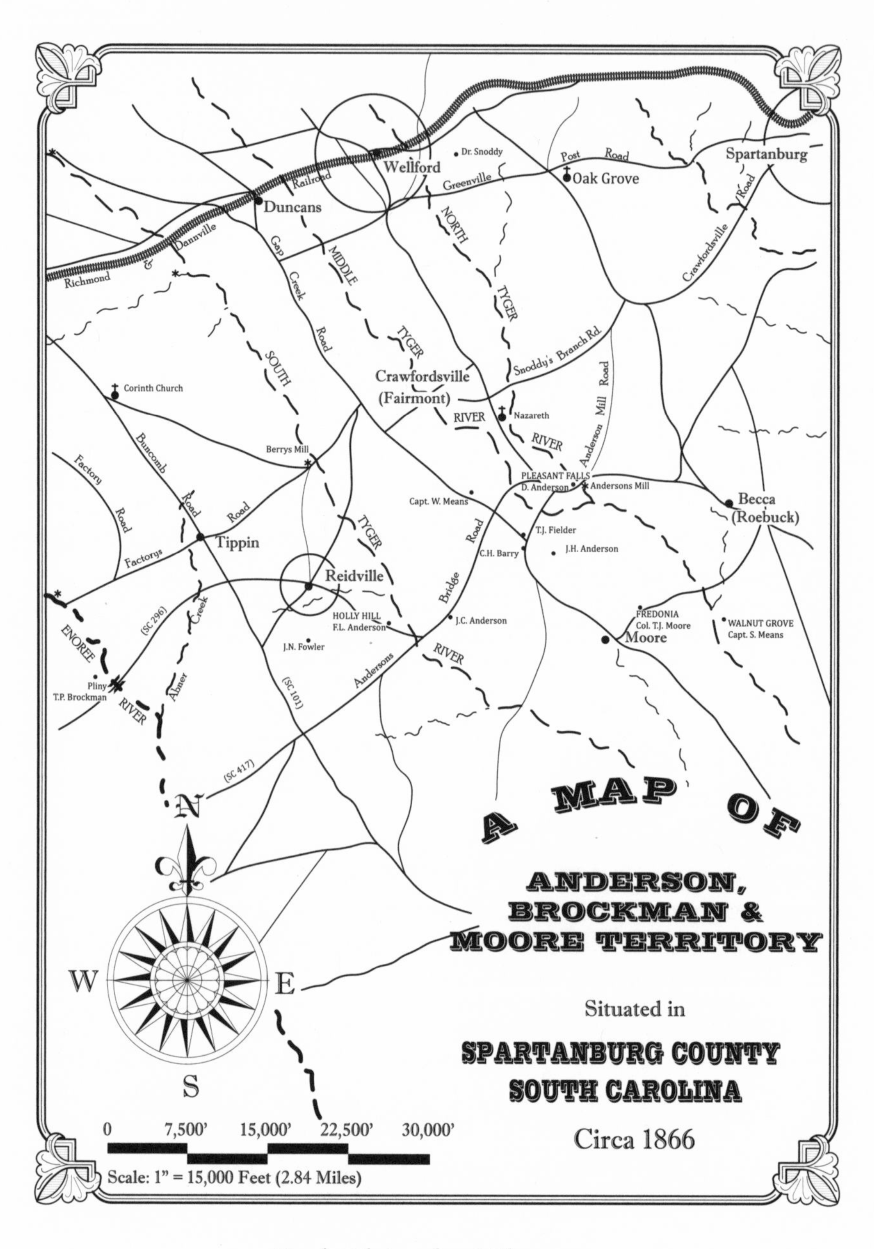

Map by Christopher S. Thompson

cotton growers produced less than one bale each, making the forty bales produced on Andrew Charles Moore's acreage in 1860 quite substantial. Half the county's farmers cultivated fewer than 100 acres.[2] It is not known how many acres the Andersons and the Moores cultivated, but the Moore family owned more than 2,500 acres at the time of the Civil War. They undoubtedly cultivated more land than the average Spartanburg County farmer.[3]

Slaveholding was well established in the county, but only 30 percent of the county's farmers actually owned slaves. Most farmers worked their own land with the help of family members and occasional hired hands. Among the county's slaveholders, fewer than half owned more than six bondspeople. As a result, landowners often worked side-by-side with the slave laborers at least some of the time, and most Spartanburg County slaves had close interactions with whites. The Andersons and the Moores owned more slaves than most of the neighboring planters. According to the 1860 census, David Anderson, patriarch of the Anderson letter-writing clan, owned thirty-seven slaves, while his brother Frank owned twenty-two. Nancy Montgomery Moore, mother of Andrew Charles Moore and Thomas John Moore, owned twenty-four. Andrew himself held title to twenty-six slaves, and Nancy's son-in-law Sam Means owned another twenty. Only 8 percent of Spartanburg County planters owned more than twenty slaves. As these numbers suggest, the Moores and Andersons were substantial upcountry planter families, although their slaveholdings were quite small compared to the most prosperous lowcountry planters.[4]

The historian W. J. Megginson speculates that the close daily interaction between slave and slaveholder and the relatively small percentage of slaves in Spartanburg County (31 percent of the population compared to 57 percent statewide) led upstate slaveowners to "operate in a more relaxed atmosphere."[5] Perhaps the "relaxed atmosphere" that Megginson describes explains the reason he found that a fair number of upstate slaves, including some of the Moores' bondspeople, could apparently read and write. (Two letters in the collection were written by enslaved men who accompanied their masters during wartime service.) In some cases slaves learned to read from the children of their owners or even from the masters themselves. In other cases they learned in Sunday schools sponsored by upcountry churches.[6]

The nearest trade center for the Moore and Anderson families was the village of Spartanburg, roughly ten miles away for the Moores and seven for the Andersons. In 1860 one thousand people lived in the village, which boasted two hotels, eighteen stores, four churches, five schools, a handful of professionals, and the district courthouse and jail.[7] For rural residents, trips to town were reserved for the marketing of crops, buying provisions, and other important business.

The daily lives of the Andersons, the Moores, and their neighbors revolved around a matrix of kinship networks that connected the families in the community. At the center of those networks were churches, the most important community institution in any upcountry rural neighborhood. Both the Andersons and the Moores attended Nazareth Presbyterian Church, the county's oldest religious institution, which their ancestors had formally organized in 1772.[8]

Like many Scots-Irish Presbyterians, the citizens of Spartanburg County valued education and invested heavily in local schools. Old field schools provided a basic education for boys and girls throughout the county; often educated farmers like Charles Moore, the original patriarch of the Moore family, taught at these local academies during the winter months. During the Civil War years, Hettie Brockman ran a grammar school for neighbor children in an old school building nearby. By the mid–nineteenth century, private academies provided advanced schooling for many of the county's children. The Andersons and Moores favored schools led by Presbyterian ministers, and they supported the founding of the Reidville schools so they would not have to send their children away to board. Many local families made the education of girls as well as boys a high priority, in part because education was believed to enhance the social status of young women and improve their prospects for a good marriage. Female academies offered courses in natural philosophy, Latin, Greek, and modern languages as well as more "ornamental" subjects such as needlework and music. Typical was the Limestone Springs Female High School[9] in what is now Gaffney, Cherokee County. Founded in 1849, the school was attended by Harriet Brockman Anderson's much younger sister, Ella Brockman, who made her home with Harriet and David. The letters in this collection also detail citizens' efforts to raise money for the Reidville Male High School and the Reidville Female College in the western part of the county; the two schools opened in 1857. Nor were the Presbyterians the only Spartanburg County residents who valued education. In 1854 local Methodists opened both Wofford College for men and the Spartanburg Female Academy.[10]

Most white Spartanburg residents were strong secessionists. The historian Philip N. Racine contends that their fear of the economic and social consequences of emancipation fueled this secessionist fervor. Once the South entered the war, young men from the county enlisted in large numbers in various Confederate units. It was common for slaves to accompany their young masters to

The Nazareth Presbyterian Church, established 1765.
This 1832 sanctuary is in use today. From the editor's collection

war where they wore uniforms, provided personal services, and sometimes did heavy labor for the army. Megginson says that the Confederate army compensated some of these enslaved men for their service.[11]

Wartime changes to local life came slowly but steadily. The prices for farm commodities soared. For example, corn sold for as little as fifty cents a bushel in 1859 but was bringing twenty-five dollars a bushel by 1865. Some farm families took on new forms of production in order to meet wartime demands. The wife of David Golightly Harris, a planter who farmed about four miles east of the Andersons and Moores, began weaving cloth. She not only supplied the needs of her own family and their slaves, but she also sold surplus cloth locally. Her husband's journal records the sale of one hundred dollars' worth of her handmade cloth in April 1863. Soaring prices for farm commodities and new marketplace activity did not necessarily translate into higher profits for farm families. High rates of inflation quickly ate up increased incomes. Local farmers were plagued by shortages of essential supplies, such as salt. The letters detail the difficulty in locating salt at any price by the later years of the war.[12]

Home-front priorities shifted as citizens mobilized to support the Confederate war effort. Upcountry families divided their attention between farm and family on the one hand and wartime concerns on the other. For example, in August 1861 the women of Spartanburg County organized a Soldier's Aid and Relief Society to provide clothing, bandages, and other supplies to soldiers in the field and to the wounded. Churches and rural communities, including nearby Reidville, also collected supplies for the troops. Local people raised money for various wartime projects. After the landmark battle between the ironclad ships USS *Monitor* and CSS *Virginia* (formerly the USS *Merrimack*) off the coast of Virginia, South Carolina women organized to raise money for additional ironclads. Mary Elizabeth Anderson reported organizing tableaux to raise money for the purchase of a gunboat.[13]

In many parts of the South, wartime disruptions led to unrest among slaves, but Megginson found relatively few accounts of insurrection plots and insolent slaves in his study of upcountry South Carolina diaries and letters. Indeed there is no particular evidence in the letters of wartime unrest on the Anderson and Moore plantations during the war years.[14]

The end of the war brought new hardships and challenges for upcountry residents. Though the area did not suffer the physical destruction by marauding armies as did other parts of the South, its residents nonetheless suffered economic problems. Spartanburg County slave owners suffered the loss of their major asset—their 8,240 slaves—often worth more than the planters' land. Many also lost savings that had been invested in Confederate securities and currency. Operating capital was hard to come by. Land values plummeted in part because of the uncertain labor supply, and some families sold land or cultivated a smaller portion of their holdings. By 1870, 98 percent of the county's farmers cultivated fewer than one hundred acres. One measure of the economic devastation can be seen in the decline in total assets for the county. In 1860 Spartanburg County residents had held assets valued at $16 million. By 1870 their assets were worth only $4 million.[15]

Families also suffered social disruptions. Many young men, such as the brilliant and promising Andrew Charles Moore, never came home from the war. Others returned maimed in body and spirit. In addition, race relations in the county were in flux. Planters struggled to forge new labor arrangements among the freed people who were a vital labor source, and as Thomas John Moore's letters to his overseer indicate, these negotiations were sometimes contentious. Freed people, too, struggled to achieve independence and economic stability in this uncertain new environment.

The Letters

This collection introduces us to the neighboring Anderson and Moore families in the 1850s, as the South perched on the precipice of the Civil War. The majority of letters in this collection were written by or to three young men. John Crawford Anderson (b. 1842), Andrew Charles Moore (b. 1838), and Thomas John Moore (b. 1843) were contemporaries, born within a five-year span. John Anderson was the Moore brothers' neighbor and a fellow congregant at Nazareth Presbyterian Church. Their military service in the Civil War drew them together in a common cause, but only at the end of the war were the families related, by the marriage of Thomas John Moore to John Crawford Anderson's sister Mary Elizabeth.

The early letters, dating from 1853–1860, find the young Anderson and Moore men away at school. Their parents, siblings, and aunts are writing them regularly. These early letters are filled with everyday concerns—about the boys' moral character and their educations, work on the family farms, and family news. We learn a great deal about daily life in the upcountry from these early letters. Many of the earliest concerned the young men's schooling, a preoccupation of the Presbyterian families. John was a student at Thalian Academy, also known as the Slabtown School, from 1857–59, which was led by Rev. John Leland Kennedy and located on the border of today's Anderson and Pickens counties, near Carmel Presbyterian Church. Later he studied at the Arsenal in Columbia, South Carolina. Students intending to graduate from the Citadel, South Carolina's military college in Charleston, spent the first year or two at the Arsenal. John's very pious mother, Harriet Brockman Anderson, offered moral lectures and admonishments to her student son. She advised him to attend church and Sabbath school regularly and pleaded with him to "keep out of such places where morals are in danger" (p. 1). John's father, David Anderson, detailed the state of his own health (ailing), his crops ("tolerably well"), and the price of corn ($1.25 per bushel; p. 5). He responded to his son's requests for money and shared neighborhood news, especially news about the community support for the founding of the nearby Reidville Male High School and Female College. In a most remarkable passage, he described the convening of a "neighborhood court" to mete out punishment to slaves from throughout the community who had gathered for a raucous night of cardplaying and drinking.

In the 1859 and 1860 letters of Andrew Charles Moore and Thomas John Moore, we glimpse the world of university students and tag along on Andrew Charles Moore's visits to Washington, D.C., and New York City, where he meets Japanese diplomats and verbally spars with opponents of slavery. Andrew Charles Moore, a student at University of Virginia during this period, also offers commentary on John Brown's raid and on the deepening political crisis. In fact, not until Andrew's 1859 account of John Brown's raid is there any mention of politics in these letters.

The rest of the letters cover the war years. Several young men in the family enlisted, following the lead of Andrew Charles Moore, who wrote his mother from Alabama in February 1861 to say "the time has come when every man must gird on his armor, & take the field or submit to despotism" (p. 40). He enlisted in the Confederate army and wrote detailed letters from the front until his death at the Second Battle of Manassas, an event related by his brother Thomas John Moore, also a Confederate soldier. John Crawford Anderson, a student at the Citadel during part of the war, also eventually enlisted and served. So did Franklin Leland Anderson, the beloved uncle of John Crawford. Frank's letters are especially vivid in their portrayal of the perils of battle and of the stupefying boredom of camp life.

Letters from women and men in the family to the men on the battlefront include details of home-front shortages, efforts to raise money for the Confederate cause, and expressions of Confederate patriotism. The old lowcountry/upcountry split is also evident in family commentary about the rude and demanding coastal refugees who have temporarily settled in Spartanburg County. The collection concludes with postwar documents from Thomas John Moore's plantation that illustrate his adjustments to the realities of a new era.

These letters are significant on several levels. Although most historical accounts would lead us to believe that South Carolinians were obsessed with the sectional crisis to the exclusion of all else in the 1850s, the letters correct this impression. On November 21, 1859, Andrew reports on John Brown's raid and on the reaction to that raid in a letter to his mother. He concludes the account with the pessimistic prediction, "I have come to the conclusion that there is obliged to be a dissolution of the union before long" (p. 19). This statement makes it clear that he has been following the growing sectional split as it has developed; his concern for the state of the union did not grow out of the single incident of John Brown's raid. Yet none of the extant Anderson or Moore letters to this point had mentioned the sectional crisis; instead their concerns were profoundly local, suggesting the extent to which their world revolved around home, family, and farm. In fact, in the very next sentence of the November 21 letter, Andrew returns to the personal, announcing his engagement to his second cousin Mary Foster and admitting, "I ought to have told you [about the engagement] long ago" (p. 19). His next letter, written December 18, 1859, inquires about the state of the crops, comments on his mother's reaction to his engagement, and reports on his plans to enter law practice the next year. He also offers advice on buying a slave and requests that his mother ask his guardian to send money to pay his tuition. He does not mention politics again until the following May when he, on a visit to Washington, hears a fiery four-hour speech by Senator Charles Sumner of Massachusetts. In short, even at this point the family's attention is engaged more by their private concerns than by the political rumblings that will soon tear their world asunder.

We learn a great deal about the economic and social history of the upcountry and about the war's impact on one particular community. The letters to the soldiers in the field detail the gradual but steady erosion of the quality of life on the home front during the first two years of the war. Many of the letters from 1861 are filled with both the mundane and dramatic details of local life: news of ill family members, social events, and homes destroyed by fire. Mary Elizabeth Anderson writes to her brother in Charleston to ask him to acquire bagging and roping for the farm operation, but she also asks for particular colors of thread and sends him lists of books she wanted to acquire.

The reality of the war sets in quickly nonetheless. In November 1861 Harriet Anderson reports the arrival of "the long expected trouble" (p. 54), the first combat deaths of local boys. Soon comments about the impact of the Union blockade and fears for the safety of the soldiers become a prominent part of every letter. Nancy Moore Evins's stepson would die of a war-related illness in early 1862.

The soldiers' letters, too, display the changing attitudes toward the war. Though the Moore and Anderson boys continue to express patriotism to the bitter end, the tone of bravado and the courageous tales of battlefield exploits in the early letters give way to hints at privation and hardship. They also attempt to keep an eye on the distant business affairs back home. John Crawford Anderson, for example, writes to his father about an acquaintance who has been successful in smuggling cotton past the Union blockade to the Bahamas, a man who promised to obtain gold for the cotton. There is no indication that the Andersons used the man's services, but the passage reveals the difficulty in selling cotton, a commodity for which there was limited local demand, during the war years. Thomas John Moore lost his older brother and his mother during the war, making him unexpectedly the heir to the family plantation, Fredonia. After 1863 many of the extant letters are correspondence with his overseer, Thomas Hill, about the running of the plantation.

Indeed as the war proceeded, the letters are less plentiful, suggesting it was harder and harder for home folks to have letters delivered to military encampments and for soldiers to save letters from home. The frequent inquiries about whether a family member had received a particular letter also testify to the difficulty in maintaining regular communications with loved ones.

The letters also provide insight into the complexities of master-slave relationships before, during, and shortly after the war. Family letters frequently detail illnesses and deaths among the slave community, suggesting close connections with their slaves. At least two letters in the collection are written by family slaves, indicating that at least some of the Moore and Anderson slaves were literate and also that the bondsmen valued ties with both black and white folks back home. For example, Tom Moore's slave Elihu wrote to his wife in April 1863 from Wilmington, North Carolina. He reported on his health. He thanked her for sending him some clothes but indicated that he could buy "more suitable ones hear" (p. 115). He also attached a brief note to the plantation overseer, Thomas Hill. Perhaps in writing to Mr. Hill he hoped to ingratiate himself with the man for the future or to help insure good treatment for his wife. Or perhaps he had a good working relationship with Mr. Hill. We will never know his motivations, but the letter certainly indicates a more complicated relationship than some accounts might lead us to believe.

These letters paint a poignant picture of the impact of the war on one particular Southern community and on two families within that community. The war's enormous cost comes home as we get to know the Andersons and the Moores.

Notes

1. Philip N. Racine, *Seeing Spartanburg: A History in Images* (Spartanburg, S.C.: Hub City Writers Project, 1999), 19–21; Laurel Horton, *Mary Black's Family Quilts: Memory and Meaning in Everyday Life* (Columbia: University of South Carolina Press, 2005), 9–12.

2. Philip N. Racine, introduction to *Piedmont Farmer: The Journals of David Golightly Harris, 1855–1870* (Knoxville: University of Tennessee Press, 1990), 2; University of Virginia Library, "Historical Census Data Browser," http://fisher.lib.virginia.edu/collections/stats/histcensus/php/county.php (accessed January 16, 2008).

3. When Dr. Andrew Barry Moore died in 1848, his will left "5–600 acres" to his wife, Nancy, 946 acres to daughter Margaret Anna, 635 acres to son Andrew Charles, and 675 to son Thomas John.

4. U.S. Bureau of the Census, *1860 U.S. Census,* "Spartanburg County, Southern Division," pp. 186, 191, and 199; Racine, *Piedmont Farmer,* 2.

5. Racine, *Piedmont Farmer,* 2, 4; Racine, *Seeing Spartanburg,* 23; W. J. Megginson, *African American Life in South Carolina's Upper Piedmont* (Columbia: University of South Carolina Press, 2006), 7–9, quote on 9; University of Virginia Library, "Historical Census Data Browser," http://fisher.lib.virginia.edu/collections/stats/histcensus/php/county.php (accessed January 16, 2008).

6. Megginson, *African American Life,* 138.

7. Racine, *Piedmont Farmer,* 2–3.

8. Racine, *Piedmont Farmer,* 9, and Racine, *Seeing Spartanburg,* 27; Horton, *Mary Black's Family Quilts,* 21–25. Nazareth's third sanctuary building, built in 1832, is in use today. The well-maintained cemetery is a major asset for historians and genealogists.

9. Limestone Springs Female High School, founded in 1845, was often referred to as Limestone Seminary or Limestone College in the letters. The school closed in 1870 and reopened as Limestone College in 1873.

10. Racine, *Seeing Spartanburg,* 26; Horton, *Mary Black's Family Quilts,* 37.

11. Racine, *Piedmont Farmer,* 10, and *Seeing Spartanburg,* 26; Megginson, *African American Life,* 192.

12. Racine, *Piedmont Farmer,* 11–12.

13. Horton, *Mary Black's Family Quilts,* 39–40. Tableaux, short for *tableaux vivants,* were elaborate depictions of dramatic scenes by motionless, silent costumed performers. Often they depicted scenes from classical or popular literature. Tableaux were popular entertainments in the mid–nineteenth century.

14. Megginson, *African American Life,* 186–87.

15. Racine, *Piedmont Farmer,* 2; Horton, *Mary Black's Family Quilts,* 45.

METHODOLOGY

The 124 letters included in this book were largely in good condition, folded and enclosed in their original envelopes. Some of the letters to and from Civil War battlefields were damaged, the ink blurred, or had pages missing due to the frequent redeployments of soldiers and the vagaries of the Confederate postal service. Many had been hand carried back and forth by soldiers going on or returning from furlough.

As there were fourteen different letter writers, the editor had to become familiar with each person's handwriting, some adorned with the many extra flourishes of nineteenth-century penmanship. The most difficult letters included cross-writing, where because of a lack of paper, a writer would turn the letter to the side and continue writing over previously written lines. The writers varied in age from early teens to late sixties.

Educational levels of the writers varied from David Anderson's very basic schooling to Andrew Charles Moore's law studies, and the quality of spelling and grammar in the letters also varied greatly. The editor wished to depict these writers as they were and endeavored to present each letter as written. In some cases where a writer constantly rehashed earlier points, portions were deleted. Each deletion begins with an ellipsis.

Grammar was not edited, nor was spelling, unless to make a word understandable, where a correct spelling was added in brackets. Capitalization, or lack thereof, was not changed, nor was punctuation. If a writer used an ampersand, it was retained.

Brief identifications appear in brackets in the body of the letter as do short clarifications made by the editor. Longer explanations are contained in notes at the end of the letter. I have added some introductory and transition paragraphs to the letters.

The editor's task was made much easier by Harriet Means Moore Fielder (Mrs. John P. Fielder), his great-aunt. Known to her nieces and nephews as "Hattee" with the emphasis on the last syllable, she was an 1897 graduate of Converse

College and a historian by avocation who helped edit the volume *William Anderson and Rebecca Denny and Their Descendants, 1706–1914* as well as various lists concerning the history of Nazareth Presbyterian Church and Spartanburg County Civil War veterans.

Hattee read each letter and in pencil wrote a short identifying clue above many of the persons referenced. Her longer annotations were written on plain unlined paper or on scraps she saved from envelopes, advertising flyers, and even canceled checks. The notes were an invaluable resource to the editor. Upon her death in 1949, the letters were passed on to her nephew, Thomas Moore Craig Sr., who kept them in a filing cabinet and transcribed only the Thomas John Moore letters.

FAMILY GENEALOGIES

ANDERSON/BROCKMAN FAMILIES

James Mason Anderson (January 28, 1784–June 24, 1870). Family patriarch. Son of Major David and Miriam Mayson Anderson. A farmer and wagoner, he lived on the South Tyger River and was called "Tyger Jim" to distinguish him from his first cousin James M. "Enoree Jim" Anderson, who lived on the Enoree River. He married Mary "Polly" Miller (November 18, 1788–May 27, 1856) in 1810. They had ten children, the oldest David. In his later years he moved in with his son Franklin Leland Anderson and ran Frank's plantation, Holly Hill, while Frank was away at war.

Capt. David Anderson (January 1, 1811–July 2, 1892). Son of James Mason and Mary "Polly" Miller Anderson. Born near Reidville, South Carolina, and studied in Spartanburg under Rev. A. A. Porter. He later studied law under Elisha Bomar, clerk of court. He preferred farming and established his farm and gristmill on the North Tyger River near its merger with the Middle Tyger. His home, Pleasant Falls, still stands today, overlooking the shoals and Anderson's gristmill. Married March 28, 1839, to Harriet Maria Brockman. They had nine children, eight surviving to adulthood.

Harriet Brockman Anderson (February 28, 1819–July 1, 1892). Daughter of Thomas Patterson Brockman and Mary Kilgore Brockman of Pliny, Greenville County, South Carolina. She attended school in Greenville and completed her education at Salem, North Carolina. She married Capt. David Anderson in 1839. A bibliophile, she read voraciously, imparting this love to her children. She devoted her life to maintaining Pleasant Falls as a hospitable place to family, friends and passing strangers, including many Confederate soldiers.

John Crawford Anderson (January 18, 1842–February 23, 1892). Born at Pleasant Falls, son of Capt. David and Harriet Brockman Anderson. Educated at Thalian Academy (Slabtown School). In 1859 he entered the State Military Academy, spending two years at the Arsenal in Columbia and graduating from the Citadel in Charleston in 1863. Entered the Confederate army and was later an adjutant in the Thirteenth Regiment, South Carolina Volunteers. Wounded at the Battle of the Wilderness. He returned to Spartanburg after the war, operated his farm, Plain Dealing, and later served as Spartanburg's postmaster and in the S.C. House of Representatives (1878–80). He married Emma Buist on February 27, 1866, and they had nine children, six of whom survived to adulthood.

Mary Elizabeth Anderson Moore (November 28, 1843–April 27, 1921). Born at Pleasant Falls, the daughter of Capt. David and Harriet Brockman Anderson. Educated at Pine Grove Academy and Laurensville Female Academy. Married Thomas John Moore on February 27, 1866, and went to live at the Moore family home, six miles south of Pleasant Falls on the North Tyger River. Mother of eight children: Andrew Charles Moore II, James Anderson Moore (died in infancy), Thomas Brockman Moore (died in infancy), Annie Mary Moore (died while in college), Paul Vernon Moore, Harriet Means Moore Fielder, Henrietta Sue Moore Craig, and Nancy Montgomery Moore.

Henrietta Alethia "Nettie" Anderson Smith (April 10, 1846–January 10, 1911). Born at Pleasant Falls, daughter of Capt. David and Harriet Brockman Anderson. Graduated from Laurensville Female College in Laurens; later studied under Dr. Ferdinand Jacobs. She married Christian Eber Smith in 1870. He engaged in farming in the Glenn Springs area of Spartanburg County until his death in 1905. Both were active in the Glenn Springs Presbyterian Church.

Major Franklin Leland Anderson (January 30, 1830–February 23, 1909). He was the beloved "Uncle Frank" of the David Anderson children. Son of James Mason and Mary "Polly" Miller Anderson, he was educated at the Poplar Springs Academy and graduated from the University of Virginia. He returned to the family land and built Holly Hill, an impressive brick home that stands today. He was noted as a very successful agriculturalist. Long active in the South Carolina Militia, just before the Civil War he enlisted in the Spartan Rifles as a sergeant and was with the first group of soldiers to leave Spartanburg County for the fighting in Virginia. He served in the Fifth Regiment, South Carolina Volunteers, until 1862 when he became a member of Holcombe's Legion, distinguishing himself during the siege of Petersburg. He served the entire war and was never injured. In 1858 he was married to Susan Knuckles Norris, who died in 1863, leaving him with three young children, Julia, Frank, and William. His second marriage in

1866 was to Ada Eppes of Sussex County, Virginia, whom he had met while stationed at camp on the Nottaway River near her home. They had nine children. Ada Eppes Anderson died in 1924.

Eloise Eugenia "Ella" Brockman (February 6, 1844–December 9, 1868). Daughter of Thomas Patterson and Mary Kilgore Brockman. Much younger sister of Harriet Brockman Anderson; made her home with Harriet and David in early 1860s. Attended Limestone Springs Female High School. Married William Henry Anderson in 1866. Lost two daughters in infancy and died shortly after the second child's death.

Henrietta Malinda "Hettie" Brockman (December 22, 1840–1877). Daughter of Thomas Patterson and Mary Kilgore Brockman, much younger sister of Harriet Brockman Anderson, made her home with David and Harriet in early 1860s. Married A. C. "Sandy" Earle.

Anderson-Brockman Genealogy

Birth order is given in brackets.

Anderson Family

(to America ca. 1742)
William Anderson (1706–1785) m Rebecca Denny (d. 1806)
  [2] Maj. David Anderson (1741–1827) m Miriam Mayson (d. 1818)
    [4] James Mason "Tyger Jim" Anderson (1784–1870)
      m Mary "Polly" Miller (1788–1856)
      [1] **David Anderson (1811–1892)** m Harriet M. Brockman (1819–1892)
        Nancy Cunningham Anderson (1840–1841)
        John Crawford Anderson (1842–1892)
        Mary Elizabeth Anderson (Moore) (1843–1921)
        Henrietta Alethia "Nettie" Anderson (Smith) (1846–1911)
        James Henry "Jimmie" Anderson (1848–1923)
        Thomas Brockman "Tommie" Anderson (1850–1903)
        Harriet Maria Anderson (Anderson) (1853–1921)
        David Perrin Anderson (1855–1874)
        Emma Frances Anderson (Oeland) (1858–1893)
      [8] James Alexander "Uncle Jim" Anderson (1828–1870)
      [9] Franklin Leland "Uncle Frank" Anderson (1830–1909)
      [10] Mason Gilliland "Uncle Mason" Anderson (1832–1882)

Brockman Family

Col. Thomas P. Brockman (1797–1859) m Mary Kilgore (1800–1861)
[1] **Harriet Maria Brockman (Anderson) (1819–1892)**
[8] Col. Benjamin T. Brockman (1831–1864)
[11] Capt. Jesse Kilgore Brockman (1839–1864)
[12] Henrietta Malinda "Hettie" Brockman (Earle) (1840–1877)
[13] Eloise Eugenia "Ella" Brockman (Anderson) (1844–1868)

Moore Family Genealogy

Birth order is given in brackets.

(to America ca. 1750)
Charles Moore (1727–1805) m Mary Barry (1733–1805)
[9] Andrew Barry Moore, M.D. (1771–1848)
m 1. Anna A. Maxwell (ca. 1788–1831)
2. Nancy Miller Montgomery (1804–1862)
[1] Margaret Anna "Ann" Moore (1834–1879) m Capt. Samuel C. Means (1830–1915)
[2] Mary Elizabeth Moore (1836–1836)
[3] Andrew Charles Moore (1838–1862) m Mary J. Foster (1841–1901)
[4] Thomas John Moore (1843–1919) m Mary Elizabeth Anderson (1843–1921)
[10] Charles Moore, Jr. (1774–1836) m Jane Barry (1783–1857)
[2] Gov. Andrew Barry Moore (1807–1873) m Mary Goree (d. 1877)
[6] Juliet Moore (1823–1864) m Dr. Robert Foster (1812–1890)
[1] Mary J. Foster (1841–1901)
m 1. Andrew Charles Moore (1838–1862)
2. William R. Barron, M.D. (1836–1917)

Moore Family

Andrew Barry Moore, M.D. (February 11, 1771–January 23, 1848). Ninth child of Charles and Mary Moore. Born at the family plantation, Walnut Grove. Graduated Dickinson College, Carlisle, Pennsylvania, in 1795. Studied medicine in Philadelphia under Dr. Benjamin Rush. Returned to Spartanburg County and practiced medicine, 1800–48. Married Anna A. Maxwell, who died in 1831, with no children. Married Nancy Miller Montgomery in 1833, and they had four children: Margaret Anna Moore Means, Mary Elizabeth (who died in infancy), Andrew Charles Moore, and Thomas John Moore. Dr. Moore made his home at Fredonia from ca. 1820 to his death.

Nancy Miller Montgomery Moore Evins (November 13, 1804–March 14, 1862). Daughter of John and Margaret Miller Montgomery of the Wellford area of Spartanburg County, near Snoddy's Bridge on the North Tyger River, north of Nazareth Presbyterian Church. Wife of Dr. Andrew Barry Moore. Widowed in 1848, she reared three children to adulthood as a single mother. She married Col. S. N. Evins on December 20, 1860.

Margaret Anna "Ann" Moore Means (December 17, 1834–May 18, 1879). Daughter of Dr. Andrew Barry and Nancy Miller Montgomery Moore. Attended Limestone Springs Female High School. Married Capt. Samuel C. Means in 1856. Their one child, Andrew James "Jimmie" Means was killed in a hunting accident in 1875, his sixteenth year.

Andrew Charles Moore (March 11, 1838–August 30, 1862). Son of Dr. Andrew Barry Moore and Nancy Miller Montgomery Moore, he was born when his father was sixty-seven years old. He graduated from South Carolina College in 1858 with distinguished honor and studied law at the University of Virginia, 1859–60. He entered the Confederate army in 1861, serving in the Eighteenth Regiment, South Carolina Volunteers, and was killed at the Second Battle of Manassas. His brother Thomas John was nearby and buried him. In 1860 he married a second cousin, Mary J. Foster of Marion, Alabama. They had no children. An elaborate marble monument at the Nazareth Presbyterian Church cemetery marks his grave.

Thomas John Moore (April 29, 1843–August 19, 1919). Born at Fredonia, in Moore, the son of Dr. Andrew Barry Moore and Nancy Miller Montgomery Moore. Educated at local schools and at Rev. John L. Kennedy's Thalian Academy, he attended South Carolina College, Columbia, and was called out twice for service in the Confederate army, including for the attack on Fort Sumter. Permanently left school his senior year (April 1862) to join Company E, Eighteenth Regiment, South Carolina Volunteers. In summer 1863 he transferred to Company A, Holcombe's Legion, serving as a private and later as color ensign in the regiment. Married Mary Elizabeth Anderson on February 27, 1866. He served in the S.C. House, 1872–74, and S.C. Senate, 1880–84. He was chairman of the Board of the South Carolina School for the Deaf and Blind for more than seventeen years.

Governor Andrew Barry Moore (March 7, 1807–April 5, 1873). The son of Charles Moore Jr.; grandson of Charles and Mary Moore of Walnut Grove Plantation. He moved with his family to Perry County, Alabama, in 1826, read law, and was admitted to the bar in 1833. He married Mary Goree in 1837. First elected to the Alabama House of Representatives in 1839, he served four consecutive terms, three as Speaker. He was a circuit judge from 1851–57, resigned to accept the Democratic Party nomination for governor, and was elected without opposition. He was reelected in 1859, defeating William F. Samford, who challenged him as being slow to prepare for the coming conflict. Moore served as governor until 1861. At war's end he was imprisoned at Fort Pulaski with other prominent Southern politicians and released in August 1865. Though referred to as "Uncle Governor" by Andrew Charles Moore (above) and his siblings, Governor Moore was actually Andrew's first cousin, thirty years his senior.

Upcountry South Carolina
Goes to War

Pre–Civil War Letters

David and Harriet Brockman Anderson were married in 1839 and established themselves at Pleasant Falls, on a hill overlooking David's gristmill on the North Tyger River in western Spartanburg County. The first of nine children was born to them in early 1840. In the ensuing years David concentrated on his business and farming interests, while Harriet was occupied with running the household, taking care of the additional eight children (born at intervals until 1858), finding the proper educational situation for each child, and supporting the nearby Nazareth Presbyterian Church. This first group of letters, written before the calamitous events of 1861, reflects many of those endeavors.

[1] Harriet Brockman Anderson to John Crawford Anderson
Addressed to him at Thalian Academy

Poolesville PO Spar March 5th, 1857

My dear son,

I now address you with feelings that are deeply interested in you. I greatly desire that you may acquit yourself with credit to yourself and to your dear parents—who you must feel have great regard for welfare and standing both at school and elsewhere. Nothing can afford us more pleasure than to know that you behave well towards your equals and treat your superiors with respect. Be kind to all and keep out of wicked company—go not in the way of the ungodly and sit not in the scorners chair . . . I wish you to attend church whenever you can and if there is a sabath school in reach be sure you are a scholar. Never stay from church or sabath school for slight excuses . . . keep out of such places where the morals are in danger . . . I remain your affectionate Mother

[2] Harriet Brockman Anderson to John Crawford Anderson

Poolsville, Spar, So Car April 10, 1857

My dear Son,

... The high schools that have been spoken of have been located at Powder Spring [renamed Reidville]. I and A Wakefield have given 100 acres of land and a thousand dollars. The neighborhood have given 4 thousand and Mr. Reid[1] says the schools are fixed facts.... Your Pa says he wants you to procure the *Life of Dr. Franklin* and see if he eat egg suppers. You must keep a minite of what you spend and what for for your Pa requires it and will make you give an account of how you spend and what for which is a reasonable demand and you must be ready to comply. We are willing to do what is right but not indulge to your ruin ... I remain most affectionately

Your Mother

1. Rev. R. H. Reid, the 1846 valedictorian of South Carolina College and a minister of Nazareth Presbyterian Church, was the founder in 1857 of Reidville Female College and Reidville Male High School. Area families supported his efforts, hoping to keep their children closer to home.

[3] Harriet Brockman Anderson to John Crawford Anderson

Poolsville PO Spar March 18th, 1858

Dear Son

... You made some requests about college. Apply yourself diligently and give proof of the fact and your Pa will give you good opportunity. We thought your last letter better than any we have received. I hope you will improve in writing and spelling because they are the only way you have of showing to absent friends that you are learning.... Be a good boy and make us proud of you. I remain your affectionate

Mother

[4] David Anderson to John Crawford Anderson

Addressed to him at Arsenal, Columbia, SC

May 13th, 1858

Dear Son

I recd yours by Charly Miller stating that I was well which is far from the Truth. I have been sick for four weeks and confined to the House pretty much all

Capt. David Anderson and Harriet Brockman Anderson.
From Edward Lee Anderson, *A History of the Anderson Family, 1706–1955* (Columbia, S.C.: R. L. Bryan Company, 1955); used with permission

the time. So Charly proves to be a Dull young man. I am Recovering slowly I am now able to walk about the Plantation and attend to a little business. My Liver and Stomach are disordered. I have taken a good deal of Medacine and not well yet. . . . Our prospects for a crop are not very flattering at present. Our cotton is up to a pretty good stand we have run around it and commenced chopping out. Our corn is doing tolerably well except 20 acres in the Fork we have ploughed it up and planted over. Our wheat is nothing to brag on Part of it is very sorry. We have peaches and apples plenty. Our corn was badly bit by the frost but has fully Recovered. We have had one mess of small Irish potatoes which helped me very much.

. . . We are driving slowly at Reidville. We intend to commence plastering the first of next month. We have finished the brick work of the Professors House. The workmen have covered it and will have it ready for plastering in a few weeks. The School is improving slowly. Mr. David has 30 Schollars some Latin and English. There will go up several houses this summer. It (will) perhaps be a grate Place.

I send you at your request Five Dollars which I hope will answer all demands at present . . . I hope you will make a wise improvement of your time and opportunity.

If you could be suited at Reidville as well as where you are I would be pleased on account of the distance. Yours truly,
David Anderson

I find I have but two dollars instead of five. D.A.
PS Your Uncle Frank borrowed me clean out. D.A.

[5] Harriet Brockman Anderson to John Crawford Anderson

Addressed to him at Arsenal, Columbia

Poolsville, Spar Jany 16th, 1860

My Dear Son,

Knowing you would like to hear from home I attempt to address you. Emma [Emma Frances Anderson] has been very sick since you left. I thought at one time she would not recover. But she has been spared. Her disease was worms She could not stand alone for a week and now can just walk a little but is improving very fast. All the rest are well and we are glad to hear that you are so well pleased and hope it will continue. My dear son I hope if you have not made your peace with your God you will delay no longer. O! Tomorrow. Tomorrow may be too late. Stop and think before it is too late. It would be a source of much pleasure to know you were hopefully converted and be assured your dear Mother presents your case at a throne of grace every day and feels that her prayer will be answered . . . I think with Dr. Baker [Daniel Baker, Presbyterian minister and evangelist]: "Let me be poor. Let me be a beggar but let me not be an unconverted sinner." . . . Now my son, you are away from the restraining influence of your parents and need the best of legacies, the religion of the Lord Jesus Christ. With this you are prepared to live and to die it will be well with you whatever your fate . . . I remain with much affection your
Mother

[6] David Anderson to John Crawford Anderson

Pleasant Falls, Feby 4th, 1860

Dear Son,

. . . I Recd yours shortly after it was written and was gratified to know you were pleased with your school and equally so to hear you speak of your safe arrival in Columbia the day after you left Spartanburg. I wish you to write me more fully about your School . . . who the Professors are and the Branches that are taught. I would recommend to you to pay attention to writing and spelling which are two very important Items in every man's education.

. . . I sent Dr. Buist flour and Corn this week also have sold 100 bushels to Williams at Clinton for $1.25 a bushel. I expect to haul to Laurens at same price as chance may offer. I see flour is advancing and I have sold out. We had quite a whipping among the negroes last Saturday. Moses Vandike and Simp Coan have had Three Parties and invited all the negroes. The party was held at Mullinax's old House and some Danced and others played Cards and all drank Liquor and eat Gingerbread. We held a Neighborhood court and gave the Card Players and Liquor Dealers fifty and the Ladies and more innocent Ten Lashes apiece which gave general satisfaction.

Old Tom Finch [neighboring farmer] is dead, his young wife took $1000 and quit the Finch family.

Let us hear from you often

Yours as ever,

David Anderson

[7] David Anderson to John Crawford Anderson
Addressed to him at Arsenal, Columbia

March 15th, 1860

Dear Son,

We have just recd your letter of the 15th Feby. We thought we would wait until we heard from you before writing. This leaves us all well and trying to get ready to do better. Some of our Farmers are planting Corn but I do not intend to plant any before the end of this month. I have been riding Betty and she has throwed me three falls and has run off from home three times and one time she got one Eye very nearly knocked out. I wish you would come and take her to the Arsenal or the Horsebreakers and trane her or will have to give her to Frank and Old Joe and see if they can do anything for her. I have hauled ten loads of corn to Laurens at $1.25.

I have all my ditches cleaned out and my Corn Land broke up the second time. The Buffaloe[1] wheat is rather thin but all the Rest is thick enough. I have a good chance for Corn this year.

Your Mother has sent you a box of meat. You will find it at the Depot as I will start it down the train today. I am sorry to think Columbia cannot feed its Boarders, however I have plenty of Corn and Bacon and if you cannot stand it come up for I expect to get in the grass this summer and will need some help no doubt. You will write me when to send more money and the amount and I will send a check for the amount.

Let us hear from you often

Yours truly,
David Anderson

1. The Buffalo(e) was the rich bottom land on David Anderson's farm between the North and Middle Tyger rivers and just north of where they converge. Cherokee hunting parties camped there before the white settlers arrived.

[8] David Anderson to John Crawford Anderson

May 14th, 1860

Dear Son,

I recd yours by last mail but you did not say how much money you wished. I presume $10.00 will answer your purpose at this time.

You will come to Laurens on Thursday the 24th and I will meet you there in company with your Mother as we wish to visit the girls [JCA's younger sisters at Laurensville Academy]. We have fine Seasons and some grass. Jimmy [James Henry Anderson] says you are fortunate in missing to help hoe out the big field over the River as it is very grassy but we will clean it out today. D. Anderson

Dr. Andrew Barry Moore established his practice in Spartanburg County in the late 1790s near Walnut Grove, the family plantation. He was married in 1813 to Anna A. Maxwell, who died in 1831 with no surviving children. He married Nancy Miller Montgomery, thirty-three years his junior, in 1834. Dr. Moore bought Fredonia, the house of his older brother Gen. Thomas Moore, on the west side of the North Tyger River, circa 1820. Andrew and Nancy Moore had four children, beginning with Margaret Anna, in 1834. Their second child, Mary Elizabeth, died in infancy. Andrew and Thomas completed the family. As with the Andersons, service to Nazareth Presbyterian Church and seeking the best possible education for their children were primary pursuits. Dr. Moore died in 1848, when Andrew was ten and Thomas five. Their mother was their sole parent until she remarried in late 1860. As women at the time did not have full legal property rights, Dr. Moore's will named his close friend, Col. Samuel N. Evins, as the children's legal guardian. It was he whom Nancy Moore married in 1860. The following letters focus on sons Andrew and Thomas as they pursue their educations in the years leading up to the Civil War.

[9] Andrew Charles Moore to Margaret Anna Moore

Addressed to her at Limestone Academy

April 24, 1853

Dear Sister

Thinking that you would want to hear all the important news from home I am now going to tell you what I know. I will begin with the affair at Mr. Fielders. There was a tolerable number of Gentlemen there, but very few ladies in proportion (as I thought). Very nearly all the scholars of our school except the smaller ones were invited and we all went and had quite a pleasant time. For my part I do not know when I enjoyed myself so well. We had a very nice dinner. Pound, sponge cake, wine, boiled custard and many others too tedious to mention as it is useless to mention only the best. The newly wedded pair looked very fine. The bride was dressed in beautiful light colored silk. The Miss Drummonds constituted the greater part of the ladies. There were five of them there, two of Jared's, two of Warren's, and one of Harrison's [large family from Woodruff]. Grandma [Margaret Miller Montgomery, Mrs. John] came down on Sunday evening last and she and Mace went down to Dr. Means the next day and brought Aunt Margaret [Margaret Montgomery Moore, Mrs. William] up with them. She had been down there a week. Grandma and Aunt M. left for home yesterday morning. Nancy Benson [Nancy Miller Benson, Mrs. Silas] went home from Dr. Means' on Friday which will be two weeks ago tomorrow. I think she had stayed long enough to catch a beau for Jo. [Oeland?] went up there Sunday after and popped the question before he left and the most generally received opinion is that their nuptials will be celebrated before a great while, and for my part I think she has done perfectly right in accepting his offer. The family is not very well at this time. Aunt Rosa [Rosa Roddy Montgomery, Mrs. John Chapman Jr.] is now sick, and Tommy [Thomas John Moore] has been unwell for the last few days but is now well. You ought to be here to eat eels, I caught three last night and intend to try them again before long. Our waggon got home from Columbia last Tuesday and is going to start tomorrow for Newberry. We got ten cents for all of our cotton except two bales for which we only got eight. Mr. Posey has gotten up from Charleston his new stock of goods. He has some very handsome muslins. Ma bought for you from the little dutch pedlar who was here last winter just before you went to Limestone a lowered poplin dress which though rather dark for the season looks very modest and retiring and I think it cannot fail to please you. It is not very fine but will do for Limestone as it requires so little washing. She says she will make it and send it as soon as possible.

As it is very late I cannot write any more and without further ceremony I bid you Goodnight. Ma and all the family join in love with you and wish you much joy at the May party. Write me a letter soon and let us hear all the good news.
Your brother
A. C. Moore

If you have any particular way you would like your dress to be made, Ma would like you to send her word. A.C.M.

[10] Andrew Charles Moore to Nancy Montgomery Moore

Greenwood, Feb. 21, 54

Dear Mother,

After having written you two letters, and not receiving an answer from either, I supposed you had not received them. I got sister's letter which afforded me a great deal of pleasure, and in it she said you was very much disappointed at my not writing. My letters must have been miscarried. I was very sorry to hear that Charlotte's child was burnt so badly that it died. When you write please tell me how it happened. I suppose you have not got your carriage yet when you get it you must come to see me, be sure. Has Thomas started to school yet and who is he going to?

How does Amanda succeed with her school? How many scholars has she? What is Davy doing?

I have succeeded in drying my books and clothes. Some of my clothes were very much injured. My gray pants have drawed up entirely too short, so short I can never wear them again. They do not reach but little below half my bootleg. My black ones which were too short before are still shorter now, so you see that I am left with but one pair of pants long enough.(my brown tweeds) I was so scarce that I went to the store today and bought me a pair of black doe skin for which I paid two dollars a yard. They are not made yet but I have given them to the tailor to make up. My satin vest is ruined and my new coat looks as bad as it can. I have not money to pay him for making the pants. He only charges two dollars which you will send me in your next letter if you please. I have bought six books since I have been here, four of which I got from a travelling barterer which took all of my money excepting a few cents. The trustees have been down upon the scholars who have not paid their tuition. I, of course, was in the number. I immediately wrote to you about it. But since you nor Col. Evins [his guardian] neither has said anything about it—I supposed you did not get the letter. The amount of it is twenty-eight dollars. Mr. Donnelley's school is still increasing, he has now forty scholars. Mr. Logan has forty-two. I am getting on very well with Mr. D. and think him a first-rate teacher. Mr. McClure the assistant, is a very clever young man. He looks very much like Mr. Holmes. I like all the boys very well. I was at a tea party at Mr. D's the other evening. There was none but school boys and girls invited. Genl. Gillam has but three boarders besides myself, all young ladies. James is my roommate.

The Baptist schools are small. There is but about twenty in each school. Please answer this letter as soon as you receive it and tell Col. Evins to be sure and send that money. (twenty-eight dollars) for the tuition and two to pay for the making of my pants, for I think it is a poor way to have all such things charged. How does Mr. H [Hill, plantation overseer] come on farming? How is Aunt Rosa? I must close. It is going on eleven o'clock. Give my love to all. Aunt Louisa sends her love to you. Good Night.
Your affectionate son
A C Moore.

Write immediately and tell Tom to write.
Send the two dollars anyhow, whether you send the other or not.

[11] Andrew Charles Moore to Nancy Montgomery Moore

October 12th 1854, Greenwood

My Dear Mother,

I have just witnessed the departure of Mr. Baker [Rev. Daniel Baker] for Nazareth, His meeting closed today at 12 and he has taken the cars for Greenville, where, (I suppose) he will be met by Mr. Reid [Rev. R. H. Reid]. He is a great preacher, and I think cannot fail to arouse the people of Nazareth.[1]

He has converted several here, some eighteen or twenty, I do not know precisely the number for it has never been publicly announced. The converts will join next Sunday at Rock[2] & those who have never been, will be baptised, John Cunningham has been converted and will join. (His mother was converted twenty-two years ago under Mr. Baker's preaching.) I know you will be pleased with Mr. B., he does not preach like common preachers. He will command attention, and if people don't behave, he will tell them from the pulpit of it. He has prayer meeting in the morning when he gives a lecture almost equal to a sermon, two sermons in the day time, and one at night. I do not see how he can stand it. He is near seventy years old and preaches almost you might call it four times a day, every day. I tell you he makes the other preachers look like small fish. & I think they must feel so. Their voices sound so feebly after his powerful voice is hushed. They really look ashamed to speak after him. I will not say this of all preachers, but this is the way the Greenwood preachers looked & I thought must feel. I will not say anything more of Mr. Baker, you can soon hear for yourself. I have a book containing his second series of revival sermons for which I gave a dollar. It contains exactly the sermons he is preaching now. I also put in a dollar to the Austin College (Texas) of which he is the President which makes two dollars of my money he got.

I have got over those bad drowsy feelings by taking blue pills. I am getting on first rate. Mr. C's [Creswell] is the most pleasant boarding house in Greenwood. It is not lonesome like Gen. G's [James Gilliam] but there is always something to cheer me up. I am the only boarder and have a fine time. Mr. C. is a man very well off and not too stingy to enjoy it. Every dollar counts him something. His table is supplied constantly with what is good, He raises plenty of everything on his farm and always plenty of pig, mutton, beef, etc on the table. Mrs. C. will keep a good table. I reckon she has got any amount of preserves, jellies, brandy fruits and things of this kind in the pantry, she puts them on the table and we just make them fly. I see into the pantry occasionally. Our room is in the basement next to the dining room.

I took tea at Gen G's some time ago. Joyed myself very well and had a good deal of fun with the young ladies. Gallanted Miss Lucy Smith to church. She is a beautiful girl and a very nice girl [part scratched out]. Frank [Leland] Anderson is taking on about her sister Ginna, I wish he could get her, she is a nice lady and I believe likes him pretty well.

I have made a poor out of studying the last two weeks. Mr. D. was gone one week to Liberty Spring, at Mr. B.'s meeting there and this week I have been attending preaching. There is preaching in the chapel tonight and every night for some time, as Mr. McLease [Rev. John McLees], assisted by Mr. Catur of Charleston is going to continue the meeting at Rock in the daytime and the chapel at night. Greenwood has been in a perfect flame for about three weeks. The Baptists have had meetings and the Presbyterians time has come and I do not know when they will stop. I reckon you are getting tired of such gab so I will close. Charles C. sends his love to sister. Give my love to Aunt Rosa, Tom, Sister all and reserving the greatest portion for yourself. Hoping you will answer this soon, I subscribe myself

Your affectionate son,

Andrew

1. Nazareth Presbyterian Church, founded in 1765 and organized in 1772, is located in Spartanburg County, South Carolina, some six miles west of the city of Spartanburg.

2. Rock Church, originally Rocky Creek Presbyterian Church, is located in southeast Abbeville District, near Greenwood, South Carolina. See George Howe, *History of the Presbyterian Church in South Carolina* (Columbia, S.C.: W. J. Duffie, 1883), 2:728–32.

[12] Thomas John Moore to Nancy Montgomery Moore

South Carolina College
Columbia
January 12th, 1859

My dear Ma:

I have now been here nearly two weeks and as I promised to write often to you I will write you a second letter. The other letter that I wrote had no news in it so you must excuse it for I had been here such a short time that I did not know anything about the place. I like to stay here very well now and hope that I may continue satisfied. I was under the impression before I left home that anyone could get through College without much study, but since then I have found out better. There are some of the worst boys here that I ever saw in my life when any of the Professors go to lecturing and anything happen that is the least funny, everyone goes to applauding and keep it up for about five minutes. Judge Longstreet[1] cannot get into the Chappel at Prayer to say anything without they stamp and scrape the floor with their feet and all such foolishness. Of course, it makes them very mad, but it is useless to say anything for it only makes them worse.

Byrd and myself have a double bed and are fixed up only tolerably well, we have a miserable room. There are some fellows rooming above us who keep [up] a great deal of fuss. I paid 45 dollars in the Library for college expenses until April and then comes 45 more until June. I joined the Clariosophic society the other night, some of the members of another society wish me to join them. I have not made up my mind yet whether to join them or not. I have not got a letter from home yet but hope that you will write soon. I don't care whether the letters are long or short, so that I get them. I have not been called to recite yet. I must come to a close. Excuse bad writing and accept of my love.

Your son,
Thomas J. Moore

I have not heard from Bud [Andrew Charles Moore] nor Sister [Ann Moore Means] since I have been here. They are lazy about writing. I wrote to both of them. I will have to send them some paper and envelops I expect for they surely have none.

1. Augustus Baldwin Longstreet was president of South Carolina College from late 1857 through late 1861. A native of Augusta, Georgia, and a Yale graduate, he had been a judge, a Methodist minister, and president of Emory and Centenary Colleges. He came to Columbia after retiring as president of the University of Mississippi.

[13] Thomas John Moore to Nancy Montgomery Moore

South Carolina College
April 2nd, 1859

My dear Ma:

Your letter has just been received and I know that you would like to hear from me, so I will write you a few lines in reply to yours.

The examination begun on last Saturday and will continue until Thursday, we have stood on two Professors and have another at nine o'clock in the morning. I have just been reading over what we have to stand on. It seems as hard now as it did the first time that I went over it. You say that you want me to stand as well as any in my class. I hate to deceive you for I am not going to do it. I have made a bad beginning this session and it is too late now. I am going to study a great deal harder from now until June than I have been doing. I did not take lectures and all I am going to do is to pass the examination safely. I do not want you to think that I have not studied any at all for I have learned a great deal since I have been here. It is no easy matter to make a good paper. At the examination the least thing in the world will throw one a great way back.

There has been an election for mayor of the city of Columbia here today. I do not know who is elected. There were three candidates, all of them very popular. I am sorry to hear about the black mare being killed. We do have very bad luck. I have never seen Joe Montgomery yet. I don't know whether he is here or not.

I have not heard from Bud in some time. I hope that June will soon come as I would like to see you. It does not seem long since I left home although it has been three months. I want you to see to Flora [his bird dog] that the Negroes do not ruin her by hunting rabbits with her.

I must come to a close as it is getting late and I want to go to bed and get up soon in the morning.

Excuse this ugly writing as it seems like writing with a stick.

Write soon and give me all the news.

I remain your son,
Thomas J. Moore

[14] Andrew Charles Moore to Nancy Montgomery Moore

Dr. Fosters[1] *May 25th, 1859*

My Dear Mother

I have been in Ala two weeks today and have fully intended writing before this. I have visited all of our kin & there is a perfect host of them. The first Sunday after I came I went to Fairview [Presbyterian] church which is in sight of Dr. Foster's house & about half of the congregation was kin.

I did not find Cousin Andrew [Gov. Andrew Barry Moore] in Montgomery as I expected. He was on a visit to Mr. Evins, where he has lived since he quit housekeeping. He was in Marion the day I arrived, got there just at dinner at the hotel and as soon as I eat went around to the Lockets[2] to see Cousin Martha, who lives at her father-in-laws. Cousin Andrew was sitting in the piazza & looked so badly I hardly knew him. Cousin Mattie [Mattie Foster Fennel] was out at Mr. L's plantation. She came home next day and was very glad to see me. Every body here was just as anxious to see me as if I had been a distinguished personage. Even Mrs. Locket rejoiced as much over me as if I had been her own son. I have spent several days at her house & they all treat me just as a member of the family. I think we ought all to be very proud of our kin out here, for they are the cleverest folks I ever saw. It seems that they can't treat me too well.

I have visited and got acquainted with all of the relations. I have been to Mr. Evins,[3] Cousin Hamilton's [Charles Hamilton Moore], Cousin Martha Moore's and am now at Dr. Foster's. Cousin Martha lives at Uncle Charles M.'s [Charles Moore Jr.] old place & is the widow of Alfred Moore, his youngest son. Dr. Foster has a housefull of daughters—five in number, & only one son, who is the youngest. His two eldest daughters are about grown; Eliza the second one graduates next month at the seminary in Marion & is quite a smart girl. Dr. Foster says that if I will remain one month he will send his daughter Mary[4] home with me & Julia Evins & Cornelia Moore also wish to go. I think they will be very apt to come when I return.

I forgot to tell you of the railroad disaster. When I took the cars for Selma at Marion we had not got more than 200 yards from the depot before one car loaded with timber ran off the track. In an hour and a half it was put on track again & before we had got 3/4 of a mile another car just in front of the passenger pulled to pieces & tore up the road considerably, scattering its load of flour bagging etc as it went. Fortunately the train was going slow and soon stopped else the passenger car would have been thrown off the track & torn to pieces. As it was no one was injured, but many badly frightened.

I am going to Eutaw next week to see E. B. Perrin [Edward Burt Perrin, S.C. College, 1858], my classmate. I shall stay several weeks with him. Give my love to all and consider me
Your affectionate son,
A. C. Moore

1. Home of Dr. Robert Foster. He was married to Juliet Moore, the daughter of Charles Moore Jr. Charles Moore Jr. was the tenth and last child of Charles and Mary Moore of Walnut Grove Plantation, Spartanburg County, South Carolina. Juliet Moore was A. C. Moore's first cousin. The Fosters lived near Marion, Perry County, Alabama.

2. Martha J. Moore, daughter of Governor Moore, married Powhattan Lockett

3. Mr. Evins was probably James Evins, the husband of Mary Moore Evins, a daughter of Charles Moore Jr.

4. Mary Foster married Andrew Charles Moore on December 11, 1860.

[15] Andrew Charles Moore to Nancy Montgomery Moore

Marion, June 27th 1859

My Dear Mother,

I have intended writing for several days, but have not got at it till now. I got Sister's letter & was glad to hear all were well. I suppose you have got the letter I wrote while in Greene County on a visit to Perrin. I enjoyed myself & have been back a week. The examinations are going on at the Judson & Howard Colleges in Marion & I have come to stay at Cousin Mat's [Mattie Foster Fennel] during that time. The weather is so very hot I don't think there can be much enjoyment.

You no doubt think I should think of coming home, as I have been away a long time. In a few weeks you may look for me. Cousin Julia Evins is sick with bilious fever & is not able to travel for a few weeks. She is recovering rapidly and can be up. Jane Anna, Mr. Evins younger daughter is quite sick also. She is improving very little.

Since my return from Greene I have been staying at Mr. Evins & Dr. Foster's. Eliza Foster graduates next week at the Seminary in this place. She is the second daughter. Mary graduated two years since at the Seminary. She is the eldest child, is very pretty. Dr. Foster has a nice wife and smart children. Cousin Julia is quite as lively as any of her daughters & if anything is even more girlish.

Perhaps I had better not come home at all; as the people here seem to think more of me than folks about home. Mr. Locket's family seem to think as much of me as if I were a near relative. This is the case with every single member of the family. My own relatives have spared no pains to make me enjoy my visit. They are the cleverest people I know, first as different from people about home as when a stranger come here every one who knows him will have him at their houses and treat him to the best. Even people who never heard of you but are friends to your friends come to see you & invite you to their houses. This is different from most countries & when our friends come to Spartanburg we will have to do our best to entertain them. *Do buy you some new horses before then.*

Gov. Moore will be here this week on his way to Tuscaloosa to attend the Commencement in that place.

I suppe Samuel has got home though Sister did not say in her letter. Andrew J. talks I guess & Flora has grown wonderfully . . .

Write some of you as soon as you receive this. Give my love to all and believe me
Your affectionate son,
Andrew C. Moore

[There is a hole in this letter where it was partially burned.]

[16] Andrew Charles Moore to Nancy Montgomery Moore

U. of Va.
October 8th, 1859

My dear Mother,

This is to inform you of my safe arrival in this place. You have heard of our being left in Greenville. However we spent a pleasant day, so much that I did not regret being left. In the morning Sallie, Hattie, Jimmy, Mary and myself visited Mr. Sam Townes and Mr. Gus Townes. The latter married in Marion and the former one lived in Marion. It was Sallie who took the girls visiting. She has the most perfect mania for riding. She rode the whole day from breakfast till dark. After dinner she struck out in the country about 5 miles & with A. Evins kept riding until after sundown. No sooner had she got home than she called out the girls & rode as long as daylight lasted . . .

I had a very pleasant trip . . . At Allston Theodore Smith got aboard & came as far as Columbia where James Kennedy and several other theological students came aboard and traveled some distance. There were some medical students bound to Philadelphia aboard & also a Mr. Underwood of Alabama who was for the last two years a student in the Seminary of Columbia, & then was on his way to Germany to prosecute his studies still farther. He knows Cousin Mattie and once brought me a message from her, which is the way I came to be acquainted with him.

When I got here on yesterday (Friday) I was emphatically among strangers & I have not seen a person I have ever seen before. In Ala I heard the Locketts talk frequently of the McKinnies who live here. Mrs. Lockett told me to get acquainted with Mrs. McKinnie and her son, Dr. McK. When Pow. Lockett was here he was sick a long time and stayed with Mrs. McK... Not knowing what else to do I enquired for Dr. McK. & found him in his book store at the University gate. He introduced me to several students & got me a room & room mate by name of Page from Clarke County, Va. He is a sober studying fellow, a student of Medicine...

I am not rooming on the University grounds but am what is called a non-resident. I am situated at a convenient distance. A walk of five minutes will take me anywhere on the University grounds.

Hoping this will find you all well & those negroes improved I must close. Give my love to all the family & tell them I would far rather be at home with you all than here...

Your affectionate son,
Andrew C. Moore

N.B. Enclosed you will find a note. Give it to Col. Evins. I did not know I had it. A.C.M.

[17] Andrew Charles Moore to Nancy Montgomery Moore

University of Va. Oct 10th 1859

My Dear Mother

Since writing two days since I have found out that my money will give out too soon. There is some more to be paid in advance than I had anticipated besides the books I will have to buy all amount to about $35.00. Please send me when some cotton is sold $100.00. Get Samuel [Col. S. N. Evins, his legal guardian] to buy a draught for that amount & send it to me as soon as possible, for I must have the money immediately.

I got a letter yesterday from Selwyn Evins [Alabama cousin]. He is at Washington College[1] in Lexington about 80 miles from here. Ally Lockett [Alabama cousin] is at the same place in the Military Institute.[2] Selwyn says of me and I give his own words, "you left the best impression on all the people about Marion of any fellow that ever has been there. I think it would be the best place in the world for you to commence practicing law" This is what he says.

But the greatest compliment paid me was by Dr. [Maximilian] LaBorde, Professor in So. Ca. College. He told Dr. Crook[3] that I had more mind than any fellow who had been in college for twenty years & that if I lived I would make a mark. These things I would tell nobody but you, for people would say I was vain & I make it a rule to keep compliments to myself; for it is best not to be one's own trumpet blower. Of course you will say nothing about it.

This morning I shall attend my first lecture. I was very anxious to get through here in one year, but find it next thing to impossible. I could do it at the risk of injuring myself by hard study & hence have concluded to stay two years.

Thomas Moore [Alabama cousin] has not returned yet.

Give my love to all and kiss Jimmie [ACM's nephew Andrew James Means] for me.

Your affectionate son, Andrew C. Moore

1. Now Washington and Lee University, in Lexington, Virginia.
2. Virginia Military Institute, Lexington, Virginia.
3. Dr. Andrew Barry Crook, a Greenville, South Carolina, physician, was the son of Katy Barry and grandson of Kate Moore Barry.

[18] Andrew Charles Moore to Nancy Montgomery Moore

University of Virginia, Oct. 23rd 1859

My Dear Mother.

Previous to going to church I have concluded to drop you a few lines which I will put in the office which I pass going to church. I will go to church in Charlottesville, one mile distant with a young Haskell from Abbeville whose acquaintance I have made since I came here & who seems to be a very clever fellow. I knew two of his brothers before.

I have now got fully straightened out in studying & have got a little more to do than I can with ease perform. When I first came here I thought of staying two years, but since I have concluded to try & finish the law in one year. This is a thing seldom done & I doubt if more than one out of an hundred ever go through in one year. I think I have capacity enough to do it; if I can hold up to study. It will require very hard work but I am willing to endure it for nine months as it will save the trouble and expense of coming back another year. Law is the only study I have. My intention was to Law & Moral Philosophy but finding that to be too much I have left off the latter study.

I have not heard from our Alabama friends yet. Although I have been looking for a letter every day for some days past. I suppose they are safe at home long before now.

Tom's [Thomas John Moore] letter came to hand & was most welcomely received. I was glad to hear that the sick negroes were improving & hope that they are now entirely well. I suppose Sam & Sister [Sam and Ann Moore Means] will start tomorrow. (24th)

I have got acquainted with some excellent fellows from Greenville. Earles Duncan & Beattie & since then have become much more reconciled to this place. Duncan & myself joined the Jefferson society last night. The other society is called the Washington & there used to be another by the name of Columbian, but which broke up last year in a row about some election, & since has ceased to exist. Cousin Thomas J. Moore was a member of the Columbians.

The Jefferson is not so orderly as the Clariosophic [at South Carolina College] & the Hall lacks a great deal of being so nicely fixed. There is generally a good deal of speaking which I expect is due to the fact that the Society gives a medal every year to the best speaker. There is considerable rivalry among the members.

The weather is beginning to get cold & we have had some frost, but not a great deal. I thought that by this time in this high latitude & among the mountains it would have been much colder than it is. Whatever way you look you see mountains at no great distance. The place is almost completely girded in with mountains. As frost is late coming here I guess it will be later with you & that we will make a good cotton crop.

Hoping that this will find you all well, I close.

Your affectionate son.
Andrew C. Moore

[19] Andrew Charles Moore to Nancy Montgomery Moore

Univy Nov 21st 1859

My Dear Mother

I write this to inform you that I am well & doing well. I find I get on much better than at first. I have now many pleasant acquaintances & can study much better since I have got used to things, I would not be surprised if I now know more about Law than some fellows who have been admitted to the bar. The study though sometimes dry is generally interesting, & upon the whole I think it one of the most interesting studies.

I have not received a line from Sister yet, though I have written to her. I have been anxiously looking for a letter from home as I am really solicitous about the fever, I hope the whites will escape anyhow.

Things in the upper part of this state look very threatening. The abolitionist are burning up houses & so on at a great rate though they have not yet burned any dwelling houses. Some abolitionists, 17 in number, headed by John Brown[1] have been condemned to be hung at Charlestowne in Dec for murdering the whites & trying to run off slaves. Charlestowne is about 130 miles from here & the people there are greatly excited, The Governor has ordered a large military force & has gone with them to Charlestowne to stay until after the hanging to guard the town from attack by the abolitionist to rescue Brown & the other prisoners. I have come to the conclusion that there is obliged to be a dissolution of the union before long.

One thing I ought to have told you long ago I will now tell you, Mary Foster & I are engaged. It is better in some respects for even second cousins to not marry, but then there is no wrong in it, & no bad consequences to result from it. I don't think you will find any person who will object to second cousins marrying. Mary told her Pa & Ma about it when she got home & they do not make any objections. Now you must write the very day you get this & tell me freely all you think about the matter. Mary is very beautiful as you know & she is certainly the most amiable & lovely girl I ever saw, & I am very sure I have never loved anyone else as I love her & never will. The more you will become acquainted with her the more you will like her. On account of her modesty she must be cultivated to be understood & appreciated. Now I don't think you will object to her as a daughterinlaw, though she is some akin, especially since both her Pa & Ma are both perfectly willing. Mary wrote me that her Pa said he thought if second cousins wished to marry he thought it perfectly right for them to do so & her Ma said the same thing. Be sure to write soon & tell me about it.

Cousin Mattie Lockett has a daughter & they make a terrible fuss over it. Mrs. Lockett says she wants Mrs. Foster to determine whether she wants me for Mary as she is anxious for me to take her daughter, Sue Lockett. Give my respects to Mr. Hill [overseer] & reply to this very soon.

Yours most affectionately

A. C. Moore

1. John Brown was the abolitionist who conducted the raid on the federal armory in Harpers Ferry, West Virginia (then part of Virginia), on October 16, 1859.

[20] Andrew Charles Moore to Nancy Montgomery Moore

Univty of Va Dec. 18th [*1859*]

My Dear Mother

I was truly glad to receive both of your letters. I had received no news from home in so long a time, that I had almost concluded something dreadful had happened. Your letters had the effect of dispelling my apprehensions. I am glad to learn that the negroes are improved so much, as it removes a great load of care from your mind & I hope no more will get sick. How are the crops turning out? The cotton crop of the *United States* is larger this year than ever before.

Your opinions about my engagement to Mary Foster are about what I expected. Her parents say they greatly disapprove of 1st cousins marrying, but do not think a marriage of second cousins objectionable. And as they have given me an unreserved assent, you may count as certain that Mary will one day be your daughterinlaw. I can see no material objection to such a thing; you are not much opposed; her parents not at all unfavorable; & the opinion of the world does not condemn a marriage between second cousins. I do not believe you will find more than one of twenty really opposed to such a thing.

You seem to think I am going to leave the University too soon. I would stay willingly two years, but then I dislike spending so much time in learning Va law, as I never shall have use for it. I am going into an office next year when I return & in December next shall apply for the bar. Then I should go to practicing immediately & not idle about until I forget what I hope by that time to know of the law. It causes me no little anxiety to know where I am to locate.

You spoke of the boy of Collins. You may tell Mr. Hill to use his own judgment. The typhoid fever has stopped, I believe & I suppose there would be no risk in buying him.

Send by the 1st of January $225.00, as I wish to pay up pretty much what will have to be paid. Give my love to all & write soon & often to
Your affectionate son,
Andrew C. Moore

[21] Andrew Charles Moore to Nancy Montgomery Moore

Univety of Va Jan 1st 1860

My Dear Mother

Being quite lonesome tonight I have concluded to relieve myself by writing you a few lines. As usual on Sunday night, I am alone, Page [roommate] is a great ladies man & invariably goes home with somebody on Sunday from church, & never returns until late at night. This has been the case every Sunday without exception since I have been here.

The weather is extremely cold & the ground has been covered with snow since last Wednesday. How long it will last is hard to say, as it does not seem to melt at all. I do abominate snow & this is the hardest snow to walk upon I have ever tried. Coming from church today I could scarcely keep from slipping up at every step.

Selwyn Evins and Allie [Albert] Lockett were to see me a week ago. They arrived on Sunday, Christmas day, & remained until Tuesday. They had been to West Point to see Sam Lockett married to a yankee girl, for West Point is in New York. They stayed with me at my boarding house We have two beds & so could accommodate them very conveniently. If they had not come, I should have had an awfully dull Christmas. The faculty gave Monday for holiday, and this is the only day during the whole nine months we are allowed.

I received a letter from Mary Foster last week. She & Eliza are going soon to Mobile & New Orleans to spend some time. I think it is well that Dr. Foster is going to send them there; for I do think nothing is so beneficial as a knowledge of the world. It makes a man or woman either to succeed better in life. for my part I think the time & money I spent in Fla & Ala the best investment I have ever made. Next time I go traveling you must go with me. Nothing would give me more pleasure than to take you out into the world a little & get your mind relieved from domestic cares. I hope you are over your surprise at what I told you about Mary F. and myself and that you are in a good humor, for I expect you thought it a very foolish thing.

When you write tell me where Sister & Sam are living. She wrote me a very short letter some time ago, & I guess it will be long before I get another. I do not see any use in being so brief as she is in her letters. Did Tom [brother] enter college? I cannot see why he does not write & let me know for I am certainly interested in it.

I have had a very bad cold since last week, though now it has nearly left me. Two weeks since I fell into a pit, dug on the railroad track to keep cows from walking along it; & hurt my leg on the shin badly. It has now got about well. It was on Saturday night I fell, I was coming home from Earles' room & it was so dark I could scarcely see the tracks let alone see the cow pit (Earle is from Greenville) On Monday night following I unbandaged my leg to see what it was doing. It looked rather badly & strange to say made me so deathly sick that I fainted. I soon revived with Page's help & hope I shall not do so foolish a thing again soon.

Nancy Miller Montgomery Moore (Evins). Portrait by Nicola Marschall, ca. 1860; courtesy of Elizabeth Moore Snowden

Write as soon as you get this & tell me about the crop & sick, for I am anxious to know how everything at home is getting along. Also tell me if you ever received that note I sent you by letter.
Your affectionate son
Andrew C. Moore

[22] Thomas John Moore to Nancy Montgomery Moore

February 3rd, 1860
South Carolina College

My dear Ma:

I will now attempt to write you a few lines to let you know how I am getting along here. I have been very unwell all the day. I have had a very bad headache. I went to recitation this morning but did not feel well enough to go at eleven. I am much better now so I will spend my time writing to you. I have heard from home only once since I left there although I have written three or four times. I know it is a great task for you to write so I will have to excuse you. You might write a short letter any time. I would not care if it was not more than a page. Aunt Hannah [Montgomery] ought to write to me if she is at our house. I got a letter from Aunt Margaret [Moore] yesterday. It was an answer to one I wrote last fall. All of them

were well. She had been visiting Mr. Moore's relations. All of the children were at their uncles and she was almost alone. We have to pay for everything we get here and very highly too. We have to pay $5.00 for a cord of wood that would make at home not more than a dozen fires. We are imposed upon by the College itself. When we come to stay for four years we pay tuition for five and for three years we have to pay for four years. That is we pay now for the half of last year and when we graduate we will have to pay for half of the next year. I found both of my handercheifs Byrd had them and as for the shirt, that is gone. I want two or three more shirts and if you do not make them I will have to bye them. It would be better for you to make them and send them to me by railroad. You say you want me to study for a stand in my class. I had much rather not study text books so much but devote more of my time to reading as I believe it would be better for me. Besides I would have to study my eyes out and then perhaps not stand as high as I would wish. There was one of the boys suspended for six months for shooting off sky rockets and a cracker. I was glad of it for they were told if they did not quit that they would be suspended and sure enough it did happen. He was the smallest boy in college and in the fresh. class. He wanted to show off big but was mistaken. I must come to a close. Excuse this dirty paper for it is all that I could find. It has been lying on the table for more than a week. Write soon to me. Accept of my love. Give my love to Aunt Hannah and tell her to write to me.
Your Son
Thos J. Moore

If you make those shirts you can put them in a small box and direct to me at South Carolina College. I wish you would send me two feather pillows. We have nothing but old cotton ones, I had as leave lay my head on a log. You may box them up and direct the same time that [you write me] a letter that I may know you have sent them. Excuse bad writing. I expect you have found work to read it.
T. J. Moore

[23] Andrew Charles Moore to Nancy Montgomery Moore

Univty of Va Feb 4th 1860
(Saturday night 12 o'clock)

My Dear Mother

Your letter gave me the greatest possible pleasure, for it was very full of news & just such things as I wished to hear. Our cotton crop has turned out rather better than I expected. When you next write be sure to tell me about the corn crop. I suppose it was good enough. Your mention of sausages, spare ribs, etc makes me feel hungry. I assure you we don't have any extra eating here.

You speak of Tom's [brother] extravagance; I think in your letters you ought specially to charge him about spending money foolishly; and also you ought to try and get him out of some of his useless habits. I think it must have been owing to nothing but carelessness, that he was so long about getting off to Columbia from Spartanburg & was left at Union after starting. He ought to know that it is too dear a breakfast to wait a day for, as he told me they left him while he was getting breakfast. I do not know that you did wrong in buying the H's place[1] considering the motives for which you took it, though as far as the value of the place is concerned, I would not have it. It was a piece of kindness in you toward your children that induced you to buy it & so I feel truly grateful as one of them. The corn and cotton saved by keeping out such a fellow as Cathcart will in a few years pay for the place, saying nothing about the moral advantage on the negroes by preventing white people from trading with them. As to the mule trade, so far as I am concerned, I am perfectly satisfied. & have no doubt that every one also will be. According to the way mules are selling, if they were young & of good size, Mr. Hill did not pay too dear. And I recommend that all the older horses be sold off, even if they have to go cheap, for the difference in the work of a good horse, will soon make up for any deficiency in the price of the old horse. I have made the acquaintance of Crook since you wrote. He is a fine looking fellow & as much of a gentleman as any of my acquaintances here. He is coming to Spartanburg next summer & wishes to arrive in time for Wofford Commencement,[2] which he will barely have time to do, as we can't leave here before the 4th of July. From what I have heard you say about Cousin Tom Moore,[3] I think his son is much like him. He is very polite, gentlemanly, dignified, & clever in every way. We frequently visit. He room about ½ mile from me. I intend stopping a while with him in Charlotte & will try to bring him home with me if possible.

The money in the check you sent me has been nearly all spent. My book bill so far has been the respectable sum of $89.00. What goes with my cotton money? Also what went with the note in Tollison & Wingo that I sent back to you? You never acknowledged the receipt of it.

We have now an abundance of snow. Most of the time the weather here has been quite warm, a thing I did not expect to find so far north. Even when it is cold I do not feel it much. I wear woolen undershirts and drawers.

I received a letter from Tom, Sister, Mary & Jimmie a few days since; they are all well. Yesterday I heard from Watson [S.C. College friend]. He is going to teach another year in Beaufort Dist.

What has become of your buggy? I hope you have disposed of it satisfactorily. Hoping this will find all well I close
Your affectionate son
Andrew C. Moore

1. Apparently an adjacent piece of land.

2. Wofford is a liberal arts college in Spartanburg, South Carolina; it was chartered in 1851.

3. Son of Gen. Thomas Moore and Mary Reagan, he married a Miss Irwin of Charlotte, North Carolina. The son referred to is Dr. T. J. Moore, who became a physician in Richmond, Virginia.

[24] Andrew Charles Moore to Nancy Montgomery Moore

Univty of Va Feb. 19th 1860

My Dear Mother

Before retiring tonight I will drop you a few lines. I have just returned from Tom Moore's [Thomas J. Moore of Charlotte, N.C.] room with whom I spent this whole evening. He and his room-mate are very companionable fellows & I always enjoy their company. The weather is now quite cold, & the ground all covered with snow. Lately we have been blessed with a snow every few days, which is anything but agreeable. The greatest objection to cold weather here is that it requires a large quantity of wood to keep comfortable fires. And this is certainly a great objection, considering that I have to pay four dollars for a common load of wood. My wood bill is enormous, as well as all other things bought here.

I am very glad to think that the session is now more than half gone, for I am very anxious to get home again. I do not think I will ever have the slightest cause to regret the session spent at the University for I do think that I will have learned more Law in the nine months here than I would have learned in two years away. I do think that a Law office is a poor place to learn a great deal about the Law. We have a Moot-court in which a Professor acts as Judge & this gives all the advantages of an actual practice of the Law in the common courts. A Moot-court is just the same as any other court, only instead of trying real cases, they are all fictitious, being prepared by the Professor for the purpose of exercising the Law class in legal practice. I flatter myself that when I leave here, I will know a good deal about Law & how to practice in a court.

I received a letter from Selwyn Evins a few days since. He is still at Washington College, just to the west of the University, in Rockbridge County, so called because the Natural Bridge over James River is in that county. The small pox has disappeared entirely & he did not catch it. Also I received a letter from his mother, Cousin Mary Evins. All our relations, she wrote, were well except Cousin Hamilton Moore, who has been quite sick for some time. His lungs are thought to be seriously affected & he is thought not to be a long liver.

As I am entirely out of money & as I might as well try to live without heat here as without money, I must ask you to send me about $50.00 as soon as possible. I have not the means now of procuring wood, lights. etc & hope you will not allow any delay. I thought I would not need more before the end of the session, but one thing, or another, has completely drained my purse. You have no idea how money disappears when almost every man who looks at you must be paid for so doing. My book bill this year will not be a dollar under $100.00. I have now quite a respectable array of Law books.

Hoping this will find you all well, I must close.
Your affectionate son
A. C. Moore

N.B. Did you not make a mistake in saying I made 40 bales of cotton. I thought it was 39. Please tell me what has become of the money for which it was sold.
A.C.M.

[25] Thomas John Moore to Nancy Montgomery Moore

South Carolina College
February 27th, 1860

My Dear Ma:

Your very kind letter was received a few days ago and now I seat myself to answer the same. I was very glad to hear from you as it is very seldom that I get a letter from home. I got Aunt Hannah's letter about a week or two weeks ago and have not answered it yet. I suppose that she will not like it, but I will write to her in a few days. I suppose that she will be at Grand Ma's . . . Sister is at home now. You must make her answer my letters . . . You will not be lonely now. Jimmie [Means] is there I suppose and it will keep you busy to attend to him. We have a very dull time here. At least I do. I do not like to be bound up in a Town. The arrangements about our rising in the morning and going to recitation before breakfast, our dinner and suppertime and almost everything is different from what I have been used to and makes me feel very much like going home. But I will get used to it after a while and will not mind it.

I suppose that you have heard of the death of Col. [James Henderson] Irby of Laurens which was caused by an apoplectic fit. His son was in college here but went home on yesterday. His son I suppose will now go to ruin as he will have his own way. He came to College last year, applied for Soph. class but had to take Fresh. Stayed in Fresh. all the year and did not take Soph. Then he took Fresh. the second time and if he comes back he will not rise. We have a good many such fellows in College as he. College seems like a common school. I can see but little difference between the boys. Do not seem to be any smarter here than anywhere else.

Byrd [roommate] says that he thought he would be elated on entering college, but has come to the conclusion that he is as small as ever. Our examination will come off in about a month. That is at the 1st of April. I do not expect to stand first nor second. I will be somewhere amoungst the middle ones. I have not studied as hard as some have and of course they will stand first. I am not a good mathematician and to stand well a man must have all good qualities. You need not think I have studied none at all by my talking as I do for I have learned more since I have been here that I have done in a long time. There are some here who study very little. I can't see how they ever get through the examinations.

I have no more news that will interest so I will stop. You must write to me often. Give my love to all.

Your son,
Thomas J. Moore

[26] Andrew Charles Moore to Nancy Montgomery Moore

Univty of Va. Feb. 29th 1860

My Dear Mother

I have just received your letter saying that you had written twice since I had. I suppose my letters have not gone as they should, for I certainly have written regularly. The account you enclosed is for some books for Tom in Columbia, as Sam [Means] & I went down to Fla last year. I will write to him & have the debt paid. They were books Tom could not get at Spartanburg.

I am glad Uncle Franklin [Montgomery] is doing well in Texas, & think Uncle Prater [Montgomery] ought by all means to go. I guess he would go were it not for Grandma. But I cannot see the great necessity for his remaining even on her account. It seems to me that if she could get a prudent man to attend to her business, & have Uncle Theron [Montgomery] to look over his management occasionally, she could get along quite as well as she does. One thing is certain Uncle

Prater will never do much for himself in the way of making money, as long as he remains where he is.

I am glad to hear you spend considerable time in visiting and receiving visits; for then I know you are not lonesome. I have been in a number of places but never have I seen a place like Spartanburg as to friendly intercourse with your neighbors & friends. Here people who live in sight hardly know each other, if we are to judge from the amount of their visiting. This is not the case in other places where I have been.

I heard from Tom a few days since. He says Sumpter told him in Ca [Columbia?] that Sam was getting tired of Fla. As for myself I do not think I could like Fla on account of the sand & chills.

The weather here is getting to feel like Spring. Fire for several days has been useless, & I hope will continue so, as it costs $4.00 a load. My wood bill & book bill has been enormous.

Send me $50.00 *without delay*, as I am in daily need of money & have not one cent. I shall expect it as soon as I can receive an answer to this.

It gives me great pleasure to think there are but four months of the session remaining. I am going to stop in Charlotte a few days, & bring Tom Moore over to see his relations in Spartanburg. He says there are some Morrisons living at Charlotte, who are related to the Moores. Their grandfather and mine were first cousins & so we are third cousins. Do you know anything of them?

The bell is now ringing for dinner & I must close. Give my love to Sister & write soon to—
Your affectionate son
A. C. Moore

[27] Andrew Charles Moore to Nancy Montgomery Moore

University of Va April 19th/60

My Dear Mother

I do not recollect whether I answered your last or not, & beg you to excuse me, if I appear to have been negligent about writing. Time passes by so rapidly that weeks seem but days. & when I think it has been but a few days since I wrote, upon counting up I am surprised to find it has been weeks instead of days. It seems to me that my time is so short, that when I use the greatest exertion in studying, I seem to accomplish nothing. Still I know that every day my legal knowledge is somewhat increased, & I flatter myself that I know more law than some of those that have been at the study of it for a much longer time. I have a case now in the Moot-court of the University. Today I filed a declaration which is the first thing done in a lawsuit. The trial will come off soon, & then I expect to make my first legal speech. This I think a bold proceeding for a six-months lawyer. Duncan, of Greenville So. Ca is my assistant, & I feel certain we will gain the suit.

Sister wrote that you wished me to buy you a watch. If you will send the money I will get it. I suppose you will wish a fine one, for I know you do not believe in things of cheap quality, & fine watches are always better timepieces.

Cousin A. B. Moore wrote me a month since, informing me that he would go North about the last of May, & asking me to accompany him. I am anxious to visit the North & as I shall never have a better opportunity in the way of good & instructive company, I wrote him that I would go. He said if I would go, he would come by the University for me. Mr. Napoleon Lockett & lady (Cousin Mat's fatherinlaw and motherinlaw), Sue Lockett (their daughter), Miss Mary Jones, their neice, Annie Moore, Mary and Eliza Foster will be in the party. I received a letter from Eliza Foster today. She says they are busy making preparations.

I think you had better ponder well before you buy Posey's land. You cannot be certain that you will continue in S. Ca., for it will not surprise me if all your children should someday move away . . . I am sure that I can not afford to live in Spartanburg for the reason that I know I can do so much better elsewhere.

I am glad to learn my nephew can talk so well. I have a curiosity to see him. You had better make some disposition of Flora's pups, sink them in the river if you think fit; for I guess they are half hounds.

Tell Mr. Hill to buy me a check for $350.00 & send it soon. I do not know how much my expenses North will be, as I do not know how far I shall travel & how long be gone & so write for probably a good deal more than I shall need. A good deal of the amount I have written for will be spent in getting away from here. Also I want Mr. Hill to buy a check for $41.00 on either New York, Charleston, or Savannah. The last check I want sent to Wm. Means, & he will pay it over to Fryer for my fiddle. If Mr. Hill has not the money in hand, Col Evins may have some. You had better buy a separate check, with which I can buy you a watch in New York. Tell me what sort of watch you like, whether single-or double cased, large or small, cheap or dear. Give my best love to Sister & Jimmie.

Your affectionate son
A. C. Moore

N.B. I shall start North about the 20th May

[28] Thomas John Moore to Nancy Montgomery Moore

April 28th, 1860 *South Carolina College*

My Dear Ma:

. . . I have been sick all this week with the Dysentary and was in bed most all the time but am getting better. I was taken with it on last Saturday and have not been out of sight of my room since then. I had a Doctor tending on me for the last few days. He came to see me four or five times. Was here night before last but will come no more. . . . You know I am subject to the disease, but this [time] had had it much more than I ever did before. The dysentery and diarrohea seem to be very prevalent disease about here. There have been several in College besides myself who have had it. One student had it so bad that he has gone home and I too felt much like going on a trip home. I have been boarding with an old negro who lives in the Campus for the last few days as I could not get anything from my boarding house. I would tell my tenement boy to go get me something to eat which he would do whenever he got ready. I think when I get able I shall have to brush him a little. Since I got sick I have been bored nearly to death by some Charleston fellers above me. I am going to take another room. Those fellers can keep as much fuss as a pack of negroes at a cornshucking if anything a little more . . . I beg you now not to be uneasy as I will soon be well.
I remain your Son
Thomas Moore

[29] Andrew Charles Moore to Nancy Montgomery Moore

University of Va May 21st 1860

My Dear Mother

Your letter came duly to hand & was perused with much pleasure. I should have written sooner but have been waiting for our friends from Alabama so that I might be able to write something definite about my trip North. They have not arrived yet, though they were to have started on the 15th of this month. I have been looking for them every day for some days & having been so long disappointed, have quit expecting them on any particular day, & now am prepared to see them, or not, at any time. I will do the best I can in buying you a watch, & do not think $65.00 will get a first rate one. One of better quality will look better & not get out of repair, as all cheap watches do, more or less.

We have had quite a crowd of people at the University & in Charlottesville for the past week, during the sitting of the Episcopal Convention, which corresponds to our Synods, & the Methodist Conferences. The Convention has now adjourned & we have our usual quiet, much to my satisfaction.

Have you any of the seventeen years locusts? They are making the woods around this place perfectly alive with noise. For several days I thought they were frogs, & was surprised to find out they were the locusts, which kept up such a constant noise.

Summer has visited us at last, though the weather is very pleasant. Everybody here has an ice house & an abundance of ice, a thing we cannot obtain. The people dam up the branches in the winter, & the weather being cold, the water freezes over to the depth of several inches. In this way they secure large quantities of ice. It is strange to me it does not melt as they use no particular mode of preserving it. It is thrown into a great pit dug in the ground & covered over with nothing but straw. The sides of the pit are ceiled with plank, & no coal dust or anything of the kind, used. Ice must be more easily preserved than with us.

Tom wrote that Mr. Hill was planting a water-melon patch. I hope he will have a fine one by the time I get home & you may tell him I will take pleasure in seeing and helping him eat water-melons. They don't grow to much perfection in this country.

I eat some cherries a few days since. They were sweet & nice, better than any I have ever eaten. Strawberries are also on hand & very good. I bought a quart the other day for 16 cents & found them excellent, especially as they were the first fruit of the season that I had tasted.

You seem to be proud of your grandson.[1] I suppose I will hardly know him. Hoping this will find you all well I close. Give my love to all
Your affectionate son,
A. C. Moore

1. Andrew James Means (b. 1859), the son of Margaret Anna Moore Means and Capt. Samuel C. Means, died in a hunting accident on March 1, 1875.

[30] Andrew Charles Moore to Nancy Montgomery Moore

Washington City, May 31st 1860

My Dear Mother

Before going to bed I will drop you a few lines. I arrived here last Tuesday with the following company, Mr and Mrs Lockett, Misses Sue Lockett, Mary Jones, Cousins Mary and Eliza Foster & Annie Moore, Gov. Moore and Mr. Phelan, a young man and private secretary to the Gov. I doubt if there ever was a more pleasant party travelling together. We will remain here until Monday next & then will go to New York. This city is full of sights. Yesterday I went to the Patent Office & to the White House. At the former place there were so many curious things that I could not look at but a small proportion. You may know that it take a long time to look over the Patent Office when I tell you that it covers two squares. It is certainly an enormous building. There I saw the original Declaration of Independence, the clothes Gen Washington wore when he resigned his commission as Commander in Chief; the writing desk or rather a little case that Washington carried through every campaign of the Revolution; and of other curiosities such a number that it is useless to try to enumerate or even to recollect.

At the White House I saw a number of people but not the President.[1] It was six o'clock and the President was at dinner. The grounds about his house are magnificent, covered over with the most beautiful green grass & pretty trees. A band of 30 musicians made most delightful music before the President's door, & the people were promenading in every direction over the grounds.

I visited the Capitol today for the third time & saw the great men of the nation. They do not look better or smarter than other people & I must confess my ideas of great men is somewhat lessened. I, as well as the rest of the party, was introduced to the Vice-President, Breckinridge.[2] He is very polite and fine looking, pleasing me more than any of the celebrities I saw. The Gov. does not go about with us but remains at the hotel, his rheumatism has become worse since he left Ala. When at Montgomery he walked all about, but at Raleigh, N. Carolina had a crutch made which he now uses.

I saw today the largest cannon in the world. It weighs 49,000 pounds, measures four and a half feet at the breech and about one and a half feet at the muzzle.

Also I saw the Japanese you hear and read so much about. They go perfectly bareheaded, all wear swords, some two and others of lower rank but one. They are anything but good looking and about the color of mulattoes. At the hotel where they are staying there is a constant crowd around the windows trying to catch glimpses of them. One of them, whom they call one of the Doctors i.e. learned men of the Embassy, had a head shaved bare as your hand. The rest of them shave the top of the scalp and comb the rest of the hair to the middle of the scalp, where it is tied a few inches from the ends, and then made into a little bundle about the size of the little finger and sticking close to the head.

The party of our friends came by Charlottesville where I got into company. The Gov. will return to the Virginia Springs and wait for the rest of us. He did intend traveling north but his complaint growing worse he has concluded to leave us and go to the Springs. His business is to buy arms and he thinks he

Andrew Charles Moore ca. 1860. From the editor's collection

thinks he can be suited in this place. We will not get back to the Springs from the North until about 1st July.

Mary and Eliza Foster send their love to you. Give my love to all and write soon. Direct to New York where I shall be next week.

Your affectionate son,
Andrew C. Moore

1. James Buchanan, a Democrat, served as fifteenth president of the United States, 1857–61.

2. Later that year John C. Breckinridge became the presidential candidate of the proslavery Southern segment of the divided Democratic Party.

[31] Andrew Charles Moore to Margaret Anna Moore Means

New York
June 8, 1860

My Dear Sister,

Though I have not recovered from the effect of today's travels and am hardly in writing plight, I will scribble you a few lines. I reached this place today, having left Baltimore in the morning. As we were steaming along in the harbor this morning, just before landing we met another steamboat. Hearing the cry of "man overboard" I looked ahead and saw just in front a human creature struggling in the waves. Fortunately the boat was stopped just in time to avoid running over her and she was caught in the clothes with a hook. After being pulled aboard it proved a woman who had fallen from another vessel. She was much exhausted, but I suppose will recover.

I remained in Washington a week and visited every place of note in the city from Buchanan and Chip Lane[1] down. Wat Phelan (Gov. Moore's Secretary) and I called upon Stephen A. Douglas[2] and his young and beautiful wife. She is a lady of greatest personal beauty and most elegant manners. She entertained us most pleasantly and before leaving asked us to walk into an adjoining room where we found a sumptuous repast of strawberries, ice cream, and champagne. I also visited General Cass[3] in the Secretary of State's department, where I saw many curious things. The original Declaration of Independence, Washington's diary, Arnold's traitorous letter, in which he offered to sell his country. Major Andre's letter in which he begged to be shot rather than die on a gibbet; the Japanese treaty that you have seen so much about of late, etc., etc.

On last Monday in the Senate I heard Charles Sumner[4] of Brooks notoriety address the Senate for four hours on slavery. He called slavery "the sum of all villainies" and slaveholders "barbarians." It was surprising to hear how he told about pulling out negroes' toenails by the roots as punishment for running away: about cropping their ears to know them, hunting them with dogs, etc.

Gov. Moore remained at Washington. He will return to the Va. Springs as soon as he has procured the arms he was to purchase for Ala. He could get them in Washington and his health he thought too feeble to go the whole ways with us. We will join him about the 1st of July on our return.

From Washington we went to the Naval Academy in Annapolis Maryland where we stopped at the identical hotel in which General Washington was quartered and saw the building in which he resigned his commission. From Annapolis we passed up to Baltimore by steamboat on the Chesapeake Bay and thence to N. York, leaving Baltimore this morning.

In Washington, I visited the Japanese,[5] smoked their little brass pipes with bowls the size of the end of your little finger and filled with genuine Japanese tobacco. They politely filled their pipes, lit them, and asked me to smoke and drink a cup of tea which had no sugar in it. Also I visited Mt. Vernon, 11 miles below Washington on the very banks of the Potomac. The Father of his country lies beside his wife each in a splendid Sarcophagus, which are seen through a grated door of the vault. No less than 200 persons visited it at the same time as myself.

We will remain here a day or so and then go to West Point. Write soon and direct to New York as I will be here soon again. My letters to you and Ma are intended for both of you and you must show her this. My best love to Darrell and Jimmie.

Your affectionate brother,
Andrew

1. Senator Joseph H. "Chip" Lane was born in Buncombe County, North Carolina, and elected as a U.S. senator from Oregon in 1859. He was Breckinridge's vice-presidential running mate in 1860. A partisan of secession, he lost his senate seat in March 1861.

2. Stephen A. Douglas (1813–1861) served as a U.S. senator from Illinois, 1847–61. Known for his debates with Abraham Lincoln in their 1858 senate campaign, he was chosen as the presidential candidate of the "pro-sovereignty" portion of split Democratic Party in Baltimore on June 18, 1860, ten days after entertaining Andrew Charles Moore.

3. Lewis Cass (1782–1866) served as secretary of war in the Jackson administration, 1831–36; minister to France, 1836–42; Democratic presidential nominee, 1848; and secretary of state, 1857–60.

4. Charles Sumner (1811–1874), who served as a Massachusetts senator, 1851–74, was assaulted on the Senate floor by Rep. Preston Brooks of South Carolina on May 22, 1856.

5. The agreement with Japan on July 29, 1858, opened additional ports in Japan to American trade and established diplomatic recognition between the two countries. Apparently Andrew Charles Moore met with the recently arrived diplomatic delegation.

[32] Andrew Charles Moore to Nancy Montgomery Moore

Fifth Avenue Hotel, New York, June 13th/60

My Dear Mother

Before going to bed I will drop you a few lines. I shall remain here for some days yet and then go to West Point, where Mr. Lockett's son lives. Yesterday I went to Bartholf's Establishment and tried to find out what is the matter with your machine. I saw Bartholf himself. He could not tell me satisfactorily what is the matter and gave me two springs stronger than the one in the feed-wheel. He thought the present spring was perhaps too weak. I think the proper plan is to send the wheel by Mr. Judd or otherwise to the manufactory and have it put in order or get one of the improved kind. I saw not a single feed-wheel like yours, all of that style being out of use.

I have examined the ladies watches at the two most reputable jewelers in the city. I could suit you exactly, but fear I have not enough money to buy such a one as I think you ought to have. I will be from home longer than I expected and besides expenses are heavier than I calculated upon. I could buy a watch such as you have named but that price is the lowest and the watch is the most inferior they have. Cheap watches look almost the same as the first rate article and for a time run as well, but they lack durability. Look at my watch. It cost a good price and a long time since and now it is as good as the day it came out of the maker's hand. And finally the main reason why I do not wish to buy the cheapest watch I have been shown is that you are very able to wear a fine watch and I want my mother to have as fine a watch as anybody else's mother. I will not get the watch now but you shall not be put to any more trouble about it for I will have one got that will suit you. I intended buying a trunk but expecting to be short of money, I shall send back by some of our merchants.

This hotel is a superb affair called from its location on 5th Avenue street, the 5th Avenue Hotel. It is six stories high, built of marble, and most superbly furnished. You are carried up and down stairs on the "vertical railway" and there is nothing you can possibly want that a servant will not bring to your room in a few minutes after the ringing of the bell. You can eat at almost any hour of the day of the most sumptuous fare. Indeed I do not see how, considering the fare and other things, the proprietors can make money boarding at even $2.50 a day. I will show you when I come home some bills of fare that you may form an idea of the good eating at a N.Y. first class hotel.

Edward Buist is in N. York studying medicine in a dispensary, a place where medicines are furnished to the poor at the expense of the city. Mr. Adger and family, or part of them, are staying at this hotel. He has not yet returned from the General Assembly.

It is seldom that I see a negro here. All the servants are white and I can now order a man as white as myself to black my boots with perfect unconcern, though it seemed wrong at first; I like them much better than negroes; they are quite as obedient; much quicker, and more trusty. They all seem to be watching an opportunity to wait upon you.

Day before yesterday I went over to Long Island to witness a trot between the two fastest trotters in the world, Flora Temple and Geo. M. Patchen. I never saw such trotting before. Patchen beat. They trotted 2 miles in 4 minutes 53 seconds. Write to me at New York care of L. H. Seawell.

Your affectionate son,

Andrew

[33] Thomas John Moore to Nancy Montgomery Moore

June 15th, 1860
Columbia

My. Dear Ma:

Your very kind and welcome letter was received by yesterdays mail and I now hasten to reply while I have some leisure moments. The time will soon be here when I shall come home and see you all once more which I am very anxious to do. Our examination will begin on next Tuesday and end on Tuesday week. I will leave Columbia on Wednesday and will expect you to meet me at Spartanburg. I am very anxious for our examination to come off for I do hate to think about it. I had far rather go to the field and plough a week than stand an examination such as we have here. It completely breaks a body down by writing all day and studying when he is out of the room. I got a letter from Sister and Bud on yesterday as well as from you. This is something unusual, that is getting a letter from each one of you at the same time. Bud was in New York when he wrote and enjoying himself finely. While at Washington he went to see Buchanan and Chip Lane. He also called on some Japanese and smoked a pipe and then took tea with them. From there they went to Anapolis, the capital of Maryland. They put up at the identical hotel where Gen. Washington once had his troops quartered. They then went to the immense city of New York as he called it. Says that he gets the best eatings that could be thought of and can tell a white man to black his boots with impunity. He says you need not walk up and down stairs of a house unless you want to but only step in a little machine which will carry you safely. I wish I had one to carry me up and down as I am on the second floor.

Gov. Moore's rheumatism bothers him a great deal. He could not go on with them but stopped at the warm springs of Virginia. Bud bought him a setter puppy in Virginia which Austin is to bring home. I think that we will thin out a few of the birds when we get home. . . .

I am very sorry that I cannot be off from here one day sooner so as to go to the examinations at Reidville. You would like to go I suppose. I must come to a close as it is awful hot. Give my love to all and accept a share for yourself. . . .
Your affectionate son,
Thomas J. Moore

On December 20, 1860, when South Carolina seceded from the Union, Andrew Moore had completed his law studies and was living in Alabama. He had married his cousin Mary Foster and was starting the practice of law in Marion, Perry County. John Crawford Anderson was in his second year at the Citadel in Charleston, and Thomas John Moore was enrolled at South Carolina College. Their lives were immediately and inalterably changed.

Letters, 1861

As 1861 dawned, John Crawford Anderson was still a Citadel cadet, Thomas John Moore remained a student at South Carolina College, and Franklin Leland Anderson was tending to his plantation. On April 12, Confederate forces fired upon the federal garrison at Fort Sumter in Charleston Harbor and controlled the small island two days later. War began in earnest. Prior to the war Frank had been a member of the local Spartan Rifles and thus was in the first group of Spartanburg County troops dispatched to Virginia, becoming a part of the Fifth Regiment, South Carolina Volunteers, in the buildup to the First Battle of Manassas on July 21. Tom left college briefly to serve in Charleston when Fort Sumter fell, and then again when Union troops took Port Royal. Andrew left Alabama and returned to South Carolina to enlist in the Eighteenth Regiment, South Carolina Volunteers. He finished the year in Virginia.

At home the Spartanburg community began to see shortages of basic goods as the blockade of the coast tightened. Salt was particularly hard to acquire.

Hettie Brockman suffered a two-month-long bout with typhoid fever. Her parents' estate was finally settled, with her older sister Lucy Earle's husband buying the Old Place. Hettie and Ella left the Andersons' home and moved in with the Earles. Ella returned to Limestone College that fall. John was often called out of the Citadel for training camps.

David Anderson began selling flour and later hams to the Confederacy, and the first deaths of neighbors and cousins in the war were reported.

[34] Andrew Charles Moore to Nancy Montgomery Moore Evins[1]

Perry County, Ala.
Feb. 24th, 1861

My Dear Mother

My last to you was dated a week since. In it I stated that I had been quite sick, & that Mary [Mary Foster Moore] was then sick, but that I hoped she would become better soon. Quite to the contrary, she is now worse than then. Her attack is somewhat like pneumonia, but is not exactly the same, and bids fair to be a serious one. She suffers a great deal, from intense sickness. I am no better myself. Really I do not know what is the matter. My whole system seems to be generally deranged. Last night I suffered a while from a pain in my left hip joint, which finally changed to my right thigh bone. This morning I feel no symptoms of it.

I have been anxious to get back to S. Carolina for some time, but have been unable to move. The time has come when every man must gird on his armor, & take the field or submit to despotism. We must fight now, or lose our all. None are more willing than myself, & before this I would have been in the field had my health permitted. I wish you would inform me if any new companies are forming in Spartanburg, or if any more are called for by the State. If so I shall hasten home to unite myself with one of them, as soon as I am able to leave here with safety. I am opposed to joining an old company, hence I ask about new ones. Col. [S. N.] Evins knows what troops are needed, & what companies are raising to supply them.

Dr. Foster's family are well. He says you are the next nicest lady to his wife & sister [Margaret Anna Moore Means] is next to Mary [in his affection]. He thinks a great deal of you all. Sel Evins has not reached home yet, probably due to the destruction of Railroads by late rains.

Give my love to all, & answer this immediately.

Your Af. Son
A. C. Moore

1. Nancy Montgomery Moore had married Col. S. N. Evins on December 20, 1860.

[35] Nancy Moore Evins to Thomas John Moore

March 4th, 1861

My Dear Thomas,

I received your letter by last mail, was glad to hear you were enjoying good health, and that you had such a clever set of boys in your tenement. I hope you are improving your time to the best advantage, nothing would give me more pleasure than to hear of your well doing.

I am very much mortified to think I do not seem to be your mother now [following her remarriage]. I do assure you that you are as near my heart as you ever were. I often think how long it will be before I can see you. I do not think you ought to complain so much. I think you ought to write two letters to my one, knowing I have so much to see to. Andrew and Mary stay pretty much to themselves. He says he is so busy reading he has time for very little else. You wished to know where I were living. I am at my own home [Fredonia], where I expect to stay, at least for some time. If I were to prefer going to Reedville, I think Col. [S. N. Evins] would build a house there. I have made only one visit to Reedville, have staid two nights at Col. He goes up to see them very often, as his business calls him there. I have not been to your Grand Ma[1] since you left. Intend on going tomorrow if nothing prevent. I suppose Andrew wrote you about Unkle Theron's [a Mongomery relative] misfortunes in getting his house and a negro house burnt. Saived but very little as there was no one at the house but Sally and a negro woman, it was a very windy day. The fire was first discovered in a small room in the kitchen just beyond the seller door, think a spark must have blown in there. He had been having some work done to the house. The men had finished and taken their tools away the day before. They have put up a negro house and are living in it. He had the misfortune to get his leg badly cut and has not been able to work since. I am very sorry for them, feel that I ought to do something for them The schools at Reedville are not large, the male is near thirty and the female numbers 33. They are pleased with Miss Galloway. Mrs. Butler and her daughter are at Spartanburg teaching. The trustees met Friday. Ann went with Mr. Means, came to Col. Evins that evening. Sam and Andy [Sam Means and Andrew Evins] went to the village to muster. Ann staid with Margaret untill Sunday and went to church. Jimmie [Means, her grandson] staid with me. He is a fine little fellow.

I cannot tell you much about the farm, are clearing on all the places, and seem to be very busy. I have been gardning some, have potatoes, peas, and cabbage plants coming on. We are enjoying good health hope these find you enjoying same . . . Col. Evins says he will write to you soon.

All join in much love to you,
Your Mother N.M.E.

1. Probably Margaret Miller Montgomery, wife of attorney John Montgomery. She died in 1882. His other grandmother, Mary Moore, died in 1805. T. J. Moore was born when his father was seventy-two.

Fredonia, the home of Thomas John Moore and Mary Elizabeth Anderson Moore (rear), Nancy Montgomery Moore (in chair), Henrietta Sue Moore (on the ground), ca. 1895. From the editor's collection

[36] Franklin Leland Anderson to Mary Elizabeth Anderson

McLain's Ford, Va.
July 11, 1861

Miss Mary Anderson
Dear Niece

I was agreably surprised yesterday morning before leaving camp upon being handed another long and interesting letter from you, I hope such punctuality will characterize our correspondence in the future and that you will continue to be liberal enough as not to be ceremonious about an answer to all your letters.

I left Camp Walker about 9 o'clock A.M. yesterday on what is called Picket or Brigade guard, which is designed to scan the country two or three miles around camp, challenge suspicious persons, and give the alarm in case of an approach of the enemy. This duty is about as pleasant as that in Camp on account of the change and recreation it gives and is considered but little more dangerous as there is a large body of troops between us and the enemy. But our last night's experience says there must be one condition to the above, viz., provided the weather is good. About an hour by sun a dark cloud came up and in a little time the rain was upon us with no shelter but our blankets and the woods. After the first shower however we remembered a house a mile off where there was a large stone barn to which we resorted and asked to shelter in it for the night to which the Landlord kindly consented and also gave us a hot coffee supper. About 11 o'clock it broke off and we retraced our steps to our posts, built up a large fire, and were this morning dry and comfortable. If we could only have a hot breakfast which we will not get until 12 m. [noon] at which time we are relieved and we return to camp. But this privation is alone owing to the rain as we had made our engagement for breakfast this morning but the grass and all is so wet that we think it will not pay to go after it. Old Abe's message is in camp and excites much ridicule.[1] We take the amount of money and number of men for which he calls as an acknowledgement to the world that we are not the handful of Rebbells that he has represented us to be, and that he could not have done a better thing to inshure our respectability, if not our recognition abroad. But the most ridiculous feature of the document is that he is not yet able to appreciate the self sacrificing determination of the Southern people to be free, but holds to the idea that upon a "fair test there is no Southern state save perhaps So Ca" in which there is not still a majority for the Union. With such delusions possessing the Northern mind it is not astonishing they persist in what they call a "suppression of a rebelion." I fear there is nothing short of a bloody war that will undermine them and establish our independence as a Confederacy and which if they persist in provoking we will as cheerfully give. But enough of Old Abe and the War. Suffise it to say we are conscious of the justice of our cause and are willing to leave the consequences to the great Disposer of events. I was sorry to hear of Dr. Buist's[2] determination to leave the College as I think he had the position above all others in which he could be most useful. He is certainly a much better teacher than preacher.

. . . Tell Aunt Hettie[3] the blue ribbon, though soiled and faded as might be expected in a soldier's keeping, still has its place on Andy's [Andrew Evins] gun and serves as a distinguishing mark from the rest. I had a letter from Uncle Mike a few days since, all well. Aunt Margaret's health has been better this summer than for several past.[4] She has done a great deal of serving for the Soldiers. He will make between twelve and fifteen hundred bushels of wheat. Give my love to Nettie and tell her to write to me. When you receive this mount the fillies if they are idle and [ride] up and read it to Aunt Sue and little Julia [his wife and daughter]. How I wish I could be there this morning to breakfast, but I expect Rufus [slave] will have something nice fixed when I get back to camp and will cheerfully

forego the pleasure. Give them my love, also Pa, Ma, and the children.
Truly yours, "Uncle Frank"

1. That summer President Abraham Lincoln finally acknowledged a state of war with the South.

2. The Reverend Dr. E. T. Buist, head of Laurensville Academy and College, whose daughter Emma married John Crawford Anderson in 1866.

3. The aunts and uncles referred to would be the recipient's aunts and uncles.

4. Here he is referring to his brother Michael Miller Anderson and Michael's wife, Margaret.

[37] Hettie Brockman to John Crawford Anderson

Addressed to: CDT. J. C. Anderson
Citadel Academy
Charleston, SC

Pleasant Falls, Oct 3rd, 1861

Dear Johnnie,

Your kind messenger has been welcomed with a heart full of gratitude. It is ever "a pleasure to love and be loved and if I understand a [illegible].

You cannot imagine how disappointed I felt when I arrived and found no Johnnie to welcome me home again with his brightly beaming smiles and kind words. I was quite gloomy for several days. But I have since revived and have taken quite a delightful trip to Columbia. Your father and I went down on Wednesday. We fortunately met with Col. Edwards [Col. Oliver Evans Edwards of the 13th Regiment, South Carolina Volunteers] in the City whose kindness I am deeply indebted during my stay in Columbia. We visited Camp that evening and made some arrangements about presenting the flag to the Brockman Guards.[1]

The next morning bright and early we arrived at Camp. Found all quite busy. I formed many acquaintances, some very pleasant, among them your friend Davidson! I was perfectly charmed with him! And Col. Edwards says he took quite a fancy to me—anyway we chatted to a considerable extent. He gathered me some wild flowers and gave them to me as remembrances. Oh! I did love to hear him talk—he uses such sweetly flowing language—at our parting he expressed a fervent hope that we would meet again.

Everything of course was around to see and it was with decided interest that I listened to explanations of the wonders of Camp life.

But the most trying moment to me was at 1:00 o'clock when the flag was presented. Col. Edwards delivered the presentation speech and of course came up to our expectations He would have me to stand beside him in the center of the square formed for the Speakers. Ben [Brockman] was very much frightened but made a few appropriate remarks rather better than I expected. He gave it to the Colour bearer who was Tom Davis (old Billy's son) who made a short amusing speech which elicited applause and a hearty laugh from all.

I feel highly gratified with my visit thought of you and wished you could have been there to have enjoyed it with me.

(Monday morning) Well Johnnie I have arose quite early this morning. I find it awful cold. I can scarcely hold my pen—do excuse all uncomliness.

I received a letter from Sister Mary on Saturday. She is coming over soon and is anxious that I should go home with her. I have only one objection—that of leaving my dear old State in this hour of trial.[2] Of course I don't flatter myself that I could be of any benefit whatever by remaining, but you know that we are prone to love the land of our birth and in times like the present would wish to share her every trial and affliction. The patriotic Mr. S. Means and A. Moore [brothers-in-law Sam Means and Andrew Charles Moore] has arrived in our vicinity to cheer us with the news of the "dreadful winter they are going to have in old Virginia" if they cannot stand it how many of the noble and brave will breathe away their useful lives in this cause of liberty and only the lazy would-be patriots to enjoy the independence who never once raised a hand to grasp it from the terrible hands of Tyranny. You know these men are mature, stout, able men. Far more better off in worldly goods than thousands of our good soldiers. But this is enough.

Our little family circle enjoys continued good health. All join me with much love to you. We are always delighted to receive a letter from you.

Write soon to me. You must not postpone writing as long as I have, you know the reason now.

Yours with sincere affections,
Hettie Brockman

1. The Brockman Guards were Company B, Thirteenth Regiment, South Carolina Volunteers, of which Hettie's older brothers Benjamin T. Brockman and Jesse K. Brockman were members.

2. Mary B. Harris, Hettie's older sister, lived in Rutherfordton, North Carolina.

[38] Hettie Brockman to John Crawford Anderson

Addressed to: Lt. J. C. Anderson
Lightwood Knot Springs
Columbia, SC

Pleasant Falls
Oct. 3rd, 1861

Dear Johnnie—

I have been very much disappointed by not receiving a word or two of remembrance from your worthy self.

But I believe you claim a reply to an unanswered letter. Anyway, I will waive all ceremony and proceed in giving you a few iotas of home life.

First of all the good Mother [Harriet Brockman Anderson] of our homestead is now on a visit of love and mercy. She left us Sunday morning to see Sister Fannie.[1] Jimmie [James Henry Anderson] returned this morning leaving Sister H

Pleasant Falls, the home of Capt. David and Harriet Anderson. From Edward Lee Anderson, *A History of the Anderson Family, 1706–1955* (Columbia, S.C.: R. L. Bryan Company, 1955); used with permission

[Hettie] with her and bringing to our hearts the sad intelligence that her span of life was rapidly drawing to a close and Sister could not think of leaving her in her last hours of suffering.

I received a letter from Brother Ben [Brockman] today. I am glad you all survived the tremendous gale of Friday last.[2] Tell him to send the flag on to Spartanburg if he thinks he can spare the time. The Ladies are anxious to see it and wish to make proper assignments about who's to present it...

But enough of this until we are once again blessed with the radiance of your countenance. Johnnie, I do hope you will be successful in securing a furlough. It already seems a long time since we parted. We have all spoken of you so frequently and we always have you associated with the bright, happy scenes of the lamented past.

But you ought to be here to witness our industry in domestic affairs. One day Mamie [sister Mary Lavinia Brockman], Nettie and I concluded to make up a whole program of articles—muslins for table use and so on. I wish you could only taste Mamie's Salad, my preserves, and Nettie's wine. I think your decision of these several virtues would perhaps be encouraging, as you are better prepared to appreciate delicacies.

We received a letter from Ella. She spoke of receiving a treat from you in the shape of an Epistle. She is in high spirits but speaks of being besieged with the "Blues" occasionally.

Oh! I miss the beautiful moonlight so much, but the music of the waters are unceasing in their melody.[3] I wish you and some other loved ones were near—we might enjoy it so much more.

We have been very profitably engaged of late in traversing the woods in search of Grapes and Muskadines. One evening we took a complete pound. We often thought of our noble Soldiers especially when our march was directed up a steep and rugged hillside. Twas then that Nettie (our Capt.) would encourage our drooping spirits and inspire life into our tired limbs by calling out in thrilling eloquence "On Carolinians. On to glory!" We encountered many difficulties such as a skirmish with "Yellow jackets" and being compelled to invade a portion of country thickly settled with "Beggar lice" which though of vegetable growth gave great annoyance. But we were doubly repaid in coming off victorious with many trophies. Johnnie please try and get Mamie and I an ounce apiece of "Gum [Tales?]" and bring it up with you. I am sorry I did not have the haversack complete to send down by Ben, it might have added a mite to your comfort. But the pattern has been misplaced and I have not been able to do anything toward finishing it for use.

Oh! I forgot to inform you of the important move made in our kitchen apparatus. The new kitchen has received the "finished touch" we are all fascinated with the delightful changes.

Give my love to Ben and Jesse I will reply to Ben's letter soon. Mamie, Nettie, and the rest of the children send an immeasurable quantity of love to you. Darkies send "Howdy do's" and so on.

Hoping you will excuse this dreadful apology for a letter and consider only the motives that prompted me to write and sincerely wishing to see you soon

I remain your devoted Auntie Be a good Boy and may God bless you.
Hettie

PS: October 4th
Friday morning

Well Johnnie I have just read over the eight pages I scribbled last night. I find that I have not told you half what I wanted to. I did not tell you of Willie Roebuck's return and that I received a letter from him saying he intended to call in a short time.

Nettie begs me to inform you of two exceedingly interesting letters received from your Camp soon after your departure. I wish you could see them. I think you would enjoy a hearty laugh over them. One from Mr. Hadden and the other from Long.

We have just received the sad intelligence of the death of Mr. Nesbit who had only a few days previous returned from Virginia on a visit to a sick son. The last accounts from his Son was desponding to the afflicted family.

Do write soon and tell if you have heard from "Lilias" [code name for John's girlfriend] recently. I hope you will be home in a few days as we can talk more satisfactorily than we can write.

Sincerely yours,
Hettie

1. Frances E. Brockman Stokes, who died October 7, 1861.

2. This implies that John had enlisted in the Thirteenth Regiment, South Carolina Volunteers, and was apparently on leave from Arsenal Academy.

3. Pleasant Falls is situated on a hill overlooking shoals in the North Tyger River.

[39] Ella Brockman to John Crawford Anderson
Addressed to: Cadet J. C. Anderson
Lightwood Knot Spring
Columbia, SC

Limestone, Schoolroom
October 6th [1861]

Dear Johnie,

I was very glad indeed to receive your letter last week, as I was very homesick at the time. It searved to arouse my spirits, how I wish I could get letters every mail I don't think there would be any use of having the blues if they contained as much life as yours, but mind I think I will give you a little scolding about it.

Your letter was full of the names of young ladies, how they looked and said and a thousand other things which I know I could not have seen if I had a half dozen eyes, but Johnie I really do think you are very fickel, but the one you mentioned, first L.L. who can she be? is it the spotted or the blushing beauty as I should have said I love her better than all the rest although you did not seem to care a cent for her in your last letter, but you were continually on the eve of asking some of the Spartanburg girls to shear [share] your lot with you but the one you love best is the one. Don't be so fickel when you get in their company. Well, Johnie, what do you think the young ladies of Limestone thought of you, I heard it spoken all around me if he was not a married man [meaning seeing someone, as John did not marry until 1866] he could win a good many hearts by his brass buttons and look but poor fellow it is a pity he is going to leave his little wife.

I received a bundle from home and am quite out of the [h]umor because they did not write a note. It does me so much good to hear from my friends.

It will soon be a month since I first came hear, how rapidly the time flies, I think I have been sader this session than I ever was before. School will be out on the 4th of December I will want to go home a few days and I will be [illegible] in perfect idleness I hope you will be home then as I expect many nice times this winter.

I have received a letter from Nettie,[1] seven pages long, this morning I am quite in a glee I have been eating fruit all day and had my hair shingled off. You might know I look like a goose, but a little better than before. I received a letter from brother Ben [Brockman] last week, I have answered it. Tell Jessie and Ben to write me when they can.

Johnie the time is precious. I dislike to write in such a hurry but pleas excuse this time . . . Give much love to my brothers Yours affectionately
Ella

Excuse the scarcity of paper[2]

1. Nettie, John's sister Henrietta Alethia Anderson, is Ella's niece, but the two are nearly the same age.
2. This reference to "scarcity" is the first of many to come in later letters.

[40] Mary Elizabeth Anderson to John Crawford Anderson

Addressed to: Cadet J. C. Anderson
Citadel Academy
Charleston, So Car

Pleasant Falls,
Oct. 19, 1861

Dear Brother,

We received your letter last night and as you did not say anything about the bagging and roping, Pa requested me to write to you this evening. He wishes you to send it up soon as he has finished his Screw[1] and wishes to try it. He says send a bill of the articles bought.

Cousin John Cuningham and Uncle Frank [Franklin Leland Anderson] were with us last night. Cousin John has been very sick, but is getting well. he seems rather low spirited, told us about the long stand the Fourth [his unit] took.

He wished very much to see you. He will return to Virginia in two weeks. Uncle Frank was very lively and told us funny occurances in Camp.

He and Net were playing Duetts this morning on the piano.

And to our profound astonishment your most interesting servant J. P. Long dropped in to dinner on Tuesday and spent the night here. I never was so tierd [tired] of a human.

At supper he said he could fight very well if the Yankees would not put bullets in their guns. Mr. Davis set him up for a coward at once and carried him high.

He said he was going back to his Regiment.

Aunt Hettie and I went to see Mary Landrum Wednesday. We spent a very pleasant day. Mr. L. had just arrived the evening before from Columbia he was unwell and came home. He told us Uncle Jessee [Brockman] had measles.

Aunt Het and I brought Ma's Fly brush[2] home and Aunt Het was holding it out of the Buggy as we got into the road near Col. Jameses when Jim [the horse] took fright and run as hard as he could to tear over the stumps, just did miss the fence, and a large Pine tree, struck the Sign Post inside the wheel, knocked it down and went whirling into the old field across the road, right to a gully when we were able to stop him, we were both pulling with all our might. I thought the old buggy was gone. I jumped out when he stopped turned him around and started for home. We were very much frightened. But Providence saved us.

I received letters from Uncle Jim and William Woodruff this week, also one from Emma, she sent her love to you. Net's friend Willie has measles at Culpepper. Our troops have all fallen back. What does that mean? . . . Did you get a Fly brush in Columbia? Ma has gone up to Aunt Sue's. All well and send love. Your affectionate Sister Mary

1. A conveyer to transport corn and wheat into the gristmill.
2. A type of flyswatter with loose strings that whistle or rustle in the wind or with movement.

[41] Andrew Charles Moore to Nancy Moore Evins
Postmarked: Tudor Hall Va

Camp Oct. 20th 1861

My Dear Mother,

I seat myself this beautiful sabbath morning while I am free from disturbance to drop you a few lines. Since my last the whole army has moved back to Bull Run. This Reg. is now encamped within one mile & a half of that famous stream.[1] The 5th [Regiment, South Carolina Volunteers] is about three quarters below us. I was

Anderson's gristmill on the North Tyger River, ca. 1890. From the editor's collection

there day before yesterday. Found John and Andrew well [John H. and Andrew M. Evins, his step-brothers] On my return I passed a house where an old lady was selling out a hog. I gave $1.50 for the head: so you see we have had the rarity of hog's head & brains to eat. A little hog is fine to one who eats beef constantly; as it is a nice relief to our monotony of diet; we have now on one hand part of a very fine gobler & as we have drawn coffee once more, our living has been what we call excellent.

On yesterday Sam [Means] & I walked to the battlefield of the 21st July. We had a tedious time. Leaving in the morning we were gone until an hour after dark, having walked near fifteen miles altogether there and back. I saw where the enemy formed in line of battle & advanced, firing into our troops as they came; the old house, litterally shattered to pieces, in which the old woman, Mrs. Henry, was killed; the dead horses & dead men & graves, which marked the spot where Sherman's Battery [part of the Union force of Gen. Irvin McDowell] was taken; the marble pillar erected to mark the spot where Bartow[2] fell; & various other things of minor importance, among the latter the stone bridge on which the enemy's cannon became jammed, so that they were abandoned. Seventy cannon were taken on that bridge. It is built entirely of stone, arched from pier to pier, Across the length of the bridge, are stone walls on either side which serve as banisters. The whole bridge is a strange, & very old looking structure. On the battlefield I saw several yankees partially rooted up by hogs, assisted by visitors to the battlefield; some of whom have actually prized the dead from beneath the shallow covering of earth which humanity had thrown over them. One fellow, belonging to Sherman's Battery, was completely exhumed, lying on his back, hands and feet stretched at full length, the flesh fallen & falling from his bones, & the head gone. His bones were still enveloped in his uniform, which seemed in a very good state of preservation. It was truly a gastly, horrid spectacle, & I could but reflect on the sad end to which bitter hatred of us & wicked fanaticism had brought him. Lying about were a number of shoes & boots & a couple of coats one of which evidently belonged to our side. Our men were decently buried, having rail pens & boards at the head to show the occupants of the grave. But I will not dwell longer on this disagreeable subject. Never, never, was I so forcibly impressed with the idea that war proceeds from want of humanity, & wickedness of heart.

We are now encamped where Jenkins' Reg[3] charged on the day of the great battle. Just at the spring from which we get water are signs of grape shot; one of which passed entirely through a mulberry eight inches in diameter.

I do not think there is any prospect of a battle soon. According to the newspapers it should have been fought long ago. They are now so hard up for news that correspondents are no[w] over-conscientious, & hesitate not to manufacture news to suit the public taste. The Yankees are now a long way off, & are said to be still fortifying. We have a large force at Centreville, & are throwing up works at that place. The armies seem determined neither to advance, judging from appearances.

I received a letter from Mary [wife] day before yesterday. She was well. Also one from Tom [brother]. Sam speaks of coming home in a few days. He is going to Florida, should William stay at home. If the latter leaves, Sam designs remaining near the old folks, as he thinks it will not do for all the boys to desert them.

Write soon and give me all the news. My respects to Col E.

Your Af. Son,
A. C. Moore

1. The First Battle of Bull Run, near Manassas Junction, Virginia, was fought July 21, 1861, and was an embarrassing defeat for Union army.

2. Col. Francis S. Bartow of Georgia, whose last words were "They have killed me, boys, but never give it up." Douglas Southall Freeman, *Lee's Lieutenants: A Study in Command* (New York: Charles Scribner's Sons, 1946), 1:81n.

3. Col. (later Brig. Gen.) Micah Jenkins's Fifth South Carolina Regiment.

[42] Ella Brockman to John Crawford Anderson

Addressed: Citadel, Charleston

Limestone
Oct. 26, 1861

Dear Johnie,

I received your precious letter a few nights ago . . . Since they have taken you back to those walls they will make you come down to it harder than ever. I have got started in at last after so long a vacation. It was very hard at first but it has become quite pleasant now.

I received a letter from sister Mary [Mary Lavinia Brockman] a few nights ago. She said that brother John spoke of volunteering. I suppose Mr. Young has an office. I am glad to hear it but think charity begins at home. And you saw sister Hettie I hope you were well pleased with her and enjoyed yourself finely.

I have been writing all day on a composition I hope you will excuse this paper as it is very scarce in these deggens [diggings].

The young ladies seems to fancy your eyes. There is something written in this envelope by a young lady that is present. You can't guess who it is . . . you must translate it in German and tell me what it is as the young lady is a German and she will not tell me . . .

I hope the time will fly fast . . . for it is only five weeks and I am getting so I want to see the dear old folks. I want to write some of them this evening. I have such a short time for leasure I can't write long letters like I wish to you.

I am getting tired of looking for a letter from home so I will start one that way. Johnie will you pleas have me one of those palmetto caps maid. I see some of them hear. I think they are so pretty if you will I will send you the measure of my head and will send you the money when I go home if you have it maid have it trimed in black.

I hope you will excuse this and write soon. We had a holiday on yesterday a very pleasant time.

Write soon to your true antie

Ella

[43] Harriet Brockman Anderson to John Crawford Anderson

Poolsville, Nov.13th, 1861

My dear son,

It is with feelings of intense anxiety that I address you. The long expected trouble has come.[1] Our friends are falling around us.—it is sad indeed but we must expect to meet with losses if we resist. Jimmy Norris has fallen now. Just think you and him were up at the same time. He has gone to his long home and you may fall in the first engagement in which you take part. I wrestle in prayer for you and your Uncle Ben [Brockman] especially but not alone for we have not a man we would willingly give up. I have you always on my mind. I regret I did not converse with you on religious subjects when at home. But I have so often entreated you to seek an interest in the Saviour that I hope it has not been in vain . . . If you could leave me an assurance that your sins were forgiven and you feel you would enter on this heavenly rest which remains for those that love God . . . And severe as would be the blow, it would be stripped of those melancholy feelings that your life had been a failure. And that you were gone to an unknown world without preparation. I beg and entreat that you humble yourself and seek divine aid to preserve you and to forgive you your sins . . . You have Father, Mother, and Sisters that go often to the Mercy Seat in your behalf. I may never see you again but you must meet me in heaven and we may be a family unbroken. I remain your affectionate Mother with sincere prayers.

1. The Union blockade of Southern ports was tightening and having an effect. Port Royal, South Carolina, fell to Union troops on November 7, 1861.

[44] Mary Elizabeth Anderson to John Crawford Anderson
Addressed to the Citadel

Pleasant Falls
Nov. 23, 1861

Dear Brother,

I have some time to write you this morning. We children have been alone three days and nights. Pa went to the "Old Place" on Tuesday to have things appraised and ready for the sale which was on yesterday. Jimmie brought Ella home on Tuesday and carried Ma and her over on Wednesday.

Net and Aunt Hettie have been at the old place about two weeks. Aunt Hettie was sick when Ma went over. Uncle Jessee was still over there, stays in a close room all the time. No telling when he will return to camp. O, he is so pettish and ill. I have no idea who will buy the place or any of the property.[1]

Jimmie left early this morning for Ma, Aunt Hettie, and Ella. We expect Aunt Mary and Uncle John to come by to see us. Ella looks very well, has her hair shingled and looks so much like you.

I received a letter from Uncle Jim [James Mason Anderson] on yesterday; he was at Centreville and anxious to get home. He thinks there is no probability of any troops leaving Va. for Carolina.

Uncle Frank expects to leave on Thursday next for Va. I am sorry he has to return so soon.

I hear Jim Stokes has joined Uncle Ben's Company. I suppose he will be promoted to First Lieutenant's place till Uncle Jessee returns as he is such a favourite of the Captain.

We received a letter from you last Saturday night was glad to hear you were well and that your Lady friends had been out to see you. Ma has had some socks knit for you. Mrs. Sams knit one pair, she has made some flannel shirts for you. They are made of homemade flannel, some very pretty mixed that Ma made. looks a little ruff but they will be worn over your linen and not rub badly. She also had some Gray Jeans off of which she gave Uncle Frank an Overcoat and wishes to know if you would like one. You must write us all your wants and we will do the best for you. Ma will send your socks down by some member of Bomar's Company. I heard Col. Stevens was in Spartanburg and that his brother had been released. All the Bagwells have volunteered. George and Alvin Dean are trying to raise a Cavalry Company. Since the Country has been cleared of men I think we girls will have to mount the Colts, Old Jim and Blaze, and join him, giving it the name of "Dean's Guards." I expect we could keep the Yankees from hurting him.

Aunt Hettie received a letter from Long the other day. If anyone has my sympathising the point of wisdom it is him.

I saw Andrew Moore on Fastday. He looks very thin and bad. (Net is here shaking my pen.) He spoke of joining the S.C Students under Col. Stevens. Who proposed calling the Legion in honor of Mrs. Pickens? Net is sewing some carpeting together and keeps talking to me. I told Emmie [Emma Frances Anderson] you had to sleep on the ground, she said, "I let Jonny sleep in my cradle." She talks a great deal about shooting Yankees and knitting for "Sholdiers."

You must write often and take good care of yourself. I hope you will guard against the vices of Camp, and remember your Creator in the days of your youth and yeald your heart to the Saviour. Our Father in Heaven preserve you. Your Sister

1. Thomas Patterson Brockman died in 1859; his wife, Mary Kilgore Brockman, in April 1861. They were the parents of thirteen children, born between 1819 and 1844. Their oldest daughter, Harriet, took the younger children into her home in the late 1850s when her mother's health declined. The Brockman home, Old Place (officially called Solitude), at Pliny on the Enoree River just inside Greenville County, was sold to settle the estate.

[45] Mary Elizabeth Anderson to John Crawford Anderson

Addressed to him at the Citadel
hand delivered courtesy Mr. A. C. Moore

Pleasant Falls
Nov. 28, 1861

Dear Brother,

I am preparing to send some things to you by Andrew Moore, and have a few moments to write before Jimmie is ready. We children have been alone for a week. Pa took supper with us on Tuesday night and went up and spent the night with Uncle Frank. Ma and Ella remained as Aunt Hettie is now very sick. Pa thinks she has Fever. Ma wrote me she was very low on Saturday and at one time they despaired of her recovery. Pa said she was very little better on Tuesday. Ma, Pa, and Ella are still there and the only ones. Jessee was going over to Solitude [Brockman home], they sold nearly everything, no comforts at all left. I wish so much Aunt Hettie was at home. Ma and Pa have to take the floor. Aunt Lucy wanted to buy a bed but Jess was determined she should not get it, so he bought it and afterwards traded it to Burnett and some other trash, so afraid Pa might use it while he stayed over there. Jess bought Gean for $1000. Uncle John Harris [husband of Mary Lavinia Brockman] [bought] Jason for $900 and something. Uncle Ben [bought] Betsy, Hunt, Aletha, Ephrum. Uncle Jule [Julius Earle, husband of Lucy Brockman] the place for $4050. Had a big split up with our Mountain Uncle. Uncle Frank left this morning for Virginia. Mr. Capt. Walker accompanied him. Sam Anderson staid with us last night. Orr Miller is very low, his father has gone on.

I send you some Cakes and Crackers. Sarah [cook] wanted me to send some sausage but it cannot be carried easily. We killed 20 hogs Monday.

We have not heard from you in more than a week, do take good care of yourself and write often.

My birthday, Johnie! have you thought of me only eighteen today (28th Nov. 1861) The children speak of Johnie very often. Tommie [Thomas Brockman Anderson] is very anxious to go to Va. He says if he can't go to Va. he can go to the Coast.

Give Net some credit for the cake as she assisted me.

Do you wish an overcoat? Let us know. Children all join me in love. Sarah and Darkies send howdy.

Write soon. Your affectionate Sister Mary

Berry Bagwell has just called to tell us goodbye. He leaves a wife and four little children.

[46] Mary Elizabeth Anderson to John Crawford Anderson

Addressed to him at the Citadel Academy, Charleston

Pleasant Falls
Nov. 29th, 1861

Dear Brother,

Pa spent last night with us and requested me to write you and ask you to call on the firm of whome you bought the Roping and Bagging and inform them he has received the bill and is still good for the pay.

Aunt Hettie is a little better, but has high fever at times, she cannot be moved this week.

I wrote you by Andrew Moore, who was to leave this morning for Charleston, and also sent some eatables .. think you were still in Camp, but I guess it will not go amiss if you are in the Citadel. I wrote you all the news in my last.

We received a letter from you on yesterday informing us of your return to the Citadel. did you see anything of Tom Moore while you were in Camp?

We hear very little from Port Royal and Virginia, they seem to be making a beginning at Ft. Pickens. Uncle Mason wrote to Uncle Frank not long since and said he thought every man in Mississippi would be ordered out soon.

Mr John Norris has brought his family to his father's and returned to Texas. He is a volunteer in Texas.

I expect the mail along soon. Write us soon.

I remain your affectionate Sister Mary

[47] David Anderson to John Crawford Anderson

Poolesville, Spt. Dis, SoCar
Dec. 2nd, 1861

Dear John,

I send you a check for Seventy-five dollars which will pay for the Bagging and Rope. Please attend to it immediately.

This leaves us all well except your Aunt Hetty who is sick with Typhoid Fever at the Old Place. Your Mother and Ella are with her and I fear it will give us a good deal of trouble. Your Uncle J. R. Earle Bot the Old Place for $4000.00 and will move as soon as possible. I Bot very little property, about $150.

I do not know what course to advise you so I will leave it with you to determine for yourself. I know you cannot study to any advantage still it may be best for you to Remain at the Citadel. But I think everyone should shut up Books and shoulder his Gun. Let me hear from you soon.

Yours affectionately,
David Anderson

I wish to enquire the price of flour. Find out what the Government is giving and let me know. I can send 200 sacks and will take $5.00 per sack delivered in Charleston. I would come down with it if you can make the trade. Look Round and let me know what it is worth and oblige. D.A. I want the highest price possible for flour.

[48] Mary Elizabeth Anderson to John Crawford Anderson

Addressed to him at the Citadel Academy, Charleston

Pleasant Falls
Dec. 27, 1861

Dear Brother,

It does seem that we have neglected writing you for some time since I think of it, but I do not think I am indebted to you a letter for I wrote you by Andrew Moore when I sent your socks etc., and do not remember receiving a reply. Tom [Moore] wrote Ma you had received the different kinds of bread she sent not seeming to understand that I then presided as head of affairs.

Ma will have been at home two weeks tomorrow. She spent nearly a month with Aunt Hettee. She has entirely recovered. She and Aunt Ella have gone to Aunt Alethea's to spend Christmas. She has not been back to see us yet, but Pa will send for them Tuesday. Aunt Lucy has moved to the Old Place Aunt Hettie thinks something of moving back. I don't know why, but Ella will live with us.

Well, Johnie, it is Christmas again and we are again seperated. How I wish to see you. I looked for you Tuesday evening, although you wrote you did not expect to come. But wish was so strong as to lead me to expect and hope.

Times are very dull with us. We remained at home on Wednesday and on yesterday, we children went to Grandpa's. Robbert [slave] drove us and we carried Sarah [cook] along on a visit. You were not forgotten. She amused us by telling us of when you were a babe. I quote one of her remarks, "He looked like a Mornin' Stair with his white dress on." We gave Aunt Mary and Uncle George a call. They treated us to some "Sinner's Beer" as it was Christmas. We then continued on till we ascended Tyger Hill[1] where we found Grandpa[2] quite sick. Spent a pleasant day with Miss Julia, (your "Aunt Sue") Mrs. John Norris from Texas and Aunt Sue. Little Frank has grown a great deal and looks like a General.

I received letters from Uncle Frank and Jim Bivings on yesterday. They were at Centreville but have since moved up to Drainsville, they belonging to Longstreet's Division.[3] Uncle Frank was quite well. Jim has been acting as Brigade Commissary, Capt. Elford being sick with fever.

Well Johnie Uncle Jim [James Alexander Anderson] left us last week after paying us a short visit. He looks a little changed but still lively and talks as much as ever, wished very much to see you. Took one of your likenesses home with him.

Holly Hill, the home of Maj. Franklin Leland Anderson, ca. 1890; originally known as Tyger Hill. From Edward Lee Anderson, *A History of the Anderson Family, 1706–1955* (Columbia, S.C.: R. L. Bryan Company, 1955); used with permission

Tommy was very anxious to go home with him and Pa might have let him go had he been well, but he seems to have had a slight attack of fever.

Aunt Hettie had a letter from Uncle Ben dated the 20th saying Uncle Jessee had not returned and wondering what had gone with him. Surely he has not come back to see his "little boy" so soon. [Jesse Brockman had two young sons, Thomas and Jesse.] I suppose you have heard of such a little "Critter"?

Since the call for Volunteers, three more companies have been raised by having drafts at their backs. Willie Roebuck has been elected Capt. of one. I do not know who of the others. Alvin Dean has been trying to raise a Cavalry Company will succeed if he tries a little harder. Eddie Miller has joined him. Neither Sam Miller nor John Crook have come out [enlisted]. Col. Evins gave Sam a talk and he tried to get up a big quarrel, but John took it like one of the Canine species.

Well Johnie our cousin William Woodruff now sleeps in Bethel Churchyard, there to remain till the resurrection morn. He had been sick some time but had recovered and returned to Camp, was throwing up earthworks, became very warm, cooled off too quick when he was taken with a violent chill. He suffered intense pain for three days when his Spirit took its flight. He died very tryumphantly which is a great comfort. It is hard to realize that he is no more.

Dear Brother how necessary is a preperation for death. Dear Johnie how I long to know the state of your soul for you have had very deep and pious feelings on the subject of your soul's salvation and can you not unfold your heart to a Sister who has not ceased to approach a throne of Grace in behalf of a dear Brother since she was lead to believe on a Saviour who so loved the world that he poured out his precious blood on the cross that all who would believe in him should have eternal life. Dear Johnie I hope you will no longer keep me ignorant of the state of religion in your soul. I hope you may now be living in the smiles of a Saviour's love and realized a pardon of all sin through the sufferings of our risen Lord.

May the Spirit direct you Think soberly on this subject my dear brother and trifle not with God's Holy Spirit. neither defer to a more convenient season. May God keep you.

Pa has gone to Greenville.

Did any of your friends suffer any from the fire? All are well and send love.

Excuse this Johnie and write soon.

Your loving Sister Mary

1. Home of Franklin Leland Anderson, later known as Holly Hill.

2. Known as Tyger Jim, James Mason Anderson (1784–1870) was the father of David Anderson and nine other children, including Franklin Leland Anderson, with whom he made his home in his later years.

3. Led by Lt. Gen. James Longstreet. Centreville, located four to five miles from Manassas, was where the Confederates planned to halt the Union advance during the First Battle of Manassas (Bull Run). Dranesville was the site of a minor action on December 20, 1861.

LETTERS, 1862

Andrew Evins, son of Col. S. N. Evins and stepson of Nancy Moore Evins, made it home from the war in Virginia with pneumonia, but despite the efforts of his older brother, Dr. Tom Evins, he died at Fredonia in early March. Nancy herself died soon after, making Ann, Andrew, and Tom orphans.

There was a modicum of normality as Hettie and Ella requested various items such as sheet music and certain threads from John in Charleston. The girls participated in tableaux that served as fund raisers and solicited funds door-to-door for a gunboat.

By late spring there were shortages of salt, rice, and sugar. Refugees from Charleston were flooding the upstate; slaves whose masters were off at war wandered around Spartanburg looking for food.

The defeats in the Peninsula campaign saw many wounded soldiers make their way back home with gory tales. The early excitement and victories gave way to a determined reality tinged with doubt about the future.

Andrew was killed at the Second Battle at Manassas in September; his brother Tom was nearby. Their sister, Ann Means, came to Virginia looking for them and for her husband, Sam.

Later that fall Tom wrote home for boots and clothes, saying he was without provisions and "almost naked."

[49] Hettie Brockman to John Crawford Anderson
Addressed: Cadt. John C. Anderson, Citadel Academy, Charleston

Poolsville, SC
Jan. 9th, 1862

Dear Johnnie,

I am so grateful to you for those letters received during my illness. You can well imagine, if you have never experienced the pleasure of reading a letter from one we love whilst confined to a sick room.

I will not go into particulars concerning the four weeks of helplessness I was called to undergo. If you could only see me now I think you would come to the conclusion that [typhoid] Fever was not a very agreeable companion.

As soon as I was able to travel, I went up to Sister Alethia's to spend a few days. Ella and I were honored with calls from several nice young gents. Altogether we had a pleasant, though not a very merry time for a thought of our dear Soldiers would bring to mind the suffering they were enduring and who could think of the old fashioned heart mirth without a sigh and bringing a feeling of sadness in our own soul.

But Johnnie I am again at dear Poolsville [Pleasant Falls] after an absence of two long months. I wish you were here for it would add so much to our "home contentment" to have you with us. I think so often of the charming times of the past Summers and wish that pleasures were not so fleeting, as they are bright. And I am going back again to live at the Old Homestead. My home at Poolsville will not be deserted by this removal, it will ever remain dear to memory: for it was a resting place for the homeless Orphans who sought shelter beneath its roof, and sympathy in the hearts of its loved inmates.

I am now assisting Ella in her preparations for Limestone—will return to Pliny next week. Do write to me often Johnnie let me know that you have not forgotten me

Direct your letters to Pliny—so I can hear from you on my arrival. Lissie, Nettie, and Ella unite with me in sending a quantity of Love to you.

Yours in bonds of affection,

Hettie

P.S. Miscellaneous

Grandfather Anderson is much better and we hope will soon recover. We have heard from your Uncle Jim since his arrival in Virginia. He enjoys fine health and good spirits. I received a letter from Jesse on Friday, Ben and he are both quite well. Jesse is very anxious to see his "Boy."[1]

Poor Lizzie Austin (Tom's wife) is no more. She died on the 5th.

I will close as Ella wishes to write you a note. Affectionately,

Hettie

1. Jesse Brockman married Kittie Bryson in 1861; their son Thomas P. Brockman is the "Boy."

[50] Ella Brockman to John Crawford Anderson

[Enclosed in tiny blue envelope and sent with previous letter]

Poolsville
Jan. 9th

Dear Johnie,

I know you will think strange of me waiting so long to answer your letter, but I suppose you have learned the cause before this, therefore it will be useless to explain all matters.

Johnie will you please accommodate me by buying me some "Terkeyred" [a thread] if you can get some in the City. Please send it in a package I will defray all the expences, if you will get some two bbs will be enough and one bbs of Yellow paint [a dye] if you can get these things please send them as soon as possible by mail.

I will write to you soon.

Yours truly,
Ella

PS Write me the price of all. Direct the package to Spartingburg C.H. in care of your father

[51] Mary Elizabeth Anderson to John Crawford Anderson

Addressed: Cadet John C. Anderson, Citadel

Pleasant Falls
Jan. 11, 1862

Dearest Johnie,

I received your interesting letter yesterday morning, the first I have received from you in a long time. It was accompanying two others one from Mary Sullivan and Mary Dorroh, two very nice letters. Mary Sullivan seems to have spent a merry Christmas, very different from what we spent. Tom did not write me any word about your visit to the Country. Do write me all about it who your friend is we could not make out his name as your letter to Pa was written in somewhat of a hurry.

Aunt Hettie and Ella came over on Tuesday evening. Aunt Hettie looks quite well again and quite girlish with short hair. We drove over yesterday evening to call on Sam Miller as we had not seen him since his return. He looks thin and has a cough but I think with that exception a Soldier's life has been the making of him. he came in and talked with us, seemed to feel more at ease, than I ever saw him. He asked for some music stood near the Piano and called for a piece or two and after tea or coffee it was a little dark so he had his horse caught and rode home with us. When we arrived home we asked him in. He came in and sat a good while.

Orr and Eddie [Miller] came in while we were there. Orr looks dreadfully is very thin and weak and has a very bad cough. he says he thinks he will rest awhile. Sam thinks of going on the Coast when he is well enough. Eddie is a member of Dean's Company which leaves soon for Camp Hampton.

There is a good deal of sickness in the 5th Regt. Col. Jenkins is at home sick with Typhoid fever. Lieutenant Col. Legg has fever in Virginia. And Capt. Joe Walker being Senior Captain has taken the Col.'s place. Thomson the Major being under arrest for firing off a gun in Camp, has been under arrest for near three months. John Evins is very sick, a dispach came for his Father this week.

Grand Pa has been right sick, but is improving, walked to the Shop the other evening. Uncle Frank was quite well when we heard from him last. Johnie, why don't you write to him? They are now at Centreville but get letters directed to Manassas Junction about as soon and then if they change position the letters are sent to them. I know Uncle Frank would be very glad to receive letters from you.

I began New Year with a little school I hear Tommie [Thomas Brockman Anderson], Hattie [Harriet Maria Anderson] and Davies [David Perrin Anderson] recite their lessons every morning. Also began reading Macaulay's *History of England*. It suits these "fussy times" very well. Now I wish all our Generals were Cromwells, austere morality was the characteristic of his army, not an oath was ever heard nor drunkenness ever seen in his Camp. We have to[o] many of an opposite character at the head command on our Coast and a few of them in Virginia. I do think the violation of the third commandment [Do not take the name of the Lord in vain] and drunkenness are the crying sins of our nation. Sometimes I despair of success in this war, because our nation needs humbling on account of sin and we have trampled underfoot unbounded privileges as a punishment for which this war is sent upon us. I do hope our Country may come through this "crucible" purified and refined.

Aunt Hettie thinks of going to Aunt Lucy's to live, she is going to teach a little school at the old School House on the Creek. Ella will return to Limestone in February.

Pa is thinking of taking a trip to Hamburg[1] and see what he can do for Sugar, Molasses, and Salt. I do not know what he thinks of going to Charleston to sell flour but know he has an idea of going soon if it is possible. I heard Ma say he would like to go down.

Johnie I dreamed the other night the Yankees were in the Up Country and we had a little fight in the Apple Orchard, a ball just did miss my nose. Johnie please excuse this badly written letter, this is the best pen I can scrape and it is not worth owning.

Ma and all the children are well. Oh! Johnie how I do wish you could be with us on the 18th there would be an end put to the existence of a certain biped known as the "Gobler."

Write often. I am awaiting a reply to a subject in my last letter. Please Johnie open your heart to a loving Sister and one who is deeply concerned for your eternal welfare.

Your loving Sister Mary

1. Hamburg was the terminus of the Charleston and Hamburg Railroad. It is now called North Augusta, South Carolina.

[52] Ella E. Brockman to John Crawford Anderson

Addressed: Cadet John C. Anderson, Citadel Academy, Charleston

Poolsville, SC
Jan, 25th, 1862

Dear Johnie,

I was very happy to receive your letter on yesterday morning and finding you are a little mistaken about the order I sent you. I will attempt to straighten it up.

The Terkey Red is a kind of thread—I will send you a sample of it, it is in scains but is sold by the [illegible] this will be found at a dry goods establishment. The Yellow paint is for dying thread yellow. I expect it will be easy to get at some painting affare, this for making homespun dresses don't send the other if you don't think it will suit and if the man will not take it back send me the price and I will pay you I dislike very much to trouble you so much but if it could be got in the up country I would not worry you.

I received a long letter from Hettie on yesterday she did not say she had received your letter but I suppose she received it yesterday.

Well Johnie I know you think this a poor scraching letter but I hope my pen will improve before I finish.

We heard last week that brother Ben had lost the best pair of his mules they jumped out of the flat while conveying some sick men to the hospital the men went in too but got out safe. Your father and Jimmie went to Hamburg last week for some mollasses and sugar. They have not returned yet but we are all looking forward to the arrival of the waggon next week.

I hope your lady flame has regained her former health. You must not treat her like the young officer treated the little queen or the pride of the village in Washinton Ervin's sketches.

Well Johnie I received a letter from a soldier in the 4th Regt on yesterday, a very patriotic little fellow Pentolton I will tell you sometime who it is but I assure you I have no particular interest in him more that he is a soldier and fighting for his country and you know we all have some interest in them. . . .

It has been very cloudy for several days but the sun comes out this morning with splendor. I wish you could be here to enjoy the comforts of home with us all.

I expect you Charleston people make a great deal of fun of our contry [country] clod hoppers, but they are the very ones that will do the fighting I do not include you in the City for we claim you as belonging to the Up Country race.

Net says she will answer your letter next mail it will be useless for both of us to write at once. Pleas send the things to Spartinburg or Poolsville I will not want them at Limestone if you can get them very soon.

I hope you will excuse this letter and when I write the next letter I hope to have more time and my brains a little better collected . . .

Write soon we Love to hear from you Yours affectionately,
Ella E. B.

Emma Buist [married John Crawford Anderson in February 1866] wrote to Sis and says she recons you had the French measles from studying your French gramma, it being extracted from it.

[53] Nettie Anderson to John Crawford Anderson

Pleasant Falls
Jan 25, 1862

Dear Johnie,

It has been many a day since I last wrote you not since I left Laurens . . .

We had one of your Charleston men to stay all night here this week He is out hunting for lether he talked about his wife how smart she was. She is the one that made those Palmetto hats you admired so much. I could not like the man because he looked so deceitful and then you gave them such a character. You know we believe everything you say. The man that was with him said Buddy Wright's body was brought up to Laurens last week. He died of Typhoid fever. Andrew and John Evins have been very sick but were better the last time we heard. I expect they are well by this time. The report is now that Andrew Moore is going to move back to his old place and go to housekeeping. and let the War take care of itself. I do not think much of him. George Dean is on hand yet. He joined his brother's company as an independent but got tired the first day and is now at home holding tight to his Mammy's apron strings. He struts in a large cavalry coat as large as my peafowl... We are looking for Pa home tomorrow night. I expect Jimmie is hartily tired of camping out. He will know how to appreciate his warm bed.

When Pa gets home we will "roll" in sugar and "lases" don't you wish you were at home. I know you do. Please excuse the most wretched manner in which my letter is written write to us every week I remain as ever your Affectionate Sister Net...

...Johnie, send me some Blockade envelopes and pens. Goodbye

[54] Franklin Leland Anderson to John Crawford Anderson

Centreville, Va.
Jan 27th, '62

Jno. C. Anderson

Dear Nephiew

I received your long and interesting letter some days since, but this is my first opportunity for answering. We have been busy upon our winter quarters and after a long time & labouring under many disadvantages, we have them ready to be occupied and the Reg. has been moving, a company at a time for several days, until I believe none remain in this, the old camp but those detained by sickness. Andrew Evins has had a severe attack of Typhoid fever and has been quite low but has been improving for more than a week. The Dr. thinks he will be able to travel in a week or ten days at which time he will send him home as he thinks he will not be fit for duty before our time is out. Until he leaves our mess will continue to occupy our tent, which so far has been very comfortable. Others of your acquaintance have also been sick Jim Drummond went off a few days since to the Hospital to [illegible] and will likely get a discharge. Our camp is exceedingly dull, all drills and duty suspended except guard and picket, but if you were here to go through a trip of the latter with us, you would conclude we have something to keep our fingers out of our mouths. We have had snow five or six times, two or three inches deep, but they disappear very soon and leave the most disagreeable of all things else in camp, the mud which [is] now deeper than when we have yet had snow. Our tour of enlistment is drawing to a close and we begin to have bright thoughts and hopes of getting to see the loved ones at home soon, my boy

Frank for instance. The proposition, with inducements by the late Act of Congress, to reenlist for the war was before us last week but was unanimously rejected by this Reg. I have not heard of one from SC that has accepted all preferring to return home, reorganize, and return after a reasonable rest spell. It is thought by many that during the bad winter weather when it is ascertained that we will not [illegible] under the act, that we will be disbanded and sent home at once in order that we may organize and be ready for service the earlier in the spring, which I think would be a wise arrangement. What a sad thing our reverse in Kentucky, all for the want of a skillful Gen. It will not only buoy them up at that point, but will inspire them with confidence all round. I fear too that we will not find these western men the same easy foe and of such easy courage as we have found the Yankees. But we have the justice of our cause upon which to rely, and my prayer is that the South will do her past nobly and with a feeling of reliance upon the God of battles. I was glad to hear that you had abandoned your ambition for position and turned your attention to study. From what I have seen of Military men, the lives they must lead, and I have concluded that their positions are not to be envied by thinking men. . . . I had long letter from Sis a few days since, all well at home but Grand Pa. He is suffering from gout or the pains and swellings in his feet and ankles that attended him two years ago. Nettie too is a correspondent of mine, she writes a good letter for one of her age. I hope I will see you during my respite in April. Will you have vacation or an intermission of any kind about that time? Write again and believe me Yours,
Uncle Frank

[55] Hettie Brockman to John Crawford Anderson

Addressed: Mr. John C. Anderson, Citadel Academy, Charleston

Pliny, S.C.
Jan. 30th, 1862

Dear Johnnie—

. . . I must in the first place congratulate you on forming such admirable resolutions and secondly wish you all the success that a truly engenious and persevering mind deserves.

I admire your taste exceedingly in the selection you have made from the myriad of Authors that throng our libraries of the present day. I have read only a few volumes of Irving's writings, but it was owing entirely to the difficulty of obtaining them, and not that I would read with pleasure so intelligent and accomplished an Author. Did you ever read the life of Irving? I would like so much to read it. I am acquainted with a few incidents of his life which I think highly interesting . . .

I have not heard from Emma Buist in some time. Of course I remember "the boquet" and a sweet little affair it was. "Oh!" a simple present of an appropriate character would not be at all out of place, but I object seriously to the "five tender words." Come Johnnie you must think twice before asking in cases of love—those "few words" might kindle a flame that would burn in all after time, and perhaps destroy the happiness of its victim. Remember that

"Loving is a painful thrill,
But not to love more painful still;
But Oh it is the worst of pain
To love and not be loved again"

I know you will take all I have written good humouredly—although every word is from the depth of my heart.

I have no news from this position of the Country to communicate. Our attention is totally engrossed by Politics and the war. We were greatly saddened by reports of the recent battle in Kentucky.

The measles have an unquestionable reighn in our little family. Of six children at present—you can imagine in what confusion I am writing this letter, as I have charge of them and so many difficulties to settle between them, so many questions to answer satisfactorily.

Sister Lucy joins me in sending you much love.

Do Johnnie write soon to your loving and devoted aunt.

Hettie

[56] Mary Elizabeth Anderson to John Crawford Anderson

Pleasant Falls, Feb. 15th, 1862

Dear Brother,

I received your letter more than a week since but as Net wrote last week I postponed writing until this week.

You did indeed spend a pleasant Christmas. I am glad to hear of you forming so many Lady acquaintances, for there is nothing that tends to improve a "young gent" more than mingling in Ladies society. But I must beg you not to forget Miss Laura's "sweet blush" and Emma's "free heart."

Yesterday was "St. Valentine's day." How we would all open our eyes when we saw the mail coming, that is when we were in good "Old Laurens."

But I hope it has brought as much or more pleasure to us this year. We expected our Volunteers that enlisted for the war from the 5th Regt. home on yesterday morning. There were about 60 from Walker's Company and over 40 from Foster's reenlisted. I do not know who they were but we do not think Uncle Frank is among them. They have rest for sixty days and a bounty, I know not how much.

Andrew Evins has not got home yet unless he came last night. John Poole was buried at Nazareth the first of this week. He has been the first soldier out of our congregation to die. Have we not reason to thank our Heavenly Father for his kind preservation of them.

I suppose you have heard of the death of Willie Howe. He died in Virginia. Mr. Bivings has lost two little children from something like dyphtheria, Mattie and Ammie, they died in ten days of each other.

"In the midst of life we are in death."

It is thought by some that Edwards' Regt[1] will be ordered to Kentucky. We have not received a letter from Uncle Ben in some time. We heard this week Uncle Jesse was up at Dr. Sullivan's. He has had mumps. His baby is named Thomas. I am very anxious to see it.

Ella has been at Aunt Lucy's this week. Uncle Jule promised to bring her home today. They had measles there. Cousin Kizzie [Keziah A. Brockman] was very low with measles when Ella went over, we have not heard from her since. What do you think Johnie! We are fixing Net up to go back to Laurens will go next week, nothing preventing. O Johnie! you do not know how badly I wished to return [to college] for I am beginning to see my ignorance, can't write, and nothing else. But I had to give up. Pa pleaded "hard times" that was the same excuse when I wanted to go to C____[2] to school the winter I visited it. So I will have to content myself and be a mere witness to the smartness of my Brother and Sister—Pa has promised Ma and me a visit to Laurens when Net goes down. Ella will go to Limestone next week.

Roanoke has fallen. I fear our officers are growing negligent. It is said our men fought bravely. But where they say "Let them land" why do they put our troops in such danger? I am afraid since Cotton has been dethroned "King Whisky" has usurped the throne.

Did you ever see so much rainy weather?

We are now reading Dr. Cumming on the Apocalipse a very excellent work. Johnie, I wish you would get Dr. Kanes's *Arctic Expedition* and Madame La Vertes *Travels in Europe* after reading them send them up to me.

All are well but Aunt Mary Will who has Rheumatism. Excuse bad writing as I must get down to sewing.

Write soon—All send love

Your loving Sister Mary

No soldiers came last evening

1. The Thirteenth Regiment, South Carolina Volunteers, was commanded by Col. O. E. Edwards. When he was killed at Chancellorsville (May 3, 1863), Col. Benjamin T. Brockman assumed command.

2. Abbreviated thus in original; possibly Cokesbury.

[57] John Crawford Anderson to Mary Elizabeth Anderson

[Transcribed by J. A. Winn]

Charleston, S.C.
Feb. 20th, 1862

Dear Sister,

Your letter came to hand on Tuesday and as I have not written any this week I will drop you a few lines. You have doubtless heard by now that Nashville is taken and a great number of Confederates. The report caused considerable excitement here and indeed was calculated to excite, but it was not believed by a great many and this morning's Paper gives confirmation to their belief of its enormousness. I have the notion that it is all done for the purpose of drawing the Yankees inland and then before they think they will get the most complete brushing that a set of Vandals ever received. I hope the next news from those parts will be of one of the most glorious Victories that ever shed honor on the "Colours" of any nation. But we have an almost completely different material to fight against in the West from that at Port Royal or on the great Potomac. Those western pioneers have been inured to hardships and trials elsewhere than on the field and are made of better blood than those of the older [part of] the country. It takes men of the bravest kind to put to flight such men as these, and that the point of the bayonett, too.

I believe in fighting with the Bayonett, for our Powder is getting very scarce anyway and the Yankees can't stand the Bayonett. A young man that left here in April to go to Va. Has returned and paid us a visit a few days since and told us about all his adventures during the Great battle of Manassa. He was in ten steps of the Yankees line of battle, run over Yankees and steped on their dead boddies and just reason to believe he killed several of them and says he killed one on Cannon wagon as it was fixing for the retreat. It is enough to make anyone's heart fire with rage and become [illegible] at the relation of the gallant deeds performed and crucial scenes enacted on that memorable day. But after looking over the gallant conduct of our countrimen at home in and out of the field we turn with defection and a sickening heart to relate the fact that in the very birth place of Secession we are compelled to resort to the draft for the purpose of upholding our cause, in the City of Charleston, as men were drafted on yesterday.

I have always said that they were a crowd of base cowards and as afraid of a Yankee as a chicken is of a Hawk. Some of the more honorable have volunteered and gone in like men, but if it was not for the country [people] what would the Yankees not do? Rhett has written a piece in the [Charleston] *Mercury* saying that the draft is no disgrace but if it had been [used] in the country, we would have never heard the last of it . . . Write soon and give me all the news from home. You must remember me to the Darkies and give my love to all the family.
Your brother

[58] Mary Elizabeth Anderson to John Crawford Anderson

Pleasant Falls
March 7, 1862

Dear Brother,

We received a letter from you this week, very glad to hear from you, and since I think of it I believe I am owing you a letter. You must please excuse this writing as it is very cold tonight and I am seated in Ma's room, writing on my lap and Jimmy, who returned from Reidville this evening (has started to school there, very much pleased) and Hattie are talking. Our home is very quiet now to what it was when Ella and Net were here. Ma has been unwell this week, had a bad cold and severe cough, but is a good deal better today.

Pa has been very busy hauling corn to Spartanburg. He has sold four hundred bushels at $1.00 per bushel, for Confederacy. The farmers have been taking a good deal of corn in to Spartanburg. Grand Pa, Maj. Strobel, Gen. Miller, etc.

Well, Johnie, some of our Volunteers are at home now, some from Walker and Foster's Companies, who have enlisted for the war. Andrew and John Evins came in near the same time. Sad to say Andrew is no more, he breathed his last on Saturday morning, 1st of March. He was not entirely well when he left Virginia, and was much exposed coming home, sometimes they were compeled to take the freight train and the Cars were so crowded, he took cold and at Spartanburg he had a chill but being at Mrs. Choices said nothing about it. His case terminated in a severe spell of pneumonia. He went out to Cousin Nancy's[1] on Thursday evening, eat supper, and sat up near half an hour on feeling tired. Col. Evins thought he could assist him upstairs, but on getting halfway, he had to call on Mr. Hill. Andrew fainted when they got to the door. he had fallen off so much [lost weight] and was very feeble. They placed him on the bed and he was never able to get out of it. He did not talk much as his lungs were much affected. He seemed delirious a great deal of the time, did not realize he was at home, thought he was in Camp and called for Uncle Jim several times. He did not talk about dying until he was past talking, he seemed so rejoiced to get home and hoped he would get well. He was speechless on Friday (fast day) Ma and me were down there on Friday night and Saturday. O, Johnie, he did not look anything like himself, was so thin and pale. On Saturday morning he clasped his hands together and laid them on his chest twice, as if to say he was ready. We were near his bedside when he fell asleep in Jesus. We know our loss is his eternal gain, for he was a true follower of Christ. "Blessed are the dead who die in the Lord for the rest from their labors and their works do follow them."[2] The family were with him all the time. We will miss him very much for he was a kind neighbor.

Bob Snoddy called on me one evening last week. Alf is still Capt. and Bob first Lieutenant, he is very popular and has improved a good deal since I saw anything of him. Jim Bivings called before the girls left us on Monday evening. The wind was very high that evening, while we were talking away, his horse broke loose. When he was ready to go home he found himself minus a horse. The consequence was he staid all night and rode Old Jim [mule] home. I have not seen many Volunteers. Young Allen died last week, he was well when he came in. Bob Snoddy is recruiting, has one man. I hear there has been another call for troops. We hear reports from Manassas that McClellan is trying to surround us. Thank you for your invitation to attend Commencement, but must decline these wartimes. The Ladies have on foot a subscription for building a Gun Boat.... Johnie, what about the books? Jim Bivings brought me pieces of Anndre's "Maryland," a battle song....

You saw the notice of Willie Hawes death. In life we are in death. Good night. All asleep. Angels guard you. With much love Your Sister Mary

1. Nancy Moore Evins, his stepmother. She died a week after this letter was written.

2. Revelation 14:13

[59] Ella E. Brockman to John Crawford Anderson

Limestone Semenary
March 10th, 1862

Dear Johnie

I know you will think I have treated you nice to pretend to corispond with you but I entended writing when I got hear but it has been impossible for me to write to anyone for I could not get my money changed to send any letters, so I take this chance of sending when I have some money.

I left home rather reluctantly as I love comforts so much. I dislike to leave home these times, but I have come to the conclusion that I will stay it out until the graduating time comes, if the times don't get two bad, and they won't let me come. Net, supose has gone back to school before this . . .

Johnnie, I wished so much to see you in vacation but it was impossible, therefore I fear many days will pass before we will se each other again.

I have just come to the conclusion never to write home only when I receive letters only on extra occasions I begin to think there is no use of taking time every time you have the blues for five cents are not so easy to be got these times. Just at the time I commenced complaining I got a letter so I am reconsiled now; it was a letter from Sis, it was very interesting, I took so much pleasure in reading it, but as I got it Just as school comenced and had to go into my class to recite, I would peep at it by chances when the teacher saw me she would make me put it in my pocket, but after awhile I was permitted to read it. I was so sorry to hear of Andrew Evins death. I was in hopes he would get well and enjoy the luxuries of home once more but he may be happier now in those realms above.

Bob Snoddie came home a night or two before I left. I did not see him, he has called on Sis since I left, she has had a happy time to herself receiving soldier's calls, I suppose she has written you the events of the day.

We have a pretty large school, I expect about the largest in the state. We all get on finely, I love to stay hear so much, I think the girls are more sociable this year than they were last. I think we all can now see the importance of studying.

I received a letter from Jessie but it was quite old as it was dated in January . . .

I have a great deal to do in school so there is not much time for me to spend in idolness.

Write me very soon and don't treat me as I have you this time.

Yours affectionately,
Ella E. Brockman.
Limestone

[60] Nettie Anderson to John Crawford Anderson

Laurensville
March 15th, 1862

Dear Johnie,

I will according to request write often for fear I forget. I was delighted to receive your letter. It was a nice one. You must make allowances for my letters being as I cannot soar aloft on the wings of imagination as you do.

I was quite pleased to receive the music *Maryland*. I thank you a thousand times for it. But Jim brought Sis one from Virginia not exactly like mine and can play it tolerably well and I *love* it because you sent it to me.

But I want to ask you for something else if you will listen to me. It is your Ambrotype. When Uncle Jim was out here he said he would have one and Ma let him have mine saying you would give me another so I beg you not to disappoint me. Aunt Mary begged me for it but I would not give it to her. So please have another one taken as soon as you can and send to me if you do not want to spend your money for it tell me what to pay for it and maybe my shallow purse can cover the debt.

The young ladies gave a Tableau for the entertainment of the State Guards. I went and liked some of the scenes very much. That is my first idea of anything of the sort. I do not think I would make an Opera-going Lady. I did not enjoy it though it may have been that I did not get to talk any. Perhaps you saw our President [Dr. E. T. Buist] this past week. He was in Charleston the whole week. I know if you knew him you would like him. I have found since I began to recite my lessons that Mrs. Jacobs lets you use your own language if you wish to but we generally use that of the book being expressed much better than we could do it . . .

I received a letter from Uncle Frank this week. He was quite well. He sent me four nice envelopes because I wrote to him in a blue home made one . . . Johnie, I will send you a list of music. If you can get any of it do so for I tell you it will not be thrown away for nothing, but if you think I ask too much of you do not get any of it. You must write often and long letters for it dose me good to hear from you.
Your loving Sister,
Nettie

List of music sought:

Home Sweet Home	Duet by Grobe
Pleasures of Home	Waltz

Happy Family Polker	
The Bonnie Blue Flag	Long
Do they miss me at Home	Variations
Let the wide world wag as it will	Song
Coming through the rye	Long
Southern Marseillaise	Long
Gentle Nettie Moore	Long
Let me kiss him for his Mother	Variations

[61] Mary Elizabeth Anderson to Nettie Anderson

Pleasant Falls
March 19, 1862

Dearest Nettie,

Rain, Rain, Rain. I am now seated in Ma's room in front of the fire, Children playing in the Sitting room. Ma and Pa have gone to Grandpa's [James Mason Anderson] today to see Aunt Sue, Mrs. Norris, etc. Miss Julia and Mrs. Norris came up on Monday, she gets very low spirited sometimes. She will spend several weeks with Aunt Sue. Ma has been quite unwell since she came home, has had a severe cold and bad cough, is better of her cold, but coughs badly sometimes, if she had not kept [stayed in] her room I have no doubt she would have had a severe spell of Pneumonia. So you may conclude that I have gotten over any severe attack of ignorant fever [her concerns about not being able to continue her education] and was glad I could be at home to wait on Ma and attend to domestic affairs.

I have heard ere this of Cousin Nancy Moore's death! She died on Friday the 14th, just two weeks after Andrew [Evins] died. She seemed to have a severe cold and was in bed, but Dr. Tom [Evins] did not consider her at all dangerous. Tom Moore came home on Thursday night and she seemed very cheerful, sat up in bed and brushed her teeth and seemed better, she seemed to sleep soundly during the night, and in the morning they could not arouse her, she was in a state of stupor, did not speak and was paralyzed, could not move one limb. She looked perfectly natural, was buried by the side of Mrs. Evins. Poor Tom and Ann take her death very hard. She will be much missed. Net did you know Cousin Ann and Miss Julia were particular friends? They were together at Limestone. Col. Evins was taken very sick on Sabbath morning, had a Chill was very sick a few days but Pa was down to see him yesterday and he was a little better. Mr. John Finch was to be buried today. Mrs. Caldwell has been very sick but is getting better.

Well, Net, you would be surprised to hear of my travel for the last two weeks. I know you have heard of the Gun Boat. I have been trying what I could do in our District. I get about two days in a week to ride, on Monday of last week I went to Maj. Strobels they all gave a dollar. I spent the most of a day there as it rained, came on back and Addie gave a dollar. On Tuesday we went to Tom Fielders, Gen. Millers, Cousin Sallies, and Fannie went with me to see Barb Switzer, back to Cousin Sallie's to dinner, around to Coans, Poseys, and Barrys. Barbara Posey gave me some information on the subject of my Valentine from Ridgeway. Says it is from a friend of hers, a Dr. Red who lives near her Uncle Johns, says he is mighty smart but not in the Army. Lizzie Bush went around in Reidville for me, Lizzie Bivings at Crawfordsville, she has $34. Nearly every one of those factory girls gave a Dollar. On Monday last Tommy [her younger brother] and I went to Aunt Sue's, she had Della fixed [saddled] for me, so after kissing Frank and that "sweet little Angel," I was on my way to Cashville, took dinner at Mr. Drummonds, saw Jim. We made $10 that day, we rode for some time by starlight to get home. On yesterday I went by Mr. Bivings. Tommy was tired when I got there so Lizzie mounted a pony and we were off for the Gun Boat went as far as Mr. Landrum's saw Cousins Mary and Lizzie, they are sweet girls. We made $15 that day which averaged a dollar a mile. So we have $100.50. Tommy and I went out this morning and made up $7.00. Mrs. Snoddy gave four, two for herself and one for Mary Simpson and one for Gertrude Moss. Mrs. Snoddy is in low spirits as Bobbie has gone. Jim left yesterday morning. He was down here on Friday evening, we tried to get up a fishing party on this river but it rained. Ma had a nice young turkey killed and I had cakes made. I had planned out a "glorious time." Jim took tea with us and as neither Pa nor Davis were at the table he asked a blessing. He sang "Bury me not in the deep, deep sea" with me to learn the air. We sent a box to Uncle Frank by him. Pam ——ding and Becca Phillips staid with us on Wednesday night after the tableaux at Laurens, told us all about it . . .

We had a letter from Johnie this week he has invited us to come down to Commencement but I can't go among such Cowards.[1]

Uncle Jesse is home said he would bring Aunt Hettie and Tommy over today to see us, but it is raining too much. I looked anxiously for a letter from you last week What are your studies? Write us often.

We have not heard one word from Hettie since she left us . . . Addie and Barb S. [Snoddy] walked over to see me yesterday and I was not at home . . . I was sorry to hear of our reverses in N.C . . . It seems I can't write you all. I have so much to tell. I hope to see you soon. Children send love, my love to Cousin Fannie, Mattie and Janie Your sister Mary

March 21st Friday

Aunt Mary Will [household slave] came very near dying last night, she was very bad and talked a great deal. She imagined she saw Johnie and she talked and laughed so much. Just like she does when any of us come home. She is a little easier this morning. I wish you were here to go with me this morning. I am going to Mrs. Bill Smiths. I feel lonely when I come up to my room at night. I am now in first Kings. [Bible reading program] Where are you? All send love. Lizzie B. says don't forget your promise to write to her. Goodbye Your affect Sister

1. She apparently felt all Citadel cadets should have left school to join the Confederate army.

[The following list of thirty-nine subscribers to the gunboat fund drive was attached to this letter.]

Mrs. H. E. Bivings	$3.00	Miss Ellen Crocker	$1.00
Misses Hattie and Addie Bivings	$1.00	Mrs. M. L. Dobbins	$1.00
		Mrs. Cohen	$1.00
Mrs. M. M. Bivings	$1.00	Miss Jennie Cohen	$1.00
Miss L. C. Bivings	$1.00	Miss Carrie Coan	$1.00
Carolina Bivings	$1.00	Miss Laura Coan	$1.00
Mrs. E. Maeris	$1.00	Mrs. M. Mauldin	$1.00
Mrs. M. Hawkins	$1.00	Miss Margaret Hadden	$1.00
Miss Sue Hawkins	$1.00	Mrs. Hadden	$1.00
Miss Nancy Hawkins	$1.00	Miss Lizzie Hadden	
Miss Lass Hawkins	$1.00	Servants	
Miss Celia Hawkins	$1.00	Bettes	$1.00
Miss Nancy Arthur	$1.00	Harriet	$1.00
Miss Sarah Arthur	$1.00	Mrs. Annie Moore	$1.00
Mrs. C. Davis	$1.00	Madora Caldwell	$1.00
Mrs. Steading	$1.00	[illegible]	$1.00
Miss E. Caldwell	$1.00	Miss Mary [illegible]	$1.00
Mrs. Mary Davis	$1.00	Gertrude Moore	$1.00
Mrs. Sarah Davis	$1.00	Jane Alexander	$1.00
Miss Eliza Crocker	$1.00	Lizzie Alexander	$1.00

[62] Mary Elizabeth Anderson to John Crawford Anderson

Pleasant Falls
March 22nd, 1862

Dear Johnie,

As Pa has procured a check and wished it sent you immediately, I will take this opportunity of writing you. Ma wrote you on Thursday and gave you the health of the family, etc. Old Aunt Mary is some better, the rest all well.

We heard from Col. Evins on yesterday, he was then very bad. Dr. Tom is still with him His time [of service] has been out sometime but he says he will not go back until the family are better if he is court martialed. Jimmie is at Reidville at school now, is very much pleased. Mr. Johnston, a graduate of Wofford, is their teacher, he was on the Coast awhile, could not stand it, got a discharge, came to Spartanburg and married. Has near twenty scholars. He drills them every day so Jim is perfectly delighted. Orr Miller is at school there. Sam expects to return to Va. as John Evins returns.

On my rounds this week for the Gun Boat I called at Mr. Drummons got dinner and saw Jim. Oh! Johnie, I have had glorious times the bright days of last week and this.... Aunt Sue lent me her pony "Della." Last week Tommy and I went round to Maj. Strobels, the next day down to see Fannie Miller and Barb Switzer, Barb Posey, etc. The next day to see Aunt Sue, then came the rain, rain. The next Monday we went to Cashville. On Tuesday I went by and got Lizzie Bivings (both on horseback) and went to Mr. Bensons and Landrums and the places between them and home. We made $15.00 that day. I made up $74.50 and together we have near $110.00. Everybody seemed willing to give. I called on John Murrys wife, she put down one dollar and said a twenty dollar bill was the smallest she had. That speaks well for a Volunteer...

Pa wants to know if you have cleared all accounts with Uncle Ben, write and let him know.

Do you read much and have you got any new books? Simses[1] works would be worth getting if your purse is heavy. I am anxious to read them....

The result of Pa's trip to Hamburg was two barrels of Molasses, two barrels of Sugar, Rice, Salt, and bagging, etc.

All send love. Your fond

Sister

Look out for my piece in the Charleston Courier. Goodbye John do try to come home I want so much to see you. Vale, Vole. [illegible] semper.

1. William Gilmore Simms (1806–1870), South Carolina poet, historian, and novelist.

[63] Mary Elizabeth Anderson to John Crawford Anderson

Pleasant Falls
April 10th [1862]

Dear Brother,

I have just finished a hearty dinner and at the table Pa said he was going to town and asked me to write you. It is on the subject of Salt—there is none to be had in Spartanburg and Pa wishes you to send up a sack for $20 or under, as we are almost out. He says you must look around and get some, he says on credit, but you can manage that.

A glorious victory at Corinth, but loss on both sides was heavy. I was sorry to hear of Gen. Johnston's[1] death. I do wonder if Uncle Mason was in it; it was only about sixty miles from Pantotoc [Mississippi, where he is]

We hope to hear particulars this evening. Rain, rain, rain again, a poor time for farmers. Pa has planted some Corn.

We had a letter from Uncle Frank yesterday. He was in the Hospital. Will Norris has lost his boy. . has been sick, was better, and dropped dead suddenly. Mr. John Norris is in from the Western Army. Aunt Sue is now on Pacolet. Uncle Frank wrote he was coming home when his time was out, which will be in a few days. Col. Evins is improving. Billy Means and lady are living at Old Poolesville. If we can get [catch] old Jim, Ma and I will call on them this evening.

Received a letter from Emma [Buist] this week, sends her thanks for your kindly remembrance of her, says your card was done up in style. All well. "Goodbye"

Your loving Sister Mary

Uncle Ben is up. Looks well. This is Net's birthday, only "Sixteen" . . . Aunt Het's friend, Mr. M. has been up to see her. Have not heard the consequences. Vale, Vole

1. Gen. Albert Sidney Johnston was killed at the Battle of Shiloh in Tennessee on April 6, 1862.

[64] Franklin Leland Anderson to Mary Elizabeth Anderson

Gordonsville, Va.[1]
April 22nd/62

Dear Sis

Yours is the only letter I have received directed to this place. You can well imagine therefore my anxiety to hear from you all particularly Aunt Sue and my darling little babes. But, oh! Just think about being pressed in for two years further service to my country with nothing but the end of this long, long service to look to save the fickle promise of our own Congress of a furlough of sixty days during the time and all left discresionary with the Secretary of War as to when it shall be given. But such is the price of Liberty one of Heaven's choicest blessings and for it there is no privation we should not cheerfully undergo and pleasure forego for the furtherance of the great work in which we are engaged. I learn this morning that it has been telegraphed here that the Yankees are in New Orleans and from every quarter we are getting bad news; from Yankee accounts we are led almost to doubt whether our Corinth fight was a victory or not considering the death of A. S. Johnson [Gen. Albert Sidney Johnston] and so many other valuable officers. I should think the victory pretty equally divided. What is to be the fate of this Army the Lord only knows, but it is evident the troops here have their minds thoroughly ready for the work; this is the spirit manifested by both officers and men. I hope that our fate here in the now pending conflict is to be the cause soon of a brighter prospect to us. I hope it is to decide in our favour the cruel injustices our enemy is forcing upon us. I am here still with the baggage of our Regt and am beginning to conclude that it is doubtful whether we can get it away. The r.road is taxed to it utmost transporting government stores, the troops that we left behind us are fast falling back I suppose to Richmond. They are so few that I suppose a stand by them was not designed by our Genls. The farmers of the country behind us are driving their hogs and sheep, droves of them, toward Richmond, to prevent them from falling in to the hands of the Yankees. It is distressing to see the Ladies [refugees] flocking thus leaving their homes those that are going to Richmond and beyond and other only keeping inside of our lines and falling back when they learn that the Army is to do so, I am only astonished that they seem almost without an exception cheerful under it. The Old

Folks generally stay behind to encounter the Yankees and take what care they can of their homes.

I sent by Capt. Foster a piece of my ingenuity in idle moments in the shape of a brest pin out of the ivy root that grew on the battlefield Bull Run to Berkley to be ornamented & finished off. My directions were only verbal to the Capt. and I fear it will not be done as I intended. You can call and get it when finished and tell him to charge the work to my act. I received a letter from Nett since she went to Laurens and she closed by saying "excuse all mistakes as Sis is not here to correct for me" Give my love to Pa and Ma and all the children. Tell Pa to sit down some day and write me all the particulars of how things are going . . . what he thinks of the propriety of my getting a Substitute and what the chances for one. I am very willing to serve [my share] but the Conscript thinks it so important for the disciplined troops to be in the field but the idea of a two years campaign is intolerable especially as we will still have a lot of clever representations in the field. Uncles James and Mason [Anderson] I am at a loss to tell you where to direct your letters but you had best direct them as before to Richmond.
Write soon and believe me your affectionate Uncle Frank

PS I have not heard from the Regt. Since it went to Yorktown.

1. Gordonsville is between Orange and Charlottesville, Virginia.

[65] David Anderson to John Crawford Anderson

[Sent together with the following two letters]

Poolesvile
April 26, 1862

Dear Son,

This leaves us all well. Mary wrote you to send us Salt. I have been looking for it for some time. We have about one Peck.

You must get a sack at any price and send soon. I will depend on you to buy me Salt as you can so look round and let us have it.
D. Anderson

[66] Harriet Maria Brockman Anderson to John Crawford Anderson

Dear Son,

Thinking you would like to hear something of your Uncles Jim and Mayson, I have concluded to write what we know of them. Your Uncle Jim is in a cavalry company and has an office I do not remember whether first or second lieutenant . . . Mayson is first lieutenant in Dr. H. Orr's Company and belongs to Col. John Orr's Regiment and is now somewhere in the neighbourhood of Corinth. If you should hear from them, let us know. Your Uncle Frank has not come home. All that did not reenlist have been pressed [required to serve] but we do not know to what regiment they belong or how disposed of.

We heard yesterday that Edwards Regiment had gone to Virginia but do not know how true. I expect at this time it will be better there than on the Coast, but it seems so far from home. I hope that we will be able to manage the enemy. I think of my country all the time and the many precious lives lost and perhaps souls which makes me feel humble and I cease not to supplicate at a throne of grace for all the Soldiers of our Army that he will spare their lives and if not consistant with his will that he will prepare them to enjoy that rest which is eternal life. O how I wish I could know that all my children and friends were the true followers of the meek and lowly Jesus. how cheering would be the thought for you. I feel very anxious and nothing would afford me so much pleasure as to hear of your conversion. Farewell, your loving Mother

[67] Mary Elizabeth Anderson to John Crawford Anderson

PS Must I not write a few lines to finish out your letter. Well, Johnie, I received a piece of music on yesterday from Columbia, a very sickening, loving thing and can't imagine who it is from. I thought at first it was *Desolation Wagon* from you. Please Johnie, send it to me. I heard Miss Alice Shelden, the music teacher at Reidville, play it. We are to have a grand tableaux there next Thursday night the 1st. Miss Carrie Drummond is to act Maryland bound with chains. But I must mail these letters.

Write soon.

Your loving sister

Mary

[68] David Anderson to John Crawford Anderson

Spt C.H. [Spartanburg Court House]
May 5, 1862

Dear Son,

I have just rec'd yours of the first asking leave to quit the Military School. I have been thinking of your situation for some time and have concluded to say to you to use your own discretion in the matter.

I am altogether willing for you to take the field and think if you can get command for Hendrixes Company you had better accept. I think it might suit you better than a higher office. But I leave the matter entirely with you. You must conduct yourself through this struggle so as not to be ashamed of anything you have done.

Everything looks very gloomy at this time. But I have an abiding confidence our cause is good and just and will prevail. And now my son you may perish in this struggle and if so I pray God to prepare you for any change he may order [to] be found at the post of duty and trust God for the Issue.

This leaves us all well except James who had an attack of Soar Throat on last week. He was so unwell your Mother could not leave him on yesterday but was better this morning and I hope will be well soon. Your Uncle James is 1st Lt. in a company of Cavalry drilling at Montgomery and Mayson is 1st Lt. in a Company from Pontecack [Pontotoc] commanded by Capt. Orr, brother of Col. Orr. They are at Corinth under Beauregard. Your Uncle Frank is at Yorktown, I think under Giles or Jenkins. I do not know which. He has been with the baggage until a few days ago. Alfred Foster will leave in a few days for Va. He has been at home some time getting recruits for his company.

We have had more rain this season that I ever saw fall in any one spring. Our crops are very backward and [water has] been high up and down [the Tyger River] all spring. We have not been able to plant [the] Bottems or even to put a plow in them for over a month. I have not heard of George since he left and I don't care much [if] I never do. Your grandpa's health is better—he was out today. Send me a sack of salt and I will send a check for the amount to you or any person you may direct. Write soon and let us hear from you often.

Yours truly,
David Anderson

[69] David Anderson to John Crawford Anderson

[Transcribed by Harriet Means Moore Fielder]

Spt. C.H.
May 9th, 1862

Dear Son,

I have just recd your Letter and am very much disappointed in the way of Salt. I send you a check for $35. thirty-five Dollars you will try to get me one sack of any kind of Salt you can find for I am nearly out and if you fail I will have to do without. so please exert yourself one time. Jimie is improving slowly, he has had Soar Throat and some Fever. We have had no Physician as yet and I hope will need none.

Your Uncle J. B. Earle thinks of going off to Virginia immediately and wishes to see your Uncle Ben. You must prevail on Ben to come home and stay a while and mind his health for he is not able for service and he may be needed more one month from now than at the present. I think the Cadets had better come to Columbia as a Reserve for you can't whip the Yankees by yourselves and if you attempt to Summer it in the Swamp you will all die soon. Discression is the better part of Valour.

We are very backward with our crops but if we can get sunshine we may get along yet. Write soon

NB see if you can get the Salt brought by Rail Road before you purchase. If you can buy 100 pounds rice do so and let me hear from you soon. Yours affectionately
David Anderson

[70] Mary Elizabeth Anderson to John Crawford Anderson

Addressed: Cadet John C. Anderson, Citadel Academy, Charleston

Poolesville. Office
May 24, 1862

Dear Johnie,

Your letter to Pa, containing two post scripts for me, was received week before last during a stay of one week with Grandpa and Aunt Sue. I spent a very pleasant week, assisted in nursing little Julia, who has had a severe spell this spring. I did not think she could ever recover, but she is now a good deal better.

We are all well and more. Jimmie had a long spell of sore throat, but has entirely recovered, still looks thin. He and Tommy have gone to town today in the oxcart, expecting or rather hoping to find salt and rice at the depot. A number of wagons have gone to Va. from Spartanburg for salt, and I do hope will be fully supplied for Cornbread doesn't exactly "harmonize" with my palate unless it is [has] salt.

I wrote a letter for Hanna Bagwell [neighbor] yesterday evening in which she sent word to Berry that she had only one tablespoon full of salt. What do vegetables taste like without salt? Enough on this subject.

Ma received a letter from Aunt Sallie[1] last Saturday morning. She seems to be in great trouble. Uncle Mason is now Capt., Dr. Orr having been made Surgeon of the Regt. he has chills and fever. Aunt Sallie said he had been home once from Corinth, perfectly worn out from drilling. Aunt Sallie was sic, Alice has chills and Quinine is $10.00 for a tablespoon full. Smallpox was in three miles of them, and measles at her nearest neighbors. Wheat has rust and had not finished planting corn. Our Officers are pressing Negroes and horses also going to smoke houses and dividing the meat, saying the Soldiers must be fed, most of the people seem willing to it, knowing the soldiers are their protectors. Uncle Jim was preparing to go on to Corinth, was then in Montgomery.

Uncle Frank has joined his old Company under Evins. Col Jenkins was sick on the 5th and Walker was in command. Evins and Kilpatrick's Companies made the attack and seemed to use the Artillery. We have not seen much in detail concerning their conduct, but in yesterday's paper it is said "Longstreet's Division covered itself with Glory." Jerry Burnett has, or was to try, to get off from Charleston and go on to Va. as a substitute for Uncle Frank, he agreed to go for $200, Uncle Ben left on Wednesday morning, took dinner with us on Tuesday, is better but looks a little thin. It is reported Edwards' Regt. has been sent to Gen. "Stonewall Jackson."

Jim Drummond and Enoree Bill Anderson have bought horses and joined a Company of Rangers in Va.

George Lester has been thrown out of office, and was trying for Captaincy in a Co. of Rangers going from Greenville. I am surprised to see such "Patriotic gentlemen" returning home. Why can't they take a private's place? Too many "Office-seekers"! it seems the panic in Charleston has some what subsided. Pa promised Mr. Fanning to take a family, a Mrs. Hayne and family, but they have not arrived, are still in Charleston, I suppose. I have heard they are among the "high flyers," "big bangs," etc.[2]

No Johnie I have not got acquainted with any of our visitors, have not been to Spartanburg since last September and then attended a Concert you remember just after you went down. Have not been to see Aunt Lucy since she moved, have not even been to Laurens to see Net, thought I would have been a half dozen times ere this. I miss Net and Ella very much. Have seen Aunt Hettie only once since her sickness, so you see my travels are not on an extensive scale. Grandpa has rented his house at Reidville to Mrs. Gibbs of Charleston. several persons in Spartanburg have sold out to refugees. Do you hear from Ella? I think we have had about three letters from her. Net writes us often. Emma Buist inquired particularly for you in her last. We have had several messes of Strawberries from Plain Dealing.[3] The corn in the Orchard is growing fast, some of our wheat has rust.

That poor Cadet how can you treat him so? Act coolly at all times.

I trust you are thinking of Ma's letters, nothing would make us more happy than to hear of your conversion, Johny how can you be content to remain a sinner for you know all sinners have their part in a lake that burns with fire and brimstone.

It seems so easy to "Believe on the Lord Jesus Christ and thou shalt be saved." "Quench not the spirit for now is the accepted time, now is the day of salvation."

May our Father in Heaven bless and save you is the earnest prayer of your loving,
Sister Mary

Tommy and Jimmy have come back. Brought Rice but no Salt. It is raining, raining.

1. Sarah Gilliam Anderson, wife of Mason, great-niece of John C. Calhoun.

2. Many families from Charleston, fearing the fall of the city to the Union troops, took refuge in the upcountry. The long-standing distrust of lowcountry dwellers by the Scots-Irish of the upcountry began in pre–Revolutionary War days when the colonial government in Charleston paid too little attention and failed to offer fair representation to the backcountry.

3. One of the Anderson farms or "places." Located near the South Tyger River in the Poplar Springs area of Spartanburg County, it became the home of Emma Buist and John Crawford Anderson after their marriage in 1866.

[71] Harriet Maria Brockman Anderson to John Crawford Anderson

Poolsville, June 4th, 1862

Dear Son,

This leaves us all well and we have been looking for a letter from you but none as yet. We are anxious to see the salt as ours is getting low.

We have the news of another battle [Front Royal and Winchester, Va.] No word of your Uncle Frank but suppose he is unhurt or his name would have been

given. John Cunningham slightly wounded, John Evins severely, and Thomas and Sam Miller not known how much. Your Grand Pa was here yesterday and took Sis home with him. You wrote about some unpleasant feeling in the Dean family against the Andersons. I suppose it is so but I do not know when or where the insult came from and I do not know that it is important anyway. There was a good many in our county that thought and said that Dean's Company would never be mustered into service but since that time I have not heard a word about them detracting from their character and they may be the bravest of the brave. As for Sis having committed herself to Addie, you need have no fears and I think it not worth while to make any investigation of the matter. Your informant has Snoddy blood in his veins. Addie told Sis that there would be a subscription to buy a flag for the Tyger Rangers but we have not heard from or seen it. If asked we would have given something. You must not let such little trifles occupy too much of your thought but read your Bible and follow the examples contained therein. Blessed is the peace maker and if this one precept was observed how much of angry bad feelings would be avoided . . . I pray for you without ceasing still hoping that you may soon be brought into the fold of Christ. I remain
Your affectionate Mother

[72] Mary Elizabeth Anderson to John Crawford Anderson

Pleasant Falls,
June 11th, 1862

My dear Brother,

I was very glad to hear from you on Monday evening. Your initiation into Camp life was a little severe but I hope may prove to be the worst you will have to undergo.

Johnie, there is much uneasiness felt on account of our soldiers being on James Island. Some who seem to know seem to be afraid the enemy might easily surround the Island and cut our forces off entirely. That might be if the obstruction is not strong.

But our greatest loss during the war has been the capture of our Forts and Islands which were "impregnable" and "perfectly secure." Since Port Royal was taken I have never had one bit of confidence in Gen. [Roswell S.] Ripley and was glad to hear he had been deposed. And do hope the new Commander will not rest so securely on the Forts but may have everything in readiness if the enemy do attack Charleston.

Some persons think the City must fall, that God has decreed it so as punishment to the slaveholders of the Low Country. It is true the Institution of Slavery has been grossly abused and I think this scourge on our Coast is meant as punishment for them.

Some of the Refugees are very much dissatisfied in Spartanburg. [They] Think the country people might put up with any and every privation for them.

Pa said old Professor Duncan [of Wofford College] talked very severely to a Charlestonian who was complaining a good deal, and at length silenced him! I think they ought to be content with what they can get just now. We have not heard from Mrs. Hayne and I do hope will not. We might take them for the sake of humanity but if they can go elsewhere, I say let them go. The lady in Grandpa's house in Reidville is very much dissatisfied and he has nice patches of Irish potatoes, a garden, and sweet potatoes. But things look [illegible]. Pa has been trying to hire some negroes from Capt. Elliott. He has sixteen at Reidville just walking about and nothing to feed them on. But "he will se his Mother about it" every time Pa sees him. You know those negroes will have something to eat. In Spartanburg they are killing up hogs and anything they can get hold of. Mr. Judd has had to lock up his hogs.

Aunt Sue received a letter from Uncle Frank on Monday written on Tuesday after the fight. He was in all the fight but escaped unhurt. He was in the pursuit ... said the Enemy made a stand at their Camp and our soldiers stopped almost in front of them to fasten on bayonets. They fought hard for their Camp but were driven. He staid in their Camp that night but not to sleep. He and William Gaston carried water to the wounded and dying Yankees. He took a portfolio from one of their tents ... had a number of photographs of Gen. Bank and others. How much he can tell us if he is spared to come Home. Cousin John C. was wounded slightly in the hand, Sam Miller in the ankle, and John Evins near the shoulder in the left arm, was doing well and cheerful on the 5th when Dr. Tom telegraphed. We have not heard one word from Uncle Jim or Mason. All are well. Grandpa is cutting wheat, he says poor.

May our Father in Heaven keep you is the prayer of your loving
Sister Mary

Confederate paper [1] you see. The salt has been received and glad to get it. It is reported the wagons that went to Va. for salt have been pressed into service. Not a word from Uncle Ben or Jessee. Tom heard they are near Richmond now.

Write soon.

1. A coarse-textured ruled paper.

[73] John Crawford Anderson to Nettie Anderson

[Transcribed by J. A. Winn]

Citadel, Charleston
June 12th, 1862

Sister Net,

We have had quite an exciting time for the last week in the Citadel. We were ordered out on the Island to take part in the fight,[1] but after remaining there for a few days, during which it rained all the time, we were ordered to return to the Citadel. It was against the will of every single Man but we had to obey the order. The consequence was the most of the Men thought themselves wronged and dishonored and on Monday evening occurred a rebellion. I was greatly tempted to join in it myself but was restrained when I contemplated the pain it would give my Parents and friends to know that I had become so lost to all sense of honor and responsibility to commit such an act. I have therefore concluded not to join any such proceeding.

I thought of leaving the Institution and still think that I will but have determined to wait for further developments of affairs. A great many have left and the Institution has received a severe blow. The Public generally are very hard down on the Men who have left in the scrape. Everything seems to be working against them now, and say I can't healp [help] but discover symptoms of regret brooding over the minds of some even as soon as yesterday and after some have met with their parents I am fearful of the consequences, for one Gentleman has already told his Son if he had anything to do with it that he would be discarded from his family.

Such a thing would strike me a death blow, and bring eternal disgrace upon me, or perhaps it would have the effect to make me rise above the buffetings of this "dim spot" and trim my pinions for a loftier and nobler flight than I would have otherwise aspired to, but such is nor ever will be my fate if left to my actions.

Well, enough on the rebellion for I know you are not as much interested in it as your brother . . . You have heard of the fight on James Island, I suppose. It was a very imprudent thing on Col. Williams' part. He might have saved all his men if he had acted upon advice of Col. Stevens.

Let it then suffice that our forces got the worst of it by a good deal. The wounded are now in the City being attended to by the Ladies. I know very little of the positions of the Enemy or his forces on the Island, but the spirit of the Men is to drive him off before he can get well fixed in his position.

I think and it is the general position that when the City is attacked it will most certainly fall; if not in the hands of the Yankees, by the torch. Everyone has determined to burn the whole establishment if the Yankees are likely to obtain possession of the City.

I wonder if Miss Emma [Buist] & Miss Corrie ever think of me. I saw Ed Miller & Lieut George Dean the other day, they look as bad as ever and were quite cool toward me. George thinks I want to cut him out of Miss Addie[2] but he is much mistaken.

I also saw Andrew and Tom Moore not long ago and was treated very warmly indeed by them. They say that they are sick and tired of their condition and live an awful life in Camp . . .

Write soon to your affectionate brother, J. Crawford Anderson

1. Union forces came up the Stono River and came ashore on James Island on June 2; there was a skirmish between the Confederate and Union troops, June 2–15, culminating in the Battle of Secessionville on June 16.

2. Addie Snoddy, who married Eddie Miller after the war.

[74] Mary Elizabeth Anderson to John Crawford Anderson

Poolesville, S.C.
June 18, 1862

My dear brother,

As Sam Anderson is going to town this morning and I can send a letter by him to the [Post] Office I will do so. We can't imagine why you have not written us—yesterday was a week since the fight on the Island [James Island, S.C.] and we have not heard one word from you.

Uncle Frank came home last Saturday night as Pa succeeded in getting McFarlin, a brother of the Masons, to go on as a substitute for $500. He looked very thin and much fatigued when I saw him but Pa and Ma were up to see him on yesterday, found him cleaned up and very happy. He brought some trophies home, letters, papers, photographs, etc. Will Norris sent me two Valentines as trophies. I wish you could come up and see Uncle Frank.

Bob Snoddy came home on Monday. He has had fever, was not in the fight. I must go up and call on him.

Well, Johnie, Mary Dorroh has been with me this week. She spent Monday with me and in the evening we went down to see Fannie Miller. On yesterday we went to Spartanburg, carried her over both Colleges [Spartanburg Female College and Wofford College], into the Society halls—was perfectly delighted—over a good bit of the Burg and then went to Cedar Springs where we perused it. Went to the Institution [South Carolina School for the Deaf and the Blind], Mr. Henderson had the Orchestra assembled and we heard some splendid music. From thence we turned homeward, Sam and Tommy our drivers. Addie Snoddie went in the carriage with us.

Goodbye as Sam is waiting. Remember [me] to Cousin Andrew.
Your loving sister Mary

Pa has cut some wheat, not his best. The mogul[1] in the Buffalo is good. Corn is growing, fruit ripening. Would like to have called on your Charleston friend. When you come up we will get acquainted.
Vale

1. Probably an annual crop, closely related to alfalfa, that can be cut for hay.

[75] Harriet Maria Brockman Anderson to John Crawford Anderson

Poolsville, June 18, 1862

My dear Son,

I received your welcome letter we were glad you were well. We have a great deal of sickness in our neighborhood and some deaths. Two weeks after Andrew Evins died cousin Nancy [Moore] Evins died with paralysis but had Jaundice also. They were not alarmed about her. Tom came home the night before and she set up in bed and talked to him and seemed cheerful but when they awoke at five o'clock she was insensible and died at two never was aroused to notice or talk. I felt for poor Tom he felt it so deeply he has lost his best friend and the night after she was buried Col. Evins took a chill and is now very sick and I would not be surprised he did not recover. He was feeble before his troubles came on him. Dr. Tom Evins has been here some time he would have gone Monday if his father had not been so ill. The measles are thick up here. Sis and I have been exposed to them but have not taken. Our soldiers have nearly all gone back to Camp. Three died after reaching home and others were sick but will go as soon as they are able. You seem anxious that Sis should come and were it convenient I would like for her to go. But she cannot at this time and I hope you will be permitted to remain in safety. The times are gathering darkness as they progress; I have almost despaired of our cause but I still pray we may delivered from our enemies and I feel I must discharge my duty and I can do no more. . . .

Sis has been getting up a subscription for the gunboat, she has been very successful and if the people felt it to be safe to build gunboats in Charleston, hundreds of dollars could be raised. I mean that they would not be in danger until completed. We can look back and see what would have been good policy but cannot look forward . . . not even the wise ones of the day.

Jessee came up last week, he was here on Sunday. He looks very well. He said the people of Charleston thought they might as well surrender the town, that it could not be defended. I hope it can and that it will not fall if attacked. Grand Pa and Aunt Sue and the babies well. I spent yesterday with them. No late news from Uncle Frank. I have to write upstairs and have no fire. It is raining now and we have it more than half the time. I hope our trouble will come to a close and we may once more be free and happy. I remain your ever-praying Mother

Dear John, I was up last night with Mary Will.[1] I thought she would die with convulsions. She was very bad. While I was applying mustard to her head she imagined she saw you and I never saw anyone so delighted she would laugh and talk to you as though you were present. She said you promised her a new pair of shoes and she wanted them. I do not think she will live long without a change. I do not know what else to write. I have many cares but if the war was over they would not be much to bear. I pray once more my son be ready to die—let it come when it will. We know neither the day nor the hour when the messenger will summon us to the bar of God. You must not neglect a Mother's admonition. You have been a dutiful son all your life and I feel grateful that I have such a son but you lack the one thing needful which I much desire you should have and will pray fervently you may obtain. I remain with much affection your absent Mother

1. Mary Will was an elderly family slave and had been John's nurse when he was a child.

[76] David Anderson to John Crawford Anderson

[Transcribed by Harriet Means Moore Fielder]

Poolesville, Spt Dist
June 28, 1862

Dear John,

I have not herd from you personally since the Battle on James Island. I have been looking for an interesting account in which I would see here the State Cadets rendered important service in the Battle or had wiped out the Yankees and demolished the Fleet entirely but to my great surprise I learn The Cadets marched out to James Island before day and back to Charleston the next night all in the Dark. I guess it was all right. I am no military man, therefore I have no right to Judge, perhaps you went out to choose your ground to fight upon or to retreat on.

I understand some of your Company got lost or rebelled I don't know which. I hope you were not in the number for I think every *good* General should look after his deserters and lost soldiers. I hope your whole Class has been kindly cared for before this shall reach you for I hold that every Soldier should be an officer and entitled to do as he pleases and fight when and where he chooses. I have no doubt you understand what I say on this subject.

This War has brought a great deal of distress and suffering on us. We have made little or no wheat in Sptb. [Spartanburg]. I have made enough for seed and my own use. We get little or none to grind because it is not made. We are very dry and need rain very much. It is cloudy but does not rain. Salt is very scarce and we all will suffer on account of it. I Recd the 4 Bushels you sent and would like to have 8 or 10 Bushels more. Try Chisholm again and Report all my shoppers, viz. 2 Rogers, 2 Burnetts, 1 Dobbins, 1 Bagwell, 1 Sam and Betty Waldrip and myself. Please interest yourself in this matter and I will send you the money in time. Try and make the arrangement and let me here from you soon. Enclosed you have a check for Seventy-five Dollars which I hope you will make a wise use of. This leaves all well, Yours,
David Anderson

[77] David Anderson to John Crawford Anderson

[Transcribed by Harriet Means Moore Fielder]

Spt C.H.
June 30th, 1862

Dear John,

I wrote you on yesterday sending a check for Seventy-five Dollars and a request to exert yourself for Salt.

I Recd yours last evening enquiring for Hams and C.—[corn?]

I can let you have 30 or 40 good hams at 40 cts. per pound and meal at $2.75 per 100 pounds. A Confederate agent has been up from the Coast and made me this offer and if you wish you can have it at the same price. I think I could buy more good hams at the same price from O. P. Earle. I think Charleston will be attacked pretty soon and you will have to fight hard to keep your Town. We hear this evening of considerable fighting at Richmond. I suppose you have herd of your Uncle Frank being at Home. We have not seen or herd of your Uncles in the

West very Recently. I think you had better come up and make those purchases if your Institution needs them.

I think it would be very difficult to purchase Flour at any price as our wheat crop is almost a failure.

Write soon

Yours Truly

David Anderson

[78] Mary Elizabeth Anderson to John Crawford Anderson

Poolsville, S.C.
July 7, 1862

Dear Johnie,

I had been owing you a letter for sometime but as Pa wrote you last week I thought it better to postpone writing until this week. This leaves us all in good health. Jimmie has a sore ankle, it looks as if it might have been poisoned.

Well, Johnie, mighty events[1] have transpired since I wrote you and many a good Soldier has fallen. I have ere this heard that Sam Miller is now no more—poor fellow—I hope he was prepared for the great change. What an awful thing to be sent off on the field of battle unprepared, there is a great lamentation all over the South. There was a distressing time in Spartanburg when the news was received—Mrs.Walker (of Walker House) [a local hotel] and Miss Free Henry have gone on [to the area of the battle]. John Walker was killed, the people in Spartanburg did everything to prevent Mrs. Walker from going on but she was determined to go on—Miss Free has gone on to see Pat who was slightly wounded in the thigh. Proffesor Duncan received a telegraph from his son in Richmond that Mr. Tom Duncan lived a short time after he was shot, was buried in Richmond. But Dr. Miller's family have not had one word from anyone about Sam's body. Mr. Oddie Capers has gone on to see if he can find it. or hear anything concerning his death. The Spartan Rifles have suffered much. Henry Thomson is dangerously ill with fever and the Orderly has now taken command.

We have had no word from Uncle Ben or Uncle Jessee but Antony Wakefield was wounded slightly in the back of the neck by a piece of shell, he wrote they came through safe (on Friday) and Col. Edwards was the bravest man on the field and Maj. Brockman next—their loss was two killed, William Davis and Benjamin Howe, and seven wounded.

I had a letter from Ella last week. Commencement [at Limestone] comes off on the 16th we want very much to go over but Pa does not seem inclined to let us go, but says he will send for Ella.

Cousin John C. has not been over to see us yet. I am anxious to see him. I had a letter from Uncle Jim on Friday. He is now twenty miles from Pensacola was well, is in 2nd Regt of Cavalry, Carpenter's Company. Direct to Montgomery if you wish to write. We have not had a single word from Uncle Mason, our Army is in eight miles of them. (Aunt Sallie wrote Ma) and fortifying on Mr. Orr's land. I have not had a letter from Mary Switzer in a long time.

Net is at home now, has been two weeks. We had a very pleasant time at the Commencement at Reidville—five graduates and very good Compositions, boys spoke in the evening, Jim did well, spoke your old speech "Give me liberty or give me death." Willie Roebuck was up and took dinner with us. O, he is a fine fellow, thinks a good deal of John. Who was the lady you gallanted from the Battery? June apples are ripening, I wish you could enjoy the vegetables with us, We are making up a box to send to Va.

All send love to you . . . Write soon to us. Your affectionate
Sister Mary

1. The Seven Days' Battles, June 26–July 2, at the end of the Peninsula campaign, saw the Confederates withdraw toward Richmond.

[79] Stephen Moore to his wife Rachel[1]

Camp on Jameses Island
July 8th, 1862

Dear Wife:

I take the present opportunity of writing you a few lines to let you know how I am getting on. I am as well as common and hope these few lines may find you all well. I was rite smartly vext until Minas come here. He said you was all well and that gave me satisfaction. Tell Minases mother that he is in a half mile of me. I can see him any time I want to. He is well. I will try come home in 2 or 3 weeks if I can get off. You and Elihu must gather me about 40 chickens when I come home. I will have the money to pay for them. I am making money every day. Tell Numer and Ransom they must sea to my children and sea that they mind theirs mother & tell Elihu likewise. Tell Elihu to make me those shoes by the time I said when I left there. Tell Elihu it was his request that we should divide our time in the War. He must write before I come home if he is still of the notion. If he is we will divide the time, not that I am tired of the war but it was the contract. Tell Syntty and Chany I am very much oblige to them for the word they sent me by Minas. Tell Lizabeth, Nelly, and Gracy I thank them for thir compliments they sent. tell Mother I will send her money as soon as an opportunity will admit. Tell

Camp on Jameses Island
July 8th 1862

Dear Wife I take the present opportunity of writeing you a few lines to
let you know how I am getting on I am
as well as common & hope these few lines
may find you all well I was [illegible]
ly [illegible] til Minus come here he said you was
all well & that gave me satisfaction tell
Minus's Mother he is in a half mile of
me I can see him any time I want too he
is well I will try to come home [illegible]
[illegible] if I can get off you & Elihue must gather
me about 40 chickens when I come home I will
have the money to pay for them I am
making money every day tell [illegible]
[illegible] they must see to my children
& see that they mind their mother & tell
Elihue likewise tell Elihue to make me
those shoes by the time I said when I left
there tell Elihew it was his request
that we should divide our time in the
[illegible] he must write before I come home
if he is still of the notion of he is [illegible]
will divide the time not that I am tired
of the [illegible] but it was the contract
tell Synthy & Chaney I [illegible]
[illegible] to them for the word
they sent me by Minus tell Lizabeth
nelly & Gracy I thank them for their
Compliments they sent tell mother
I will send her money as soon as
an oppertunity will admit tell [illegible]
[illegible] I want to see him as well as any
body else tell him to please take
this letter & read it to Rachel

Letter dated July 8, 1862, from Stephen Moore, on James Island near Charleston, to his wife, Rachel, at Fredonia. Courtesy of the Thomas John Moore Papers, South Caroliniana Library, University of South Carolina, Columbia

Mr. Hill I want to see him as well as anybody else. Tell him to please take this letter & read it to Rachel. I will thank you to take this letter and read it to all my people. Tell Rachel I have bought a fine watch for her I have no way to send it & will keep it and bring it when I come. Tell them all I have been on the Battlefield where the Yankees was slain. Neither of my Masters [Andrew C. and Thomas J. Moore] has not spoken a cross word to me since I have been with them. I like them as well as any boddy I ever had anything to do with. Tell Rachel if she needs any money to write to me when Elihu write. The money is not to be made it is already made. I have 3 meals of victuals to cook a day and the rest of the time is mine. If you don't spend the money I send you keep it for me for when I come home. Rachel pay Gracy 30 cts for me, pay Noah 25 cts for me, pay Numar one dollar & a half & I will settle the Ballance when I come. Write sone.
Yours husband,
Stephen

1. It was very unusual for slaves to read and write, and it was in fact illegal to teach them to in South Carolina. Both Stephen Moore and Elihu Moore (see his letter of April 9, 1863 on page 115) clearly had some mastery of written English.

[80] Stephen Moore to Thomas W. Hill

[Enclosed in same envelope with the note to the plantation overseer, Mr. Hill, that follows]

Mr. Hill:

Please give the $1.00 to my mother, Fannie. Tell Rachel & all the rest not to forget me in their prayers & I will always try to remember them when I try to approach a throne of grace. We have preaching in camp twice every Sunday & prayer meeting every night almost. I will add nothing more this time. Stephen Moore

[81] David Anderson to John Crawford Anderson

Addressed to Cadet John C. Anderson, Charleston, So. Ca.

July 14th, 1862

Dear John,

I Recd your last on Saturday acknowledging the Rect of check and you state you can get Salt at $5.00 per bushel by waiting 3 or 4 weeks. Try and make the arrangement as soon as possible you must put in Berry Bagwell's wife's name. he was brought up [drafted] on Saturday last. his wife you know is very poor and I

Ben Moore, son of Stephen and Rachel Moore, in 1937. From the editor's collection

will have to give her salt for she will have no money to pay for it. I understand Dr. Coan has purchased 30 bushels for the family. You must try to get 20 or Thirty for me. We are dependant on the salt works in Va for salt and by the time we go there and get 2 or 3 Bushels to the horse and give ten dollars for the Ballance of a load I find it will be very dear Salt. I had much rather give $5.00 in Charleston and think I had made a good trade. I do not want it just now as I have some on hand. I wish to be certain of it for Killing Hogs and if I can get in Charleston I will not go to Virginia so you must be certain to let me know what you do and I will send you the money in time. I still have my Bacon on hand and will take 33⅓ for 1000 lbs. hog bound and will have some flour soon. I do not know how much until I thrash wheat.

Dr. Dave Miller is at his Mother's on the way to Richmond to see Jeff Davis. his mission is to get up a Squadron of Partisan Rangers.

Cousin Tom's foot is getting well slowly. Your Uncle Ben and Jesse have come through the fight unhurt. Col Edwards and Uncle Ben are said to have distinguished themselves. Our Victory at Richmond has been dearly Bot. We have a great many wounded men in our midst and goodly number will die from wounds Recd in the fight. I am sorry to know your fare is so poor but I think you cannot do better than to stick it through.

I think it a wise arrangement to keep the Cadets in the Citadel for it would kill the most of you to put you in the field at this time.

We would like to see you at home soon. Our Corn is promising but needing rain at this time.

Let us hear from you soon,

Yours Truly,

David Anderson

[82] Thomas John Moore to Thomas W. Hill

Ft. Johnson, N.C.
July 17th, 1862

Dear Sir:

As Stephen starts home this morning, I will write you a short letter. Stephen has been sick for two or three days but is now improving. When he starts back you & Lou [the cook at Fredonia] must fix us up a nice box. I want you by all means to send me some good ham and also butter and a good amount of both. Honey would be nice here if we could get it. You must rob a box [hive] or gum and send it to us. Tell Lou she must bake us a good nice loaf bread to eat with it. These I believe are about the only things that we especially want unless it be some chickens. If Lou has a good supply on hand you must send a coop of them or if she has not got them you may bye them and send your bill by Stephen.

Our mess has got quinine to take for the prevention of fever. The Surgeon recommends that it be taken in brandy or whiskey. I want you by all means to send some of this brandy if you have it. Two or three gallons would not be too much. If it is not at home, bye it and send by Stephen what you paid for it and I will send you the money. Be sure and not forget this as we cannot take our quinine until we get the brandy. You need not let anybody know this for they will say that we have turned out to drinking. The best way to send it would be to put it in the box of provisions.

Thomas John Moore ca. 1862. From the editor's collection

Huder[1] and myself are well. Stephen can tell you all other news.
Yours truly,
Thomas J. Moore

1. A nickname for his brother Andrew.

[83] David Anderson to John Crawford Anderson

Addressed to Cadet John C. Anderson, Charleston, So. Car.

Poolesville Spt. Dist
July 26th, 1862

Dear Son,

I Recd your letter a few days ago and I am glad to know that you have made the arrangement with Chisholm for Salt at $5.00 per bushel.

It is much the cheapest Salt I can purchase and if it is as good as the Salt I have Recd., I will be well pleased. I send you a check for One Hundred Dollars and you must get me Twenty Bushels.

Your Uncle Frank has gone to the Virginia works for Salt at this time. He started on Monday last.

Uncle Mayson is at Vicksburg in command of Company and quite well. Your Aunt Sally writes She has a great deal of sickness in her family, measles, and fever. She has lost 3 or 4 small negroes. Your Uncle James is at Bluff Springs, Florida and is very well.

You asked for the *Express* [newspaper] to be sent you. I am sorry to say it died out Two months ago.

I have sold my bacon and corn to the Confederacy. I get $1.50 for meal delivered at Spt. depot. sent to Maj. Garrren Charleston. This leaves all well. Your Mother has gone to Rutherford on a visit [illegible]. Yours affectionately, D. Anderson

[84] Mary Elizabeth Anderson to John Crawford Anderson

Addressed to him at the Citadel

July 26th, 1862

Dear Brother, I was just reading Gen. Johnston's official report of the Battle of Seven Pines, when Pa called me asking if I wanted to write you a few lines.

Ma, Ella, and Net have gone to N.C. so I am Mistress and a little lonely sometimes as the Children are now going to school at Nazareth to Miss Col. Coan—Cousin John Cunningham spent last week with us, his finger is almost well, but is much bent the bone was broken and a piece came out—he will return to Virginia in a very short time. He went with us for Ella, who is at home for two weeks, had rather a dry time but the Concert was good.

Cousin Sammy Switzer dined with us this week. he is in for a month, looks very lean, his family were well. Mary has a school. Dr. Dave Miller has been in from Texas, been absent eight years, has gone on to Richmond trying for an office. Cousin Tom does not improve fast Have you heard of Berry Bagwell's death? His family are left very helpless.

We have a good many apples. I wish you could enjoy them with us also butter and Chickens—I was surprised to hear there were 400 Conscripts from Spartanburg. Someone reported John Beusan, who was lounging about. It made him wrathy. John Evins is expected home in a few days—You see Col. Jenkins is now Gen. and Walker Col. but eight of the Capts. have asked him to resign. I see Mr. Shaw was slightly wounded, he is in Uncle Ben's Company. I have written aunt Het, but have not heard a word from her. Uncle Jule is exempt from weak lungs Enoree Bill has been at home, was wounded in finger, I did not see him. Mr. Reidville Davis is in from Tennessee—was preaching within four miles of Yankees.

I remain your loving Sister Mary Excuse writing

P.S. Have you ever looked for Dr. Kane's *Arctic Expeditions*? We are now reading *Horse Shoe Robinson* and *Armageddon.*

[85] Hettie Brockman to John Crawford Anderson

Old Homestead, SC
August 1st, 1862

Dear Johnnie—

I owe you a thousand apologies Johnnie for not replying to your kind letter written a month ago and received during my stay in Abbeville . . . I really believe you think a good deal of your "old Auntie" to write twice in succession. I am so anxious to see you must never think of slighting us even if you come home on a very short visit. We will look for you and I, for one, will be awfully disappointed if you do not come.

I had a charming visit to Abbeville—fell dreadfully in love with a nice Soldier, of which I will tell you when we meet. But, as is the case all over Carolina, ladies were much more plentiful than gentlemen. I formed a great many elegant acquaintances—nearly all had brothers or Cousins in the Service . . .

Five of Tyger Jim Anderson's sons, 1855. From the left: William Washington Anderson, David Anderson, Mason Gilliland Anderson, James Alexander Anderson, and Michael Miller Anderson. From Edward Lee Anderson, *A History of the Anderson Family, 1706–1955* (Columbia, S.C.: R. L. Bryan Company, 1955); used with permission

I am anxious to know what you can have for me—but I hope I will guess rightly when I say it is "Johnnie's Type" [ambrotype] aye . . . But use your own taste as you have already—but you know when anything of the kind is in anticipation, we like to conjecture and generally we judge according as our wishes dictate.

Harry Goldsmith is now at home on furlough. His whole of one side was paralized by a shell in the last engagement, or series of battles near Richmond. He is improving now and rides about a good deal; he is the same Henry of old. You know Jack Austin died last Spring. Manning Austin, jr. died on the 28th of July. He came home on a few days furlough, was taken with Typhoid fever, and died. So many of the brave, noble spirits of the South passing away. How sad to think of the death of Seaborne Sanford, William Woodruff, Baldy Wright and many others. Oh, how tired I am getting of this war! It is a continual prayer with me for it to cease.

I hear that Ella is now at Sister Harriet's. I am very anxious to see her—and the other girls too, as I have not seen either of them since Jany. I wish you would come home and bring them over. I would go over to see them, but you know I am entirely dependent on the kindness of friends for conveyance. I wish I had a nice horse—I think I would feel so much better. But I have met with kind friends since I have been left homeless. But it makes one feel so humbled sometimes. as I have always been accustomed to go where my desires led me. I think though Sis might have thought enough of me to visit me once in six months . . . Don't you think so?. . .

Mr. Earle says to try to get him some salt and bring it with you if you have to smuggle it in barrels or boxes. He says if you haven't time to receive money from him before your leave the City to get it from Jeffen or Watson on his credit for a few days. He will forward the money immediately after he gets information on the subject. By so doing if it lays in your power you will oblige him exceedingly.

I received a letter from Taluhlah[1] a week since, she is having a gay time in Wetumka [Alabama] I think from her last letter she is quite popular with the soldiers. She speaks of coming out this summer. I hope she will come during yours and Ella's vacation.

Watermelons and other kinds of melons are just making their appearance in Greenville. They are a great treat. I expect you have had them sometime.

Sister Lucy unites with me in sending you happy greetings—Hoping you continue in perfect health and bright spirits.

Yours truly and devotedly.

Hettie Brockman

1. Tallulah Brockman (b. 1843) was the daughter of Hettie's brother James Henry Brockman of Alabama. She married John H. Bankhead, who became a U.S. senator from Alabama. Their son William Brockman Bankhead (1874–1940) served as Speaker of the U.S. House of Representatives. His daughter Tallulah Brockman Bankhead (1902–1968) was a noted actress.

[86] Mary Foster Moore to Andrew Charles Moore

Home, August 26th 1862

My dearest Husband[1]

Your most welcome letter was received a few days since and it is with pleasure though with a sad heart that I seat myself this morning for the purpose of responding but fear my letter will prove very uninteresting as I have no news whatever to write. I am dreadfully upset and may say perfectly miserable as I expect by evening's mail to hear of a bloody battle being fought between Jackson and Pope,[2] which, if such be the case, I hope it will prove a complete defeat for the latter General as they are such devils [illegible] I feel as if I could call them by every [illegible] the Cousins last night where the infamous Battle of New Orleans had the remains of Colonel ____eux disinterred and stole from the coffin the sword he was buried with. And I am almost confident the Almighty can never be with such outrageous people as the Yankees who commit such unpardonable acts among the people of the South. Ma and I were in Greensboro yesterday, trying to purchase some things, but they were so scarce and so very expensive that we returned without anything except this paper which you see is so very inferior as it is almost impossible to write with ink upon it and my pen was so dull I had to resort to a pencil which I hope you will excuse as I cannot do any better at present.

By looking at the date of this letter you will see that exactly five months have elapsed since we last saw each other which is the longest period of time that we have ever been separated and Oh God if that would only be all of it but sometimes it seems as if my heart would break when I see no prospect of an early peace and you must stay from me such a long time.

I must close begging you to excuse this letter being written with a pencil. I have not yet received the paper you subscribed for. I hope it will soon come and I will take the greatest interest in reading it not only for news but because you sent it to me. I think an abundance of anything you do or sent to me. All send much love

Your devoted wife

Mary

This letter was written in haste so please excuse all mistakes. Mary
Give my best to Thomas and tell Sis prized his letter very highly

1. It is doubtful that this letter from Alabama was received by Andrew Charles Moore before his death. It was likely received by his brother, Thomas, and brought home from the war.

2. The Second Battle of Manassas (Bull Run).

[87] Thomas John Moore to Margaret Anna Moore Means

September 2nd, 1862

My Dear Sister

Knowing that you are very anxious to hear from us all I will write you this in hopes that it may get started you in a day or two. I have not seen Sam [Means] since the battle[1] but have heard how he is & that he is well.

Bud [Andrew Charles Moore] was killed on the field. He was shot in the head with a very small ball. I think that it struck him in the right temple. I myself could not find the place but others say he was hit there. I did not see him fall and did not find him until the next morning. he was shot a little before sun—down while charging a battery. I had him buried on Sunday as decently as possible. I dug his grave myself and put him in it about 12 o'clock Sunday night. I could not procure a coffin but wrapped him up in two blankets and marked his grave so that it could be found hereafter in case we wish to remove his remains. O, sister it fills my soul with grief to think that we should lose him so soon after our dear Mother,[2] but God willed that it should be so and we should not mourne or grieve

He was fighting bravely when he fell being near the battery and among the front men. I have preserved a bunch of his hair for you and his wife. I have just written to her I was knocked down by a grape shot but not seriously hurt as it was nearly spent and besides it struck the belt of my cartridge box. It struck me on the left shoulder collar bone. I am truly thankful that it was no more. I will go and see Sam as soon as I can.

Our Regt [Eighteenth Regiment, South Carolina Volunteers] suffered terribly, we must have lost nearly 200 men lost 11 from being killed. Capt. [F. Marion] Tucker [of Co. E] was killed, Col Gadberry and many other. Willis Brewton was killed Frank Landrum wounded in Foot. I saw Belton today who told me about Frank. I must close as there is a chance to get this off now.

Your affect. Bro.
Thomas J. Moore

I am sorry that I could not write more but will write you another letter in a few days. Excuse haste
T.M.

1. The Second Battle of Manassas (Bull Run), which occurred on August 29–30, 1862.
2. Nancy Miller Montgomery Moore Evins died March 14, 1862.

[88] Margaret Anna Moore Means to Thomas W. Hill

Culpeper C.H
Sept. 26th, 1862

Mr. Hill:

You will be surprised to hear I have not seen Thomas or Mr. Means [her husband, Sam Means]. I got to Warrenton Sunday evening, hunted everywhere for Thomas. At last found a Poole of the same Company. Said he saw him next morning after the battle on his way to bury Bud.[1] He was not wounded. Lee Smith told us on the way he was wounded and at Warrenton. I feel almost sick about not seeing any of them. I would try to go to the army but can't get there. The Yankees are very near us. Troops are coming and going all the time. I have seen thousands of men but knew none. We are almost starved. The Yankees have destroyed everything. Mr. Nesbitt left Wednesday for the battle field. Don't know when he will get back. The Yankees were there a few days ago, burying their dead. Every place in Warrenton is filled with wounded. I have seen many horrible sights. The wounded are going home. Mr. Emory is going home this morning. I don't know when we will get home. Soon I hope.

The people here have no conscience. I can't hear anything from the last battle.

I will not write to Grandma if you see her you can show her this but not to Col. Evins.

Excuse this. Louisa [a slave, the cook at Fredonia] wants to get home to work. We will get there sometime next week.
Yours truly, M. A. Means

1. Family tradition holds that she was in search of her brother's body to bring home.

[89] Thomas John Moore to Thomas W. Hill

Near Winchester, Virginia
September 29th, 1862

Dear Sir:

I suspect that you have begun to think me a very negligent fellow about writing home and truly it seems so for I have not written to you in two months or more the reason of which is that the mail facilities are so bad that it is almost impossible to send off a letter. Our brigade has no mail carrier so we have to depend on sending our letters to the office by some one who happens to be going that way. I hope that in the future such neglect on the part of our Generals will be avoided so that we can write home when we choose to do so.

Since I last wrote to you we have been having a pretty tough time. Have been on the march almost all the time since the middle of July and have had some pretty hard fighting but I did not participate in the whole of either the marching or the fighting for after battle of Manassas I got sick and stopped at Leesburg and hence did not go into Maryland where they had the hardest fighting. I only joined the army at Martinsburg and the next day they moved back this way making me travel over the same ground that I went to them. I think that we are now bound for Staunton from the simple reason that all the sick and wounded have been ordered there from Winchester. I suppose they are falling back to the head of the railroad so as to get supplies more easily. I am very glad of it for we can then get to bye some articles very much needed.

I am now in good health with the exception of sore feet—but am almost naked, my clothes are nearly worn out and if I do not get some soon will be entirely naked. We left all our knapsacks in our travel which I suppose are lost forever to us. The shoes Col. Evins sent were in my knapsack and are lost too. I never had them on, I was almost barefooted but after hard work bought a pair of boots which have nearly ruined me.

This country in entirely eat out, you can not bye a thing and as for myself I have not the wherewithal to bye having lost my pocketbook. As soon as you see Sister tell her what a fix I am in about clothes and tell her to send them by the first opportunity.[1] Stephen [Moore] went into Maryland. He is greatly dissatisfied and wants to get home. While I was sick he started to run away from the army but some one saw him and persuaded him to come back. If we ever go into Maryland again he will be sure to leave. I think though now since we are started back that he is more satisfied. Tell Sister he must have some clothes too also a pair of shoes. I would like to see you and know how you are getting on. You must write to me and let me know. You will have to carry on matters as best you can which will be all I ask of you. I could write about Bud but I suppose you have heard all from Sister. I will close for the present but will write again when we stop so that you may know where to direct your letter and besides I have not written half what I wanted to.

Tell all the negroes that I am well and tell [them] howdy also. Tell Lou I want to see her and have her to get me something to eat.
Yours truly,
Thomas J. Moore

1. Ironically his sister had been in Warrenton, about thirty miles away, looking for him and her husband three days before this letter was written.

[90] Thomas John Moore to Thomas W. Hill

Kingston [Kinston], N.C.
November 30th, 1862

Dear Sir:

I have been thinking for several days of writing you a letter but have postponed it until this morning. It has been a long time since I heard from you and I am sure getting very anxious to get a letter from you. I have nothing worth writing to you only that we are much nearer home now than some time ago and are faring that much the better. We live finely here, have almost everything we want, get sweet potatoes in an abundance. We also get rice, peas, soap, vinegar, candies which helps a good deal after living on beef and bread so long. We mostly draw corn meal as this is a great corn country. A gentleman told me that the county raised one hundred fifty thousand barrels of corn this year and has only eight hundred voters. There are a great many rich men near here, they are all shipping their corn towards Raleigh for fear the enemy might get it.

It is not many days now until the sale [settlement of his mother's estate]. I would like very much to be there but cannot get a furlough. I will have to look to you and Col. Evins to bye for me what I need. Col. Evins wrote to me that I ought to have Numa and Hansom. I also want Elihu; Sister may think that I want to buy him thinking by that means that I will get Lou but tell that these are not my motives for I am willing for her to have Lou but I want Elihu. You must show Sister this letter and you must tell Col. Evins what I say. If you bye Elihu I want him sent here as soon as you can. The cook we now have will leave us in two weeks and I must have one. If you don't get Elihu send me Alec though I don't much like him as a cook. Tell Lou that she had better teach whoever comes a few lessons in the art of cooking. Don't delay to send by the first opportunity and send some butter by him, etc.

Col. Evins spoke of renting the land. I leave that to you. Do what you think is right about it though I think it had or at least a part of it ought to be rented. If there is anything that I need or you think I ought to have you must speak to Col.

Evins on the subject and have him to bye it. They will need some mules on the place. I am very sorry that I cannot be there. I hate to see the negroes sold but cannot help them. I hope none of the Alexanders will get them. Tell Steve [Stephen Moore] to get Sister to write who owes and I will collect for him. Tell him I miss him very much. You must write down who buys the negroes and what they have for them and send it to me, after the sale I will look for a long letter from you giving all the particulars. I have got to be Assistant Commissar of the Regiment and like it very much.

I must close this letter as I have nothing more to write. Show this letter to Sister and tell her I will write to her before the sale. Excuse haste as I have to go to Kinston for provisions and am in a hurry. Hope that you will get on well. Have you got salt? Write soon to me at Goldsboro, N.C. Gen. Evans brigade, 18th Regt. SCV.

Yours truly,
Thomas J. Moore

N.B. get money from Col. Evins to send the boy up here. It will take about 15 dollars.

Letters, 1863

In early 1863 Tom's unit moved from Virginia to eastern North Carolina, and his living conditions improved. John was still at the Citadel and urging his father to try sending some of his cotton to Nassau on a blockade-running ship.

In late April both Tom and Frank were on James Island near Charleston, and John graduated and enlisted in the Thirteenth Regiment, South Carolina Volunteers, as an adjutant, serving with his young uncles Ben and Jesse Brockman.

Tom became increasingly aware that he was now the senior male of his immediate family. In a year he would be twenty-one, and he stayed in close touch with the farm overseer, Mr. Hill.

Andrew's widow, Mary, in Alabama worried about placing the proper monument to her husband and had portraits painted of him.

John finished the year near Orange Court House, Virginia.

[91] Thomas John Moore to Thomas W. Hill

Camp near Kinston
January 30th, 1863

Dear Sir:

. . . There is nothing new about here now. We thought a few days ago that the enemy were advancing on us but find that the report was incorrect and now we know not what they intend to do.

Your brother Baylis is quite well and seems to be doing finely. Elihu likes camp pretty well though he says it is the laziest work in the world. He says he had rather split rails than to have so little to do. I have vaccinated him two or three times but none have taken any effect. The small pox is all around us but only one case has appeared among us. The case proved fatal in a few days. Proper precautions have been taken to prevent its spread. I would not be surprised if it did not get all over our country from the soldiers. I wish you to get some matter and vaccinate the negroes on the Middle Place by all means and if you think proper on the others. You can get a scab from some Doctor who will give you directions how to put it in. You had better vaccinate some small negro and also a healthy [adult] one and vaccinate the others from it. You had better vaccinate only a few at a time as it may make them sick a day or two. I think that all should be vaccinated for if the disease once gets started it will kill nearly all.

I see from the papers that Congress has passed a law not exempting overseers. You must try by all means to get an exemption because I know that you would be of more service where you are. Do not go headlong into the army without giving the matter due consideration. If there is any pretext upon which you get off honorably do so for you will never regret it and besides it is now no dishonor. Should you be compelled to leave, write me what you think had best be done.

I also hear the Gov. has ordered out half the negroes. If this be so and they take them by Districts as before, I think that it would be better to hire hands even if you had to give twice the usual price, for they are more liable to disease in Camp and moreover they would contract bad habits and perhaps run off to the Yankees or be captured. I leave it entirely with you but think what I have said is best but perhaps Col. Evins may think different.

Frank West is now at home on furlough or rather on a recruiting expedition. He will probably remain at home two or three weeks. Tell Lou that she must send me some knives and forks, say two or three knives and four or five forks. We have about lost out and they cannot be got here at all. I suppose that there are old ones about home which will suit me very well.

If Sister has anything to send she had better see Frank and let him bring them on.

Look among my books and you will find an Olmstead's *Philosophy* which send me by him. Also you will find an English Grammer among some old books, perhaps in the Cylinder [a round rotating bookcase] which you may also send and if there is an old dictionary there let it be sent too.

It may look strange to some that I send for such books but as I am getting quite rusty in the two last named and I wish to brighten my memory and moreover having nothing to read here, I can study the first named book which will be of great value to me.

Yours truly,
Thomas J. Moore

[92] Thomas John Moore to Thomas W. Hill

Topsail Sound [*N.C.*]
April 9th, 1863

Dear Sir:

I received a letter from you sometime ago and another one yesterday and will now answer both at once. I have no news to write you. I and Elihu are both well. Elihu has had a bad cold but is now quite well.

I do not find any fault with you for not buying the mules of which you spoke for I believe that you did the best you could. If you cannot make out well without another mule, you had better buy one if it is a small one but you know better about this than I do. So you can do just as you think best . . . You wrote to me about clothes for the negroes. You had better let things go on for you know that it will make a fuss if anyone should object. If you cannot clothe them by Lou's and Lindy's work and you say you must hire someone to weave, you are in a bad fix but I hope that you may make the best of it. As said before any other thing would cause a row . . .

I wrote something about a substitute. I am determined to have one if I have to give 2000 [dollars]. I want you to try to get me one. If I were anywhere outside of the army I think I could get one. If you think of anyone go to see them immediately . . . you can offer as high as 1500 if they won't come for that find out what they will come for and write to me immediately . . .

I would think the money spent would be the most profitable that I have ever spent. A man who comes to this Regt will get in an easy place and will not have much to do. Let me know what you have done as soon as possible.

Tom Kelly asks me to sell him six bushels of corn. He says his wife cannot get it. I want you to let her have the six bushels at one dollar per bushel. I have not the heart to charge a soldiers wife 2.50. We should be good to them and besides I will never miss it. He says Watson will come for it and will pay for it. If you sell to a poor soldiers wife hereafter anything of mine let her have it very cheap. A man who imposes upon helpless women and children should be drummed out of the Country.

Enclosed you will find a letter from Elihu to Lou also [$]20.00 which hand over to her.

I must close for the present. Elihu sends howdys to you.

Yours truly,
Thomas J. Moore

[93] Elihu Moore to His Wife, Lou

Camp Near Wilmington [*N.C.*]
April 9th, 1863

My Dear Wife:

I seat myself this morning to drop you a few lines to inform you of my good health and Where Bouts and hoping these few lines may find you and family joying the best of health. Lou I hav no nuse uf intrust to rite you. Mars. Thomas is well and gone up to Town today. Wee Recdt A Letter Last night from you. Wee was glad to hear from you all and to know that you all wer injoying good health except a few bad colds. You all may bee thankful that you may come off that well. Lou you wantied to know if I wantied any cloth[e]s. I am very glad that you quit making them cloths as cloth is so high for I can buy more suitable ones hear. Lou you sead in you letter that I hav not sent you but one leter true a nuff I hav not and I will tell you my resuns of doing so is because I hav never recd. A pen scratch from none of unes only what few words Mr. Hill written to me and I am mutch a bilge to him for riting to me though I hav not forgotten youall yet and never will as long as the sun rases in the East and sets in the West. Lou I will rite to you in less than agin five days.

Mr. Hill Dear

Sur I am mutch a bilge to you for writing to me. I was glad to hear that you was well. Mr. Hill you said that you wished you had me up plowing with Mary. I will go you halves there for I wish I wer there a plowing with Mary with tite line for you Mr. Hill. I want you to give my love to all with no exception and take part to your self an remember my love.

Yours as ever,
Elihu Moore

[94] John Crawford Anderson to David Anderson

Charleston, S.C.
April 20th, 1863

Dear Father,

Being somewhat engrossed with a project which I chanced to suggest to you sometime since and being encouraged by the favorable response, but at the same time I think, remembering, I have been induced to make some enquiries and find

John Crawford Anderson. From Edward Lee Anderson, *A History of the Anderson Family, 1706–1955* (Columbia, S.C.: R. L. Bryan Company, 1955); used with permission

out the chances of a trade. I know young Horsey, who has a brother now in the employ of John Frazier and Co. and who has been successful in running the Blockade seven times and will haul out in the stream tonight to try it his eighth time. He says he will get any reasonable quantity of cotton from here to Nassau for part of the profits.

The only way of getting Cotton on these vessels going out is by means of some of the firm or a friend of the firm.

And I propose for you think about the matter and see if you are willing to allow me the chance to try my hand in the game. If you say ten bales you see at the present prices say 20 cts [per pound]—it will bring you $800, while at

Nassau the price varies it is true, but Horsey has been selling Upland Cotton from $2.00 and upwards—the same cotton will bring you $8000.00 in gold or Exchange. The premiums on gold will at once show what an enormous profit will be made. Gold sold here last week for 600 per cent and Exchange is as good and does not stand the same risk in returning. The expenses on the Cotton from home here and here to Nassau will be trifling in comparison to the profits, from here to Nassau it is 10 cts on the pound. But the main risk is yet to be considered, that is the running [of] the Blockade but when you consider that one out of twenty of the vessels going out and coming in this port—you will see the risk may be lessened in a two-fold, three-fold, or even fourfold degree by dividing the cotton among so many vessels or even the same vessels and so many trips. I know not what kind of trade I can make with Horsey yet for he is going out tonight and sent me word that he could not come up to see me today, but would as soon as he returned from Nassau. This trip which he expected to make in at the greatest ten days if fortune attended him.

He has been trading in that way and has a trade of that kind on hand this trip.

By giving him a third or even half of the profits you will see that it will handsomely pay the trouble and if a part is lost and part gets on safe you will make more than you could make off of the double quantity here. Besides the investment in such things as you may desire in return.

I wish to know immediately the chances. You can do as you choose in disposal of the profits if made or of the loss if sustained which will not exceed $1200 or $1500 at the greatest. I write thus early in order that I may know positively whether to give Horsey ground for the expectation of a trade or not. I have not fully detailed the conditions which are expected in such a trade. But they are simply these, I furnish the cotton, pay the freight, lose everything if lost, if made he shares the profits and has the general supervision of the shippage and selling.

Creswell has gone into a similar trade with the son of one of the firms and gives him half and at the same time makes money, but if the profits can be made to preponderate on my side of course I will make the necessary efforts. Excuse haste and write soon. I am no longer Sergt. Anderson but have the title of Capt. prefixed to my name. I have not seen Uncle Frank if he has returned. I understand Uncle Mason is in.

Give love to all the family,

Your obedient Son,

J. C. Anderson

[95] Thomas John Moore to Thomas W. Hill

Charleston, S.C.
April 29th, 1863

Dear Sir:

... You see from the caption of this letter that we have at last got to Charleston after many trials and troubles. We left Wilmington last Friday night at 12 o'clock and by 9 o'clock the next night were in the vicinity of Charleston. We got off the train at the six mile house on the S.C. railroad and then moved down to the four mile house where we staid only one day. We then got orders to move across the Ashley River into St. Andrews Parish. We are now camped about one and a half miles from the edge of town but now the regiment is packing up for another move three miles further still from town. It seems that they intend to keep us moving all the time but I hope that we will soon get settled down again. We are now about a mile from where we were encamped when I joined the Regiment over a year ago. Everything looks so natural here that it makes one feel as if he had got back home. There is a great difference between this place and Wilmington. Here it seems that a man can live there he would be likely to perish. At the latter place there were no signs of a crop of any kind, no vegetables, and in fact there was nothing. Here we can get what we want. The market house is as full as I ever saw it. Green peas, potatoes and all kinds of vegetables are in abundance which at Wilmington not a bit of such things could be bought. Upon the whole you may rest assured that we are highly pleased with the change. Cook's Brigade of N. Carolinians has gone to take our place, in other words we swaped with them. It is all well the talk now that we will go to the west but I think not for we will stay here during the war or at least in S.C. somewhere. Gen. Evans says that we will be kept as a kind of reserve force in S.C. to be sent where we are most needed and besides if any troops are sent from here to the West it will be those who have been here ever since the war began. Some regiments here have never seen the enemy yet and I think it would be nothing but right to give them a showing. I saw Uncle Prater [Montgomery] a day or two ago. He was tolerably well though he had been complaining a day or two before. He likes camp finely and do not blame any body for liking it when fixed as well as the Charleston's Battalion. Sister went through Wilmington and staid all night there but I did not see her as I did not know that she was there until the next morning when she was gone. I was in three miles of town and could have gone to see her so easily had I known that she was there. She intended to stop when she came home but will not now do it as I am gone. Was very anxious to see her . . . I shall have to stop writing for a few hours as the wagons are here to move us.

We have made our move. Have a beautiful camp but bad water and gnats in abundance . . . I saw Haslan's cavalry today. The company is just from Pocataligo. Bill Means was with it. he was looking well. They think that they will go to the west. I can hardly write the gnats are so bad. Sandflies are also very bad. I want to get to a place where such things are unknown. I had hoped before this to have got a letter from you saying that you had procured me a substitute. What is the matter? Have you tried or are none to be had? I have just learned today of a man who is anxious to substitute. His name is Billy Edwards. He [lives] near Buck Bennets. I want you to go and see him immediately for if I get one the sooner the better and if I keep waiting long enough the war will be ended. Maybe I do not offer money enough. In price you may go as high as 2500. dollars. Perhaps you may strike a trade with Edwards. Some men will come for the money or land or whatnot you promise to give. Perhaps you can get him for a good deal less. I want you to go see [him] the first day you get this letter and write me so I may know what to expect. Make everything look as favorable as possible. Tell him that our brigade will be apt to stay in S.C. til the war ends. If he won't come tell Charles Barry what I have written and maybe he could get me one. I hear also that Elison Casey would like to come to the army. If Billy Edwards won't come give him a trial. I could not endure these biting insects for a thousand dollars or so.

Yours truly,
Thomas Moore

[96] Mary Foster Moore to Thomas John Moore

Home [Marion, Alabama]
September 11th, 1863

My Dear Brother

Recently I have been expecting one of your welcome letters, of brotherly love and affection, but have been much disappointed. Months ago I answered yours, but never received a reply. Why have you not written? Is it possible dear Tom that you are about to forget the heart-broken wife of your dear dead brother, whom you promised should retain a sister place and love in your memory? No, no, such I hope can never be the case, unless some officious persons, who seem to think a great deal less of me since the loss of my *gallant* and *noble husband*, have been working upon your kind feelings with regard to me. Such an intrusion, I hope will prove unsuccessful, for I have always spoken of you in the most eulogising terms, and heartily thank you for the kindness, courtesy, and love, particularly in my deep affliction, that you have uniformly extended towards me, which I can assure you is sincerely reciprocated.

I regretted very much indeed that you did not succeed in procuring the monument,[1] as I wished so much for one, and am fearful now that we will not be able to get one in a long while. I hope you visit *that precious grave* frequently and attend to it, to prevent the growth of weeds and grass, which I wish was in my power but therefore as it cannot be, I entrust it to your care when at home, and request of you not to neglect it. I have a splendid picture from which I intend soon having his noble portrait painted. We have one of the most elegant Artists [Nicola Marschall] the county affords, and I have an excellent picture of your Ma [see page 22], which if you would like to have one painted also, the price I think one hundred and twenty-five dollars, I will have it done with pleasure, and take the greatest care of it, which I know you will value very highly.

Dr. Effinger's[2] family are still in the neighborhood, though they think of leaving the latter part of next week for Georgia, finding it perfectly impossible to procure a place for his negroes, and his brother having two plantations there very kindly offered the use of one. Cousin Emma Henderson and Mary Effinger[3] are two lovely girls, and spend most of their time with us.

Every one is anxiously awaiting the fate of Charleston,[4] which I am persuaded will ultimately fall in to the hands of the merciless Yankees, and then what will become of the South Carolinians. The outrageous vandals will inflict more brutal chastisements upon the people of the birth place of rebellion as they style your city, than any place in the south.

What has become of your sister? I wrote to her several months ago, but have never received a line in return, which was the case with several others. I know not what to attribute it to, but hope you will explain all things to me when you write.

The family send much love, and wish you a safe and happy return from the Army.

Affectionately yours,

Mary

1. A very substantial monument made of Carrara marble was erected in the cemetery at the Nazareth Presbyterian Church after the war.

2. Amanda, the daughter of Gen. Thomas Moore, married a Henderson first and Dr. Effinger second.

Base of monument to Andrew Charles Moore, Nazareth Presbyterian Church cemetery. The broken palmetto symbolizes the broken dreams of Confederate South Carolina. From the editor's collection

3. Emma Henderson, age nineteen at time of this letter, was the daughter of Amanda Moore and her first husband; Mary Effinger was Emma's half sister, the daughter of Amanda Moore and her second husband.

4. Charleston did not fall until February 18, 1865.

[97] John Crawford Anderson to Emma Buist

[Transcribed by J. A. Winn]

Camp "Orange," Orange C.H., Va.
Dec. 7th, 1863

Miss Emma; Esteemed friend:

I must ask your forgiveness for not answering that long and interesting letter of yours which has been to Charleston and back to "Camp Orange" this the second time. I rec'd it a few days before we left this Camp on our last "tramp" after the Yanks, and had actually begun a reply when the order came for us to be in readiness to move . . .

Let me tell you some of the little adventures in which I have been engaged since the 27th of last month.[1] If it proves a conglomeration of concatenated events I hope it may be interesting in a few points at least.

The night of the 26th last we received orders to be in readiness to move at four in the morning, every man provided with three days rations. As a matter of course that night there was very little sleeping in the Regt. And by half past three we were ready to move. At four we left. Day-light found us at Orange C.H. a distance of 2 miles.

That morning was bitter cold and the ground frozen as slick as ice. On the hills between here and Orange many a good fellow caught a sweet fall but as he rose to his feet the first thing he thought of was his pipe and tobacco, while everybody else was in full rise of laughter. That morning I was suffering from cold, but in as fine spirits as if I had been at a wedding party. We went down the Orange and Fredericksburg Plank Road about sixteen miles . . . the march was very rapid and the day cold all the time . . . The grandest sight I have ever seen was on that day. I saw all of A. P. Hill's [troops] in motion. The country after leaving Orange some two miles was almost level, now and then a gradual rise. At one time I surveyed the line as far as the eye could reach.

Being on horseback I could see a long way back and before, but as I rose one of these little eminences I had the crowning view. It was a charming sight to see the guns glistening in the noonday sun and became grandly sublime when associated with the thought that that great host of men were moving on to Liberty or to Death.

I have long been anxious to see an Army in motion, and since my desire has been gratified in that respect I have a still more eager one to be amidst the whistling of balls and the rolling thunder of artillery.

When the Infantry and the Cavalry came in contact some amusing confabs would take place. There is a spirit between the Infantry and Cavalry which is not desirable nor to be approved.

The Infantry frequently ask them to "come off of that horse," "come out of them boots," and sure as we get near the enemy, we meet the Cavalry going to the rear. Then you hear the cry from the Infantry "Cavalry to the Rear, the Yanks are in front." It is truly amusing to hear the flashes of wit on each side when they meet.

About four in the evening we arrived at Verdearsville about fourteen miles from Orange. After remaining there some two hours we went on about two miles farther down on Mine Run and went in Camp on the other side of the Run. I thought we would get in a fight that evening, as the fighting was going on in our front and the whiz of shell could be distinctly heard. Some wounded and dead were brought out to the rear that evening, but the fight did not amount to much as we only had a few Cavalry in it. That night I got very little rest and was cold all the time, but in the morning (the 28th) at three we began to fall back on the other side of the Run and after some time were at our positions in Line of Battle.

We had not been there long before the trees began to fall and the wood rang with the sound of the axe.

The rain was falling beautifully and to tell you in short it was a [illegible], but the men did not seem to mind it, and in a little while the Breastworks began to go up on the whole extent on the line. Gens. Lee, Hill, Pendleton & many other less shining constellations reviewed our Line, as we were on the Road, it was the point of great interest. E're the sable curtain of night began to fall from the East we were in waiting for the Vandal foe. And truly behind that Line of Logs lurked death for many a Yank, and had they advanced to the conflict that beautiful Sabbath morning as was our expectation, many a death knell would have been sounded, and many a Yank been tortured with agonizing pain.

Our men were in the most appropriate of spirits. Every man felt confident of victory . . . On Saturday night (the 28th) after drying by a large fire I fell asleep on some pine tops and had a sweet sleep, which continued till about sunrise Sunday morn. I was going to say that I arose and made my toilette, but no not exactly, for out in Line of Battle the soldiers don't have much toilette to make. But at any rate I did wash my face that morning if I did not the morning before.

Gen. Lee came along down the Line just as the sun began to tinge the beautiful forest with a golden hue, as he neared the 12th Regt Rev. Mr. Watson from York [S.C.], a young seminarian, was leading in morning prayer. The General halted and took off his hat and waited till the prayer was finished. It was an imposing scene, and seemed to impress every one in sight of the great solemnity of the occasion. Few conjectures were at first made by those at a distance why he halted, but in almost one instant the whole crowd was quiet and respectful. It was a grand sight and one which I will long remember. The day was all beautiful and quite quiet until about three o'clock. Then the news came that the Yanks were trying to flank us on the right. We at once began to trot at "double quick" and from that till night we kept it up. After "double quicking" about one mile and a half to the right we were halted in an old field and had not been there more than five minutes before the Yankee Sharpshooters began to give us a touch of the minie-ball music. The consequence was one man killed in the 14th Regt. And two wounded in the same Regt.

There was a great deal of firing on the Line that evening both Infantry and Artillery. The Skirmishers were firing all the time and every minute we expected to get in a fight, but all in vain. Night came on and no fight. That day one of Gen. Lane's men was out in the Skirmish Line and a wild turkey flew upon a tree in front of him. He fired and killed the turkey and when it fell he was afraid to go and get it, so after waiting some few moments the Yanks began to come up to get the turkey. The Reb drew on him and killed him, then went and got his turkey and fifteen dollars in greenbacks and a good over coat besides [from the fallen soldier]

That night was one of the coldest and we suffered accordingly. Next day we stayed in the same place all the time, and were in expectation of a fight every moment. One of our men from the Brigade shot an Officer on some Yankee General's staff while they were spying at us. Some few prisoners were taken. That and the firing were going on all day. At night one fourth of the Army was at the Breastworks all the time. Gen. Lee expected the Yankees to make an attempt to gain our lines under cover of night. But all went well till in the morning about three when we were ordered to the right to support [illegible] in case of a fight. For three hours there we stood in the bitter cold without one sign of fire and not a stick of wood in five hundred yards. I thought I would freeze and to get rid of the torture dropped on the frosty grass and went fast, yes "double quick" to the Land of Nod.

After sunrise squads were sent out to the woods to cut and haul wood on their "bone carts," a new invention perhaps to you home folks, but a cast of familiar acquaintance to all the men of my present association.

Still fires did little good that day for the cold came from all sides and the fire but from me. The firing on the right and left continued all day, more or less, and at nightfall Gen. Wilcox, a generous, noble and kind man, sent us out in a pine thicket and told us to make ourselves comfortable. Well, it is needless to say we did so and that night I had a good time. Next morning, Wednesday the 2nd, we awoke only to find the Yankees had gotten out from our front and soon we were on trail of some of them down the Plank Road. Prisoners were coming in from the woods and from the front and we were pushing on in full expectation of being on them in the next half mile till we heard the Yanks had moved at nine the night before. After going some seven miles we came to a halt and soon after turned about to come back to our Winter Quarters.

Many a heart was made glad by the tidings that the Yanks had crossed back on the other side of the river. I had a conversation with one of the prisoners and found him to be a very intelligent fellow. We came back to our Breastworks and stayed all night and on the next morning. That day the 3rd set out for Camp Orange which we reached before night a distance of 18 miles. On Tuesday evening Gen. Lee and Stewart were round in rear of the Yankees and found that only one Corps, the 2nd, were in our front on the right, and he at once determined to attack them the next day and gave Gen. Wilcox, our Maj. Gen., orders to make the attack at 11 o'clock in the morning, and Gen. Anderson (no relation of mine) at the same time to make a flank movement on them but in the morning there was no Yank to be found. We would have given them a good one if we had been permitted to attack them. Gen. Lee saw Gen. [Wassen?] the Yank while in their rear. After turning round to come back, Gens. Lee and Hill came dashing up from the front and as they passed the different Regts. The shout of applause went thrilling from the lips of every man, and it was a splendid sight to see them dashing along with hats off and Hill's beautiful standard of colors flying to the breezes.

Lee is quite a venerable old gentleman. His beard is nearly white but some dark in it yet. Stewart is a dashing fellow and has a large streaming black feather in his hat. A. P. Hill reminds me much of Stewart. Gen. Pendleton is very much like Gen. Lee and can only be distinguished at a distance by the horse he rides. The shades of night have long since fallen around me and now the stillness of the night tells of its hour, so with a few more lines I will close and ask your pardon for being so lengthy. The night I reached our old Camp again I was blessed by a good supper and a walk in the fairy land of dreams amidst beauties and pleasures which have not been unseen by me, and strange to say there was a Greenville out there as well as in So. Car. . . .

Nothing more just now.

Truly your friend,

J.C.A.

1. This letter describes the Mine Run operations, an inconclusive series of engagements that took place November 26–December 2, 1863. Mine Run was a creek.

LETTERS, 1864

On January 19, 1864, John wrote from Orange Court House, Virginia. Tom and Frank were camped near Savannah. In April their unit headed north reaching Tarborough, North Carolina, later that month and the Richmond area by midsummer.

Ben and Jesse Brockman were both killed as a result of the Battle of Spotsylvania, May 8–12, where General Ulysses S. Grant futilely tried to flank General Robert E. Lee. John remained with the unit.

Frank Anderson, Tom Moore, and Sam Means had a relatively comfortable camp on the Nottoway River that summer and fall and met many of the local people. They were being held in a reserve position. Food was scarce and inflation rampant. Ann Means ventured north and visited their camp.

In November and December John was in the trenches near Petersburg.

[98] John Crawford Anderson to David Anderson

Letter sent to David Anderson, Poolsville P.O., Spartanburg Dist., S.C., "Politeness of Mr. Huchison to Columbia," then mailed post due.

Orange C.H., Va.
19th Jan. 1864

Dear Father:

Yours by Miles Knight reached me on night before last the 17th. Peter [slave] came through all safe, but caught a severe cold and was coughing a good deal on the night of his arrival, but now seems to be recovering and is getting into this harness of Camp. The Turkey was very acceptable as it was the charming dish of my birthday breakfast, and today at dinner it was left to me to take the last morsel.

Together with Uncle Ben's box I think we will fare fine for a week or two to come. He received double the amount of butter that I did, consequently we have a good supply on hand. . . .

I don't admire the distinction you make between Ed Willis and Miles Knight. Willis is a reliable man as well as a sober and honest man; but I can't say the same for the other, perhaps I may be prejudiced by remembering that Miles stole a Whip from me about twelve years ago. As we went on Picket yesterday I have not had a chance to make a settlement of Pete's expenses, but will in the morning.

The Overcoat I like very much and is quite the idea. I find it impractical to wear woolen shirts on account of the body lice, more familiarly known here as I. F.W.s. (In for the War). I have been troubled with them at least while we slept with Brother Bouchelle but since I have left him and wear the cotton, I have not been troubled at all.

Pet [Peter] tells me the girls got home on Sunday, but Knight says Net did not come home but had the measles down the Country and that some young lady came in with Sis and Ella. I am puzzled to know which to believe. Pet saw them at the Village and certainly knew them.

We have no news of importance in Camp. Yankee Congress seems to be making Herculian efforts to arouse the Northern hordes to a proper sense of the sufferings of their bretheren in Rebel prisons. [John S.] Mosby continues to harass the enemy and is in their Lines all the times. . . .

We had some very cold weather about ten days ago. We were on Picket and rode back from the Picket Line at night, crossing the River the water froze as it splashed on my boots and pants and when I got to Camp my boots were frozen fast to the stirrup and the ice on the bottom of them no less than an inch thick. Since then it has turned warm and been raining a good deal but tonight it blows off cold and freezing.

[Rumour?] says Gen. [Samuel] McGowan will be in soon and will take command of Evans' Brigade and make an exchange with McGowan of So Car for Va, but such news can't be relied on. I will see what I can do in buying a horse and will let you know. I think an appeal will be made to Mr. S. [Simpson] Bobo to come out for the Senate next fall. I have heard several talking of it in this Regt.

A number of cattle were driven in for the Army this evening. Men are getting a little more meat now, about a quarter of a pound a day.

I am enjoying fine health and getting in good condition for the Campaign.

Your son,
JC Anderson

Mary Elizabeth Anderson (Moore).
From the editor's collection

[99] Mary Elizabeth Anderson to her sister Nettie

[This letter is in very poor condition.]

Poolesville, S.C.
Jan. 20th or 30th, 1864

My own dear Sister,

This is a beautiful winter morning. I have dressed myself in my prettiest homespun, attended to my "dairy duties" and returned finding all [children]—and Ella just out of bed. We are all very well, my cold much better so that I can sing some but have not had time to practice much. Fallen sings a great many pretty pieces and plays very well. I so hope you have been learning "The Maiden's Prayer" and some of Cousin Hattee's pretty music. I must tell you how Johnie's [John Crawford Anderson's twenty-second] birthday was celebrated.

I wrote you Uncle Mason and family were expected also Mrs. Smith and Mrs. Means.... O, we had a splendid dinner. After the first table, the table was filled by little Children, from Tommy down to Benny and Theodore, only twelve not including Lizzie and N__nnie. . . . The remains of the Feast were reserved for Uncles Mason and Frank, who did ample justice to the dinner at supper. They spent the night so you know we had a pleasant night. . . . Before dinner Uncle Mason came into the dining room and we made a "splendid eggnog" He is so pleasant. He sent Johnie some cake and after Uncle Jessee came yesterday morning, we made some candy and sent him. I hope he will get it. . . .

Dr. Coan was married last night to Miss Amanda Otts by the Rev. R. H. Reid. . . .

Fallan and Ella join me in much love to Uncle Jessee's family and my friends. . .

Your loving Sister Mary

I must tell you a compliment was placed on me the day of Johnie's dinner. You know I am loth to take compliments, but Aunt Sallie said the custard I made was the best she had ever tasted in her life. Tommy is going to town for Uncle Mason's overcoat and I am sending this by him. I weighed 130 lbs yesterday morning.

[100] Thomas John Moore to Thomas W. Hill

Savannah
March 21st, 1864

Dear Sir:

I write this note and will send it in a letter to Mrs. Barry. It is in reference to sending provisions. Mrs. Barry will send down something to you which you must pack up in our box and turn over to Tom Fielder at Spartanburg or some other place. Charles [Barry] tells me that he thinks you can get a jug from Mrs. Barry for sending some molasses. In sending eggs, fix them up as you did in that box sent to James Island and they will be sure to come safely.

Look over the books and see if there is one there titled Kanes' *Elements of Criticism* send it in the box.

If you are ever over at the rolling mill buy me a spider [a long handled iron frying pan often with legs] or round [base] and a frying pan if they have such things. We need just such.

There is no news of interest. We are all well. Jno. Switzer will probably get off on furlough before long. He has already sent one [a request] up to the General. I will write you again by him.

Yours truly
Thomas J. Moore

[101] Franklin Leland Anderson to Mary Elizabeth Anderson

Oatland Island, near Savannah, Ga.
March 29th, 1864

Dear Mary

I received your letter day before yesterday while on picket. Yesterday was occupied in moving back to camp. I am on camp fatigue today, but the duties are not onerous and I will fill in the time writing. Your letter came unexpectedly but was more welcomed on that account. When I received yours I was in the midst of a long letter to Sister Julia[1] in answer to one received the day before. You can imagine what my anxiety had become from such tardiness in waiting to hear from those precious little ones of mine, But the letter revealed the cause, Hill, the idol of her heart, had come, and of course she was excusable for forgetting my anxiety for a few days. I was glad to hear that Hill thought enough of his Tiger [Tyger River] friends to pay you all a visit and hope his stay though short was pleasant. Frank had had another attack and had been quite sick but was well again. Your Pa wrote me that his last account of Willie[2] was that the house was not sufficient space for his perambulations and that he had taken the yard. What a pleasure it would afford us to see him on some of his jaunts. Capt. Bert gives a gloomy account of things up the country, the backward wheat crop, the snow and all things combined gave a mid-Winter appearance. The long winter too I suppose operates against your school but I hope your dilligence with that of your pupils will reduce any timé that may be lost. I enjoy my life in camp much more than I expected I could. The great reason is that it is so thoroughly occupied; induce if we had no boy to attend to the culinary department, to draw the rations, etc, we would not have an idle moment, but a week in camp and one on picket is the regular routine; of the two though the duty is a little more severe we greatly prefer the picket week, one great distraction at the picket post is that the oister [oyster] banks are accessible, and this I enjoy beyond measure, I like them best fried but the can of lard I put up is nearly exhausted and when it is, it will detract very much from the luxury, but we still have bacon that will answer as a substitute.

Barry and myself have asked for a pass to go to the City tomorrow, four miles. We go with a view of taking a view of the city, visiting the Cemetery, which Uncle Mike says is well worth a visit. I have not seen Mike for two weeks, but he was quite well then. Our greatest annoyance is the gnats, which are swarming the moment the wind ceases to blow, we better appreciate the annoyance when we sit down to read or wright, in fact it is impossible without first making a little smoke which they can't stand.

[Illegible], Tom Moore and Barry have learned to sing *The Private's Serenade*, and have worn out the verses we have and want it all complete. Please send me too the words of the *Poet's Sigh*. Has Nett any notion of a visit to Rutherford for Mrs. Lee's benefit? Love to all, write often,
Your Uncle Frank

1. Frank's wife, Susan Nuckles Norris Anderson, had died April 16, 1863, and her sister Julia was helping with Frank's three young children.
2. William Norris Anderson (b. 1863).

[102] Franklin Leland Anderson to Mary Elizabeth Anderson

Envelope: F. L. Anderson Co. A.
Hol. Legn. S.C.V.
To: Miss Mary Anderson
Poolesville
Spartanburg, South Ca.

Tarborough, Edgecomb Co., N.C.
Saturday, April 23rd, 1864

Dear Mary,

Your kind letter has been received. Today week ago we left Savannah and the Regt has traveled at the rate of seventy five miles a day since. We arrived at Weldon day before yesterday and everything seemed to bid fair for a good long rest. and as such yesterday we went to work fixing up a brush tent. I worked three or four hours at it and before it was quite completed we had orders to prepare to march. In two hours we were again aboard the train came back fifteen miles took a branch road leading coastward to this place, the end or nearly so of the R.R. Where we will go from here is as usual unknown to the lower officials like myself "private," but one thing I do know, that although the Legion stiles [styles] themselves Gen. Evins' [Brig. Gen. Nathan George Evans] foot cavalry we can't make as long days drive as we have done from the past week. Three other Regts. of the Brigade at Weldon before we left and the rest were expected. The men have not shed many tears from Gen. Evins late misfortune, but rather hope it is serious enough to inspire some other Brigadier to take command of us, one reason as to the object of our being sent here is that we are to march and guard the prisoners of the late capture at Plimoth this to their destination. Gen. Ha—— [Hagood?] official dispatch this morning prisoners is sixteen hundred, the rest of twenty-four hundred as first reported are supposed to be negroes, but I think it more reasonable that those who took the prisoners will guard them and we will have a chance before long of trying our own hand for a like booty, if so I feel assured we will do our duty, and trust the God of battles will crown our efforts with a like success. Moore, Barry, and myself[1] have just taken a stroll over the town of Tarborough, and find it quite unlike its name, one of the most handsome country villages I have ever seen. The place reminds me very much of the village of Greenwood though it is on a much larger scale and a great deal more elegance and stile about it. No one would have dreamed of finding such a place in N.C.

I wish you great success at the Oak Hill Seminary. Hope Bennie's foot is so he can cross the trenches. I see by the papers the Enemy are occupying east Tennessee. I think Morgan's men would do you all the greatest good to go and drive the scoundrels back. I mean no reflection upon your *gallants*, but the enemy there getting pretty close home. The drum beat and I must close. The foot cavalry will move soon some way. I wrote to Sister Julia on the 16th the anniversary of my dear Sue's death. Sad were the recollections of that day. Is the rose bush and the violets at her grave living? Write soon—direct to Weldon, NC Your affectionate Uncle Frank

Send me the words of the *Poets Sigh.*

1. Thomas John Moore, Charles A. Barry, and Franklin Leland Anderson had shared mess from April 1862 until the war's end.

[103] Thomas John Moore to Thomas W. Hill

Tarboro, N.C.
April 30th, 1864

Dear Sir:

I wrote to Sister yesterday. I did not know where to tell her to direct her letters. We have now received orders to move to Kinston where you can inform her to direct. We march 16 miles today. Take the rail road for Goldsboro and then march to Kinston 25 miles. The object of this move you see in Sister's letter and as I have but a few minutes to write, I not rehearse it here. I said yesterday I was unwell. Today I feel much better.

My object in writing this short letter is to get some money. My mess has not five dollars. Tobacco is five dollars a plug here. Everything else in the same proportion. Some have sent home for money but have countermanded the order as they did not know where we would be. I presume you have never sent the 25 dollars I wrote for. I now want 75 or 100. Money buys very little here especially the old issue.

You can mail it in a letter to me at Kinston, N.C. Company "A," Hol Legion, Genl Evans Brigade and it will come through same. Do it immediately.

I must close for the present. Will write you another letter in a few days giving you the news.

Yours truly
Thomas J. Moore

Send enclosed note to Mrs. Barry.

Ben and Jesse Brockman, two brothers of Harriet, Hettie, and Ella, had volunteered for the Confederate army in August 1861. They were instrumental in organizing Company B, Thirteenth Regiment, South Carolina Volunteers, a company known as the Brockman Guards. Ben was named a colonel and Jesse a captain. Both were killed as a result of the Battle of Spotsylvania, Virginia, May 12, 1864. Jesse was wounded and left to die on the battlefield; Ben lost an arm and died of gangrene in a Richmond hospital a month later. Ben had never married; Jesse left a wife, Kittie, and two young sons, Thomas and Jesse. In later years Jesse was reared and educated by Thomas John Moore.

When John Crawford Anderson graduated from the Citadel in 1863, he joined their unit as an adjutant and shared mess with his two uncles until their deaths.

J. B. O. Landrum, in his *History of Spartanburg County* (1900), included this letter on page 400.

[104] Col. Benjamin Brockman to His Older Sister Mary Brockman Harris

Richmond
May 24th, 1864

Dear Sister Mary: I have been unfortunate in losing my left arm in the battle of the 12th of May, the bloodiest fight of the war. Jesse was wounded, I expect dangerously, and fell into the hands of the enemy. Poor fellow, the only brother I had is now, perhaps cold in death, but we have to submit to these things. He was, as I am informed, acting with distinguished valor when he was shot. Excuse short note. My respects to the Doctor [Mary's husband] and a kiss to Edgar [her young son].

Truly your brother,
B. T. Brockman

[105] Thomas John Moore to Thomas W. Hill

Nottoway River, Virginia[1]
July 16th, 1864

My Dear Sir:

. . . I write merely to let you know of my health and whereabout. In regards to the former it is good, and the latter, it is the same as formerly.

Since I wrote you last stirring scenes have been acted near us. The fight at Sappony Creek Church is one in which 5 Companies of our Legion were engaged and was fought principally by these though I am told that Hampton's Cavalry gets all the praise. I am almost tempted sometimes to write a piece for the newspaper on this matter. "Give the Devil his dues" is my motto. But of this I cannot here speak for want of space and time.

Our Company was not engaged though the greater part was at Stoney Creek some two and a half miles from the place. I myself with our Pickets and a gun detachment of 25 men were left to guard this place which is only five miles from Sappony.

The Yankees were scattered in every direction. The woods being full of them. We at this place captured more than twice our number. They have now all gone and some are nearer than 16 miles. I hear cannon in direction of Petersburg but this is nothing unusual.

Capt. Jesse K. Brockman in the uniform of the Company B, Thirteenth Regiment, South Carolina Volunteers. From J. B. O. Landrum, *History of Spartanburg County, 1900* (Atlanta: Franklin Prtg. and Pub. Co., 1900)

Col. Benjamin T. Brockman in the uniform of the Company B, Thirteenth Regiment, South Carolina Volunteers. From J. B. O. Landrum, *History of Spartanburg County, 1900* (Atlanta: Franklin Prtg. and Pub. Co., 1900)

We are highly elated at the news from Maryland.[2] Have just heard of our victories and the capture of Baltimore, all of which we hope will prove true. We have no fears of an attack from the enemy here now for their attention is drawn to other points.

We get no news from the South and very little from Petersburg. The trains run very irregularly and always go through from Stoney Creek in the night for between that place and Petersburg the enemy are near the railroad.

I have just received the papers of yesterday and day before from a lady friend. They are quite a treat. We are living finely. There is a family which takes particular interest in us. So far so good.

I want a pair of pants. Send me a pair of those I sent home from Savannah in Lt. Pinson's trunk. Tell Sister to make my shirts. I want the tails made longer for I am thoroughly disgusted with these I have. I cannot keep them in my breeches. Don't forget this. I am in bad need of pants. Write me about crops, etc. and particularly about Taxes. Direct to Petersburg as before.
Thomas J. Moore

1. Nottoway, Virginia, is approximately thirty-seven miles west of Petersburg.
2. Gen. Jubal A. Early struck into Maryland in early July, exacted tribute from Hagerstown and Frederick, and came within five miles of Washington on July 11. The Union had to pull two divisions from the Petersburg front to drive Early back into Virginia.

[106] Thomas John Moore to Thomas W. Hill

Nottoway Bridge, Sussex Co., Virginia
August 1st, 1864

My Dear Sir:

. . . My health, I am happy to say, is good, and has been so from the time I left home. I am truly grateful for this great blessing, which is so contrary to what I expected upon leaving you. While here in the enjoyment of good health, we are amidst pleasures that are denied our brother soldiers. While they are in dangers, we are in comparative safety, while they are performing laborious duties ours are quite easy. While they have labor, danger, and toils, we have pleasure, ease and comfort. Surely so great good fortune cannot last us long, but yet, I see no probability for a change. When we go to Petersburg and there see what our friends are suffering and enduring, we are the more grateful to the Giver of all mercies for His kindness to us, and have our desires to remain here, so much the more strengthened.

Even now we have just heard that our Brigade, at least portions of it, have been blown up by the enemy, that Genl. Elliotte has been mortally wounded, that Ed Dean and his company (the one in which I was elected a Lt.) were destroyed & etc. Of this, however, you will hear before this reaches you. Can you blame us when such is the case with them there to desire to remain here. We have lost many friends in the late battles. I, only a few days since, heard of the death of your brother Baylis and the wounding of Body. Let me here offer you my heartfelt sympathies. In him you have lost a dear brother, I a faithful friend, and our Country a good and faithful soldier. All who knew him loved and honored him for his honor, his justice, his upright and moral character, his kindness to everyone and his devotion to his country. How sad to think that such good men should fall by foul hands of a despicable foe! Heaven grant that we may yet live to inflict punishment upon such wretches as have snatched him from us! But we hope it is all well with him now for we think he was a good man, that he is at rest with "just men made perfect" above. Since then he is gone from us forever let this thought be our consolation, that he died nobly and in noble and holy cause. I cannot say let us forget him for his memory's too dear and sacred but I say let us soften our grief and misery by the recollection of the above written thought.

Our only troubles here are that newspapers do not come as often as we like and the shortness of rations. Our boxes have given out and we are now thrown back on our Gov. Rations which are not fit for any use other than to be thrown away. We drew four days rations day before yesterday consisting of corn meal and bacon, the former black and dirty and even seemed as if the cob had been ground up with the corn; the latter almost spoiled, at least smelling very badly and about enough, if it were good, for a day. Were it not for the fruit that we get we would fare rather badly. Could we buy, we would not suffer, but here it is almost impossible to get anything owing to short crops and Yankee depradations during their raids. Since matters are thus, I desire you as my last letter to Sister said to forward me a box by the first opportunity to consist of the substantials: flour, bacon, lard, and hominy, etc. If no other way can be found, send by "Central Association" at Columbia. The other men of my mess will also have boxes sent at convenient times. So long as we can get anything from home we intend to live even if it does look extravagant and the Gov. rations may go to Guinea.

I would like to hear from you on your crop. I learn that you have had rain in abundance. Write me about the wheat. How your corn looks, your cotton, etc.

I would like to know something about Taxes, what they are or are likely to be. Don't forget to tell me all about these, when they are to be paid, etc.

I have to frank this letter for want of a postage stamp, hence I beg you to look over this breach of epistilory correspondence. Direct to Stony Creek, Va.

Yours truly,
Thomas J. Moore

[107] Franklin Leland Anderson to Mary Elizabeth Anderson

Nottoway Bridge, Va.
Aug. 4th, 1864

Dear Mary,

Yours came to hand a few days since and although I felt that I was in arrears both with yourself and Nettie I could not leave off reading *David Copperfield* to answer letters. This, I've no doubt, you will think a very candid confession for one so dependant as I am upon you both for the news and all the tidings I get from home, but if you have read it you are no doubt ready to excuse me knowing how completely captivating it is when you have once entered into it. If you have not, read it, both of you, though I would admonish you against novel reading to any extent. I would advise you to procure a copy and read it. You will find some of the most admirably drawn characters ever portraied by any writer. If you want a model take Agnes you will find her a perfect child of nature and free from all those ambitious deceptions & desires to please common to your sex. But when I say this you must not conclude that I am not sensible of the weaknesses of my own. I am proud to hear of your wonderful success in teaching the young idea how to shoot. Tell Benny the story of the falier [failure] of the immortal Geo Washington when it was said to him "sit down Mr. W. your modesty exceeds your valor and that surpasses the power of any eloquence that I possess" . . . I hope you will continue to have the same great encouragement to the end and that you will not weary in well doing. Then too you are acting the part of the Good Samaritan, in leading the poor refugee woman on over the trenches, doubly deserving because she was a Soldier's wife. So far you are rivaling "Agnes" in the strongest and most lovely traits of character.

There is no news that I could write but what you would have seen by the papers before this reaches you. Our Regt still holds its quiet position on the R.R. which favoured privalege I was not able to appreciate until I went to Petersburg on a visit to Will Norris and my old Co. in P.S.S. [Palmetto Sharpshooters]

I found them in the trenches with the enemy's running parallel and only from two to four hundred yds distant. on parts of the lines they had mutually agreed not to fire; here they were sitting about quite composed and unconcerned but on other portions there was incessant firing and neither party dared show their heads above the brest works. Here they had been for more than a month, during all that warm weather, inconvenient to water, and without protection from the sun and dews except such as they could make with their blankets, there is no estimating their suffering and privations and yet they seem to endure it with a patient cheerfulness. Will got a leave of absence and came over to the City with us and got a good supper with Cousin Jno Montgomery, who is Comisary of the 18th Regt. Tom Moore and myself were together. Too much cannot be said in praise of the brave defenders of Petersburg. The 18th Regt you will see were among those that suffered by the late blowing up and assault of our lines. From what I can learn no material advantage has been gained by the enemy, save the slaughter of some of our brave men. I consider we are always the sufferers in point of morral worth when we fail to kill less than five to their one.

My health has been very good though I with nearly the whole command have been troubled with what we call itch, but I don't think it is the regular itch, there is a slight eruption on the skin and at times a most amazing itching. I tried the sulpher and [land?] last week with good effect, in fact I felt I was well of it but the experience of others is that it returns again. Tell Mrs. Anderson (your Ma) she can suggest and send on, a remedy it will be very acceptable. I wrote to GrandPa some days ago to send me a box, Shoes, etc. Tell him I am very hungry and nearly bearfooted and will expect them by the 1st opportunity. The meal we draw is of the poorest kind, the bacon bad, and insufficient in quantity. We are trying now to buy a bus. of wheat for which we will have to pay 30 to 50 dollars. but with blackberries and other fruit we can make even that pay [rest of letter missing]

[108] Franklin Leland Anderson to Mary and Henrietta Anderson

Nottoway Bridge, Va.
Sept. 18th, 1864

Dear Mary and Nettie

Your letters of the 1st and 9th have been received and I know you will pardon my answering them jointly when you consider the exorbitant price of paper, the scarcity of news, and more than all what an onerous task it is for me to communicate in an epistolary way. I would [have replied to] yours Nettie immediately "if not sooner" having old sores to heal up. if paper could have been had in Co. A. Hol. Lgn [Holcombe's Legion] Sutter [sutler] Mr. Gannett came to my relief yesterday, but somewhat to my disappointment I did not get what I sent to your Pa for. I suppose he did not see him as he was in Spartanburg but a few days. heretofore he has stayed a week or two home. Wm Means passed at two yesterday but I was sleeping when the train stopped and it was only long enough for him to put off a box he brought on for Tom Moore and I did not get to see him. I was much disappointed in not seeing him even for that short time. Tom's box will be quite a treat to the Mess and I am only sorry my friends were not so thoughtful for my comfort, but Father I know has enough to do without thinking of me, and all of you no doubt are joined to your idols. I see an editorial puff in the [*Carolina*] *Spartan* [September 9, 1864] to Father's enlarged patriotism and enterprise in his old age and hope the object of it will have the desired effect, to wit., to induce others to bring in their supplies to feed the hungry multitude at Spartanburg.

I have no Army news worth communicating. Gen [Wade] Hampton with a body of picked Cavalry went down in rear of Grant's right a few days since and captured twenty-five hundred cattle that had been transported. Large and fat they were, and between three and four hundred prisoners. It was a valuable capture as it is not necessary to have the Weldon R.R. to take them to Petersburg. The expedition is still not ended, what more may be accomplished you will see by the papers. You make no allusion, either of you to the many wants I made known in a previous letter. I fear you may not have received my letter. I wrote for Ma to get me enough of the Confederate grey cloth for a vest and have it made up to send with my coat and pants. Then the undershirts is your own job. You must have Aggy prepare the yarn for you. Tell her too to prepare enough for three pairs of socks and have Mrs. Mullinax to knit them. The shirts and drawers I have will do me several months yet. I threw my cravat away when warm weather set in, if Aggy can find one send it to me, if not tell her to get you one of the black silk kerchiefs and you can make me one and send it in one of yours letters. My chance for a furlough will not come for two years at the present furloughing rates but I trust the War may stop or that something will turn up to bring it around before that time. I envied you Nett your pleasant visit to Pacolet and would have enjoyed seeing those dear boys in their Sunday cloths and good behavior. As it is impossible for me to get a furlough can't one of you with Julia bring them out to see me, among the good friends I have made here I could find you comfortable quarters nearby but reckon you had best not venture as the Yankees might make a raid and my boys might fall into their hands saying nothing of my niece and sister-in-law. Pa's letter was very short and had to employ his private sec—tell him I would like to have one in his own handwriting. Read all your letters to Grandpa. My love to all

Write often Your Affectionate Uncle Frank

[109] Franklin Leland Anderson to David Anderson

[Sent together with the previous letter]

Nottoway Bridge, Va
Sept. 18, 1864

Capt. David Anderson
Dear Brother

After finishing a letter to the girls I have concluded to say a word to you on a subject in which I feel not a little interest, I heard sometime since that Tim Fortenberry [Frank Anderson's substitute] had reached home in a low state of health. I would like to hear of his recovery or of his condition whatever it may be. If he has recovered I feel somewhat interested in his not going back to his command or into the service anywhere until the men of his age are called for. The circumstances under which he went into the service were very peculiar and I have no idea he would under any other circumstances have gone into for another person for ten times the amount I gave him. As you have heard me say I see no justice in my furnishing two men to the cause while others furnish only one. I want you to see the Enrolling Officer and see if he won't tacitly consent for him to remain at home, explain the circumstances, mention his large and dependant family and their maintenance being one of the conditions upon which he became my substitute. If it all does not avail then tell Tim for me to take a violent pain in the back or wherever else it will most avail him and play disabled until it is *just*

for him to go into the service. He has a disease with which with some management with the Surgeons he might get a discharge, but it would require some management. I hope you will give him any assistance you can and tell him for me to stay out if he can. I have no scruples about giving him this advise. "Let justice be done though the Heavens fall" ... I have enjoyed excellent health during the summer but I dread the Winter. My love to Harriet and the children,
Your brother Frank

[110] Thomas John Moore to Thomas W. Hill

Nottoway Bridge, Sussex Co., Virginia
Oct. 3rd, 1864

My Dear Sir:

... I want some information as to what arrangements are being made for carrying on the farms, etc.—whether or not you will be detailed [drafted], & if so, if the State authorities will let you stay there?

I also want to get your advice, believing you will give that that is good. I do not like the way matters are arranged. Sam's [Means], Dr. Foster and my business are too much mixed up.[1] It seems to me that it would be better if Dr. Foster's negroes were taken away and a divission of negroes, hands, stock or in fact everything that belongs to Sam and me was made and have his affairs seperate from mine. I know Sam would not wish to see me lose anything nor do I him and unless we do something matters will become so entangled that a dozen lawyers could not unravel them. Suppose you were to die, be taken from us in the army, or leave us of your own accord, what sort of a predicament would it leave us in? I do not know what belongs to me and I believe Sam is in the same situation. Now if we had each man his portion such would not be the case. Do you not think it had better be done this fall? It is true that I will be away but I am willing for you to act as my agent or attorney, because I believe you would see me have justice & in this you can do better than I who knows nothing, because you are more conversant with everything—the nature of lands, etc. Now as regards everything but the lands there need be no difficulty. The negroes have been divided & hence that matter can be settled satisfactorily. So have hogs, horses, cattle, etc. It remains then to divide the lands & there is the difficulty. I want to accommodate Sam as well as myself. But how to do it I am unable to say. I want you to write me and tell me what is best for my interest & for that of Sam Means. In the first place we must get Foster's affairs seperate from ours and you can tell Col. Evins, who is agent, that he must make some other arrangement. This, though, I do not wish done unless it meets with the approbation of Sam Means & I know he wants it unless something has occurred since I left. The only difficulty in making a division is what we shall pay the Government for your exemption but this we can arrange satisfactorily.

Now about the division of the lands. I want it fixed so we can get our plantations in a good shape. How can we do it? I cannot see unless I give up a part of my place let Sam have Hatchet Tract & me take "Home Place" and "Upper Place." This will then leave me a small part of my own tract to tack on to my other places. Now this "Home Place" is not of much value, neither is the Hatchet Tract & hence they will offset each other so far as they go & by giving up my own I get as good on upper place. I want you to write and give me your views on this matter fully for I know you know much more about it than I do. I wish it had all been done last year when we were at it. Another thing: I want you to make a list of the negroes drawn by me & preserve it for really I cannot tell which are mine & which are Sam's & it may cause a squabble some day.

I think it would be best to select three disinterested men & let their decision be binding on both parties. Let us hear from you on the matter. I will write to Sam today and ask him if he does not think it best to divide and if he does why then we will try to make some arrangements by which to effect it. In the meantime I expect to hear from you.

I have no news. Everyone seems to expect a fight soon between Lee & Grant. Crops are very bad here. I don't see how the people are to live. The chills & fever is prevalent in our camp. Tom Fielder has had several & quite bad ones. A good many have them. I have escaped so far but would not be surprised if I got to shaking. Grandma [Margaret Miller Montgomery] is making me some clothes. When they are finished send them to me. I wrote Aunt Kate [Catherine Goudelock, Mrs. Prater Scott Montgomery] some time ago proposing pecuniary assistance as well as provisions, etc.[2] If she calls on you let her have what she wants. I feel it due to my Mother to take charge of her brothers family while he is in Yankee dom.

Write immediately.

Yours truly,
Thomas J. Moore

You need say nothing about this letter.

1. When Thomas John Moore's mother died, her husband, Col. S. N. Evins, administered the inheritance of her three children, Ann Moore Means, Thomas John Moore, and Andrew Charles Moore. When Andrew was killed in 1862, his father-in-law, Dr. Robert Foster of Alabama, entered the picture as custodian for his daughter Mary, Andrew's widow. In this letter Thomas is trying to simplify this complex situation, settle with Dr. Foster, properly

divide things with his brother-in-law Sam Means, and assert his majority status, as he had turned twenty-one in April 1864.

2. Prater Scott Montgomery was captured near Petersburg, Virginia, on June 24, 1864. He was imprisoned first at Point Lookout, Maryland; then in August he was sent to a prison camp in Elmira, New York. He was released in an exchange and made his way to Savannah, Georgia, in November 1864 where he was hospitalized. His wife, Kate, finally received a letter from him notifying her of his whereabouts, and she went immediately to accompany him home, but he died on February 9, 1865, before reaching Spartanburg County. He was thirty-seven years old. This information gleaned from letters in the collection of James David Turner, his great-great-grandson.

[111] Franklin Leland Anderson to Mary Elizabeth Anderson

Nottoway Bridge, Va.
Oct. 7th, 1864
9 o'clock A.M.

Dear Niece,

As I am just from the picket post and find no one at home of the Mess, and having finished my breakfast of cold buisket and gravy, I have concluded to improve the short season of quiet to your benefit. More especially as you all are disposed to quarrel with me for my slow writing, but don't understand me as acknowledgeing the transgression, for I answer the letters I receive promptly or see nothing hear worth communicating even, and what we hear is long after event transpires and has been made stale by the newspapers. If I was on either of the scenes of action around Petersburg and Richmond, witnessing and taking part in the events that are of so much interest to us all, I imagine my disposition to write would be much greater. With you it is different, you have always around the subjects in which you know I feel a lively interest ... Moore and [Charles A.] Barry are on picket this morning. [John D.] Switzer is out building molasses mills and [Thomas F.] Fielder left two days ago to go to the Hospital at Stony Creek with chills and fever, Dr. Russel only has Quinine for the most stubborn cases and will have them go to the Hospital so that he can administer it himself. I think F will return to duty in a few days. I will go down tomorrow to see him. No Army news except what I know you have seen, to wit Grant's last move on Lee's right wing, by which it seems he gained some advantage in point of position, in other words he gained some ground and from the small cumpas [compass] now being disputed between him and the R.R. (South Side) Gen. Lee had none to spare. Grant is reported to be receiving heavy reinforcement and if it is the case we may begin to prepare ourselves for the fall of Petersburg before the winter.

To your inquiry as to how I spend my time, I will answer by giving you the programme for a week, taking it for granted I go on Picket every third day if it strikes me on Sunday I am apt to swap off with some one and that day attend church at Zion, a Presbyterian church near camp, supplied by the Rev. Mr. Murry, a young man 30 or 35, highly educated, quite an interesting preacher and I have found him very companionable. He is a widower with one little boy and sometimes inquires of me if I know of any lady in S.C. that would suit him, from the description, can I venture to send him down to Pleasant Falls? At church I am apt to meet at least three families, with whome owing to their kindness and familiarity some of us are upon as easy terms as if we were at Nazareth, never failing to receive repeated invitations to dine with some and or all of them, which invitations Tom Moore and I sometimes accept. Well, if I have made an exchange for Sunday I go on Picket Monday and while this is my best time to read, be quiet, and out of the noise of the camp, here too do nearly all of my letter writing. Tuesday and Wednesday then are apt to be dull days, occupied mostly of late by making some little improvement in the quarters, drilling, etc. In the meantime with some friend I may go one of these evenings to tea at the Eppses'. He is a nice man, practicing physician, prominent man in this part of the State, the only Elder of the church and makes every one feel at home in his company. His wife too is an exception and has to a high degree the happy task of making herself entertaining and agreeable. they have one son in service, a daughter grown, 20 I suppose, and highly accomplished, though not much pretty, in music . . . Miss Ada[1] the young lady was in Richmond when we came here staying with a cousin and never came home until some six weeks since, since her arrival our visits have been less frequent, as she attracts more company, particularly the gay birds of the Regt and we don't like to impose. The other members of the family are juniors except Mr. Murry the minister who is boarding with them. Then we think it not amiss on one of those days we are off duty to pay a visit to Mrs. Dillard, she is the female Elder at Zion and . . . one of the most garilous old creatures I have ever met, has two sons in service and two interesting daughters with her, Miss Lucy and Mary. Wednesday evening 4 o'clock is prayer meeting at Jones, a Methodist church one mile from and the other side of the bridge. Some eleven people attend but none with whome I have become intimate except Mrs. Chambless and her interesting family of two daughters. Mrs. C. is the most accomplished and intelligent old ladies I have ever met, kind to a falt. she took a fancy to our mess soon after we came, gave us repeated invitations to visit her, which we have done, some two of us, as often as twice a week on an average since we have been here. Her daughters are interesting ladies. Mrs. Field whose husband is in service is married two years since, is the finest looking lady I have seen in Va. and she is not surpassed for beauty often anywhere. I sometimes find myself almost wishing that General Lee would put the Husband where David put Uriah.[2] Miss Kittie the other daughter is a superior lady, but rather homely, is fond of playing Backgammon with Tom Moore, in fact it is questionable which of the two, the man, or game, she is most fond of, but I am satisfied nothing more is meant on his part than pleasant pasttime. T. Moore is just in and says the above is correct. I went on to say you had been complaining of my not writing.... He replied Tell Cousin Mary to write to me and I will satisfy her with long letters. I replied by saying that it would be a delicate matter for you to solicit the correspondence, he then said if you signify it in one of my letters it would all be "requisite" He writes readily and think you would be fortunate in having such a correspondent. But this is a digression from my programme. Friday afternoon I attend prayer meeting at Zion. We have organized a choir in the meantime, led by Mr. Bush, a member of our Regt. and you would be astonished to know what prayers I have made in music. An occasional visit to Mr. Field, a widower without children, who was wounded at Spotsylvania CH and has been at home ever since, Capt. Eppes and Capt Simmons, all clever gentlemen will fill out the program of the week with the exception of the many pleasant little incidences that occur which I would not have room here to enumerate. Well, you say if you call this Soldiering, what would you call the service being rendered by those brave fellows that have been in the trenches around Petersburg and Richmond all summer? True I feel sometimes like I am doing nothing for the cause, but this post had to be occupied and as well by us as any other troops. but I guess when we do go to the front we will pay up for some of it. Sam Means said in a letter to Tom Moore some time since that it was currently reported that he, Tom, and I were courting strong and would likely marry in Virginia. You can see very readily from my account of how I spend my time what the report has grown out of. But I protest against being otherwise than general in my associations with individuals or families and think it will be time enough for me to look for a wife when I have out-lived the war. This comes in incidentally for such things are so naturally and easily reported that I never thought I would waste paper contradicting. Col. Evins thought Miss Epps was Tom's flame, but wanted him if he had not committed himself to hold on for Miss Blain, who had been up from Fairfield on a visit to Cousin Ann Means. This last must be "sub rosa."

Sunday morning, Picket post at
Mrs. Chambliss Oct. 9th, 1864

I left off writing Friday afternoon to go to prayer meeting and was in no hurry to finish my letter and postponed until the morrow. When it came Switzer and myself went down the River in search of a birch out of which to get a [—uggle?] to make us a bread tray. We found it soon and after many hard licks with got a timber out and molded it into the desired shape as near as we could with an axe, whereupon he waded the river and started with it to a neighboring habitation, I taking the iron wedge and the axe and some pine knots and went towards quarters. I soon arrived and with my load, walked in deposited the pine under the bank, and looking around there sat Cousin Ann Means [Sam Means's wife, Tom Moore's sister], silently witnessing my maneuvers., waiting to see if I would recognise her, which I did in an instant. I had heard the train stop but was little expecting her or any other acquaintance. She had the company of Miss Brewton as far as Raleigh, N.C., where she found her son sick, but convalescent, and came the rest of the way with Jimmie [Means] and servant man. Tom was on picket at this post but was soon relieved and came to quarters and after dinner brought her to Mrs. Chambliss. Mrs. C. sent me an invitation to dine and there I don't often decline. I have gotten many little interesting items of news from Cousin A., such as I wish you could think of to write. Cousin Ann is the fourth S.C. lady we have with us. Mrs. Mason Finch and R[——] the two latter Mr. Quinn's daughters, they will all leave for home the last of the week. Now as there is not more room than I will occupy in answering directly your last and as I can't afford the 5th sheet, if you want particulars, just let me know in your next and I will write more full accounts. . . . I am sorry to hear of Father complaining and hope as he complains so often of swimming in the head that it was not serious. What you said of Frank was meager. If you like to dwell upon the most interesting subjects write more full accounts of the children. Cousin Ann thinks Willie very promising and as prettie a child as she ever saw. I was sorry too to hear of the death of Dallas Chamblin. He was by far the most promising of the family. Give my love to Jimmie[3] and best wishes for his success as a soldier. Write me if you hear anything from any of your Uncles. I forgot to put grits on the list of articles I sent Father, I hope you will get everything ready so that you can send upon short notice for there will be great doubt as to whether I get them unless I do before I leave here. Tell me who are elected to the Legislature and all else you can think of. My love to all. Your Affectionate Uncle Frank

1. Franklin Leland Anderson married Ada Eppes on November 28, 1866. She became stepmother to his three young children and together with Frank had nine more.

2. A reference to the story in II Samuel. King David coveted Uriah's wife, Bathsheba, conceived a child with her, and then contrived a way for her husband to be killed in battle so that he could marry her.

3. James Henry Anderson (1848–1923) was the fifth child of David and Harriet Anderson. He entered the high school department of Wofford College in the summer of 1864. That fall the Confederate government began drafting sixteen-year-olds, and he left school to join the Confederate army. After the war he returned to school and in 1871 graduated with honors from Davidson College.

[112] John Crawford Anderson to Mary Elizabeth Anderson

Envelope: JC Anderson, Adjt. 13th S.C.V. [South Carolina Volunteers]

HdQrs Jones' farm, Va.
Oct. 17th, 1864

Dear Sister:

The mail comes but no letter for me yet, still I'll write you. We have been very quiet on our line since the battle of the 30th until yesterday when we had a "great excitement" and a perfect "stampede" of McGowan's Brigade for the Boydton Plank Road just in rear of our camp. We got an intimation that we were being largely reinforced by troops from "Stony Creek" and and that the "Legion"!!! the Holcomb Legion!!! the Legion of So. Car. was passing up this road bound for the City of Petersburg. We all went out and sure enough this Legion did pass this road, but a worse heart-broken, low-spirited, set of chaps you seldom find. Uncle Frank and Tom Moore want to be transfered to the Cavalry but they will get over it by and by after they get on the line. They all look in fine health and able to do good service and probably will have the chance of it before the 1st of next month. Tom Moore has been boarding [eating] out all the time since his Sister has been out, and it has been intimated that Tom was engaged or would probably be to a young Lady near Nottoway. I know of no more forces coming in but the Legion but hear that we are getting men from Whiting's Divn. Gen. Lee is evidently making preparations to meet a grand attack of Grant. Able-bodied men in every "harmproof" department in this Army are being put in the Army of fighting men. We will get a good many men by the operation. Your good friend Mr. Bivings will have to face the balls again and prove his formerly reputed valor in arms. It will be like the rending of the hold of a drownding man to many of them, but Gen. Lee has given the order and obeyed it must and will be.

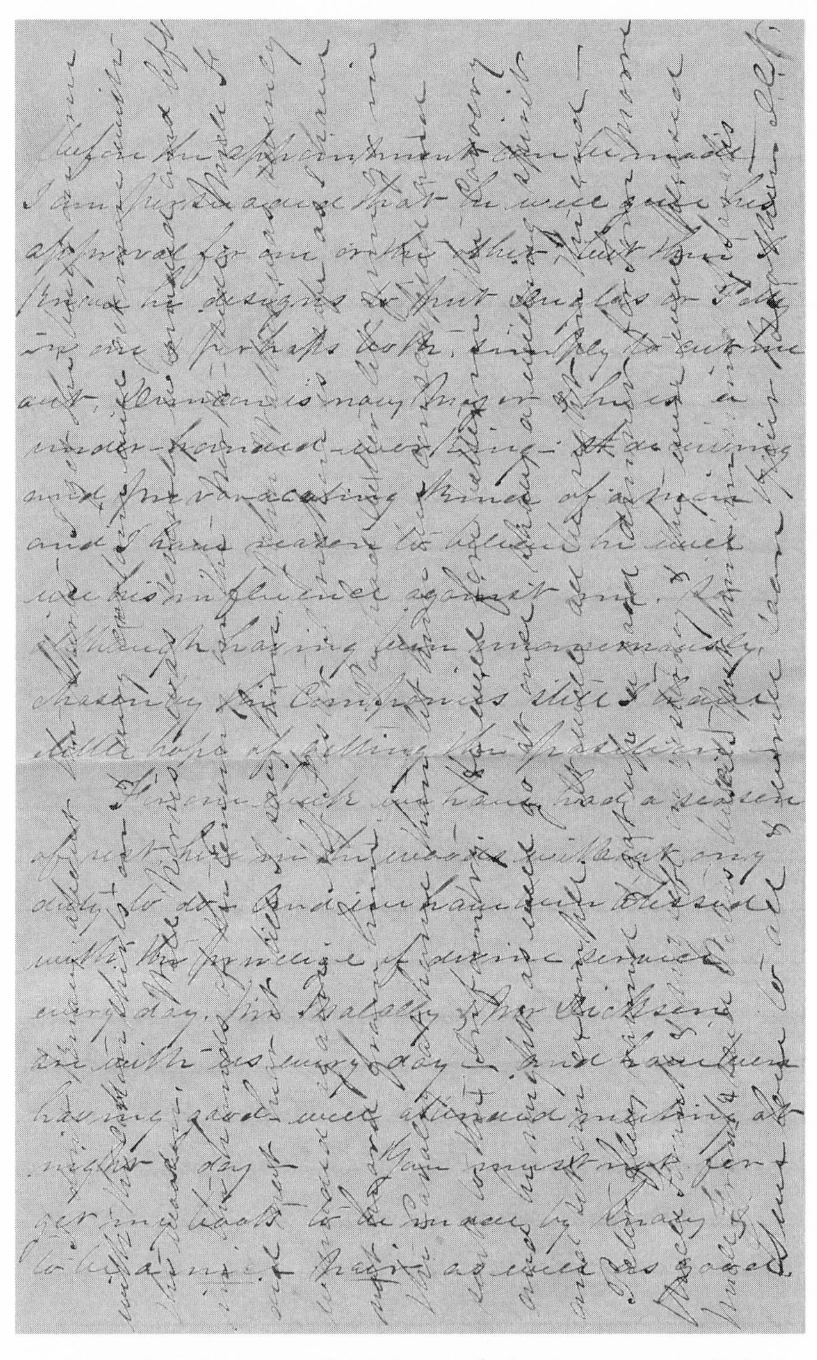

before the appointment can be made.
I am pretty aware that he will give his
approval for one or the other. But then I
know he designs to put [illegible] or [illegible]
in one & perhaps both, simply to cut me
out. [illegible] is now Major & he is a
under-handed-working—[illegible]
and prevaricating kind of a man
and I have reason to believe he will
use his influence against me. So
although having been unreasonably
treated by the Conference still I have
little hope of getting the position—
For one week we have had a season
of rest here in the woods without any
duty to do— And we have been blessed
with the privilege of divine service
every day. Mr [illegible] & Mr Dickson
are with us every day— and have been
having good well attended meetings at
night & day— You must not forget my book to be made by Mary &
to be a nice [illegible] as well as good.

Letter dated October 17, 1864, from John Crawford Anderson to Mary Elizabeth Anderson showing cross-writing. From the editor's collection

A good deal of desertion is going on among the Yankees. They come over continuously to our lines, but will invariably get some Confederates in exchange. S.C. though stands pretty fair in that respect we have had but few instances from our Brigade and none from our Regt.

We have just heard of the election . . . were sorry to see Mr. Bobo left out. I am about out of correspondents, they have proven unfaithful some of them I mean and I have concluded to drop them. So you see I have little encouragement to letter writing. I having been enjoying my box along with Dr. Coleman's which came after he left for home, his Sorghum will beat your[s].

I have been tendered the command of two different companies in the Regt.—the first Co "H" Leitze's old Co on the 20th August and the 2nd Co. "I E" Capt. Caughman's old Co about two weeks since but Hunt is absent on furlough and I will have to obtain his consent before an appointment can be made. I am persuaded that he will give his approval for one or the other but then I heard he desires to put Douglas or Tolly in one or perhaps both, simply to cut me out. Duncan is my Major and he is an underhanded weakling, a deceiving and prevaricating kind of man and I have reason to believe he will use his influence against me so although having been unanimously chosen by these companies I still have little hope of getting the position.

For one week we have had a season of rest here in the woods without any duty to do. and we have been blessed with the privilege of divine service every day, Mr. Macally and Mr.Dicksen are with us every day and have been having good, well-attended meetings night and day. You must not fear. . . .

I don't know about the shirts. I get the bugs on me with the cotton shirts and very certain will get more with the woolen. Will Norris was severely wounded and left in the hands of the enemy in the North-side. Uncle Frank did not hear it till I saw him. John Walker was severely wounded again. Alf Foster I reckon is safe as I have not heard from him. Pa had better let Jim go in the Cavalry at home than let him be conscripted and sent to the Infantry. He will fare better in the Cavalry and he might as well go at once. Show a willing spirit and set an example. It will all work out right in the end.

Peter [Anderson family slave] flew around and got up a good dinner for Tom Moore, Uncle Frank, and myself yesterday and they seemed well pleased. Uncle Frank said that Peter's vittels put him in the mind of Sarah's. Give love to all and write soon, Your brother,
JCA

In October 1864 John Crawford Anderson was part of a long line of troops set up to defend Richmond. Grant had arrayed his troops in a line parallel to the

Confederate forces. It was a stalemate at this point, and all attention was on Gen. William T. Sherman, who had taken Atlanta on September 2 and was on his "March to the Sea," reaching Savannah on December 12. Sherman's successes that fall helped Lincoln win reelection, quieting his Radical Northern critics. Anderson's Thirteenth Regiment, South Carolina Volunteers, had been in several engagements earlier in 1864, such as the battles at the Wilderness (May 5–6), at Spotsylvania (May 8–12), at Cold Harbor (June 1–3), and at Petersburg (June 15–18).

[113] John Crawford Anderson to Mary Elizabeth Anderson

Boydton P.R. [Plank Road], Va.
Oct. 21st, 1864

Dear Sister,

Yours of the 14th came to hand on yesterday and was very gratefully received.

Still the time passes swiftly by and the grand battle has not yet been fought. In fact we have come to the conclusion that the Lincoln party are unwilling to risk a battle just at this time. Lincoln's election is pretty sure now as it stands and to risk a battle would perhaps be to suffer a defeat which would be injurious to the Lincoln party.

A considerable calm has existed for some time on our line, in fact, since the 30th we have been quiet. Preparations for the grand trial may be going on and then probably only recuperation the Army is Mr. Grant's object and cause of quiet. Of course we think there will be a revolution in affairs as soon as this election comes off, let Lincoln or "little Mac"[1] be the elected.

I wrote you about the [Holcombe's] Legion coming to the City. They have been getting on fine. I heard from them on yesterday and will try to get up there to see them in a few days.

We are now on the extreme right of the Infantry line, joining Cavalry on our right, full five miles from the lines of the City. Our line is now at least 25 miles in length, with the men strung out at the distance of two feet to a man. The line extends from here to the Machanicsville Road on the other side of Petersburg. You can imagine the strict watch of the Genls. on the movements of the Enemy. We move about now and then but manage to get the good of our boxes. I have been doing fine of late. Col. Lister and a Sergt are in my Mess and I have everything to get and everything to provide. My box feeds all, but they get none [from their homes] Coleman wrote me after he left to take charge of his box which is still on hand.

You must not let Mr. Labord keep you from sending boxes, just put up the sorghum so it will not run out and let it be "a coming" for we can live on it with plenty of bread.

The pistol I left at Richmond to be repaired has "gone up." The workman was sent to Ala and I guess took the pistol with him. I find them quite a useless weapon here in the Army by the side of shell and minie balls.

The weather is pretty cold in this part of the country—we have been having frost by the whole-sale and you may be assured that "the Soldier, in his blanket on the ground" does not have the most pleasant of feelings. But I am pretty well to do with my blue blanket and two heavy Yankee blankets. I gave Peter one white blanket and Mr. Darby one and am now left with three. I bought one during the fight of the 30th for $10.00—

Good many of our Officers and men are now returning and we will soon be stronger than we were six months ago. Gen. Lee has been reinforced beyond a doubt since they still return to the Army and every man ought to return . . .

I don't mind but you had best keep the suit of jeans till I will want them more than at present. I have more clothes now than I have got any use for. The Dr. did not inquire of me, I suppose? I'd tell Miss E. [Evins] if it comes to long division, I am lost. I don't know who could have informed Capt. Evins of my working for him, unless it was Duncan, but I did all for Evins, Bobo, Foster, Carlisle, and Woodruff. . . . If we had any idea that Bobo would have been left out we might have cut Walker out.[2] I was uneasy for John Evins and gave him more assistance than any other.[3]

I have not heard anything from Will Norris yet, and in fact can't hear from that side of the lines. I did not send the cartridges and caps for the pistol but have some which I will send by some chance. Give love to all and write soon—remember me to Aunt Sallie and the children, tell her I often think of the times when I had Alice, Corrie, and Hennie on my lap and how delighted they were to have someone to play with them and humour them.

I would be delighted to spend a sixty days furlough at home about now.

Your affectionate brother,
John C. Anderson

1. Gen. George B. McClellan, who had been removed from command by Lincoln in 1862, was Lincoln's Democratic opponent in the 1864 presidential election.

2. Apparently a reference to local elections for the South Carolina House. In the Forty-fifth General Assembly (1862–63), Simpson Bobo, John Hamilton Evins, and William Moultrie Foster were part of the Spartanburg County delegation. In the Forty-sixth General Assembly (November–December 1864), the five Spartanburg County members of the House

were Henry Hopson Thomson, James Henry Carlisle, Barham Bobo Foster, John Hamilton Evins, and Joseph Walker.

3. Col. John Hamilton Evins, after injuring his arm at the Battle of Seven Pines in 1862, served on light duty. He came home in 1864 to stand for the General Assembly. He was a lawyer in Spartanburg after the war and was elected to the U.S. Congress in 1876, serving until his death in 1884. He was the son of Col. S. N. Evins.

[114] Thomas John Moore to Thomas W. Hill

Oct. 27th, 1864
Trenches near Petersburg, Virginia

Dear Sir:

I merely write now to let you know that I am well and also to give a short reply to yours of late date. I have been at this place one week and a half and am thoroughly disgusted with it already. It is certainly the worst place I have found since I have been a soldier. I have been at work like a hero making a bomb proof [shelter] for the last several days. You will have a good idea of it when I tell you it is exactly like our milk house with the exception of the cover which in this is logs laid across the top of the ground and covered with dirt. We enter by a ditch one and a half feet wide. We all live underground. You have no idea how much ditching has been done here. There is a ditch (deep as my head) to carry you to any part of the line and one-half mile in rear. One need not expose himself at all if he is disposed not to do so. The Yankees are between a quarter and a half [mile] in front of us. A large ravine passes between the main lines. Also between these lines are the picket lines, distant from each other about one hundred yards. The picket line is well fixed. The different posts are about 20 paces distant from each other and are square holes 6 feet deep and the same width in which three men are put at a time. These posts or holes are all connected by a trench or ditch and from our line where we stay when not on duty is a deep ditch to run out to it and in some cases where the ditch could not be made above ground it is done underground. I have noticed several such. In front of us there is but little firing during the days but at night it is pretty constant. We have had to report no casualties as yet. Company E 18th had a man shot yesterday while looking over the breastwork. The 22nd has lost several this way; on one occasion two at one shot, one through the head and another through the breast. Sometimes the enemy shell but it is at batteries 200 yards in our rear but bad shooting makes some of them fall rather near. There is not half the firing along the lines as was the case a short time back. I can see Yankees at any time I look and when on picket can talk with them. They call us "Johnny Rebs" and we call them "Billy." Thus we get attention from them. We nor they ever fire at night without cause [rest of letter missing]

[115] John Crawford Anderson to Mary Elizabeth Anderson

[Transcribed by J. A. Winn]

"Cosy Cottage"
Jones' Farm, Va.
Nov. 20th, 1864

My Dear Sister,

Glad to see you up and about again but would advise you to be very careful in this very inclement weather. If you could take a peep into this "Cosy Cottage" tonight and abstract thought from this sleeping Army round about, you would little imagine that War was the direct cause of such an effect as your eyes would fall upon.

First imagine yourself in the hollow just behind Sarah's house and in the side of the hill were to cut a "something" simalar to the Sellar under the kitchen with one end knocked out. Dig down til you get a horizontal plane of ten by twelve feet, say. Then in the bank cut out a chimney place which bank is in the upper part of hill of course and about four feet deep. Then extend upward the vertical plane of the side in which you cut the fire place by means of a post at each corner putting puncheons against them one on the other and pulling dirt against them to hold them secure. Then run the funnel of the chimney up outside of the extention of this vertical plane til you get it some ten feet aboveground. Now cut an entrance on the right hand side, turning out down the hill. Then pitch your wall tent on the horizontal plane about six feet from the fireplace, which remaining space will be covered by a "fly tent," a "fly tent" is simply a Wagon sheet. The wall of puncheons extending the vertical plane of the upper side serves as a habile end to the fly. Now you have the "Cosy Cottage." The inside is multiformical confusion and intelligently indescribable, but our beds, two in number, are on forks two feet above ground, small nice poles for slats and leaves of pine trees for feathers. Well now we are just as comfortable as men could wish in war times and can spend the winter as comfortably as at home. Our cottage is equally as comfortable as your sitting room if not more so.

We have a good favor and will be fixed up better when time affords. We got in just in time for the bad weather and feel we are very fortunate. All that is wanting now is a keg of sorghum to set in the corner and a cubbard of corn bread above it. By the bye my box is not here yet. It is on the way too long to suit me. The Association must spur up. . . .

Well have you seen Uncle Frank I hear he is off on furlough & did not let me know a word of it if he has gone he is a [lucky?] fellow. We have no news on our line and since the weather has turned bad we think all operations will be at an end. But we are looking for Sherman to create some news in the South. Well everything is looking about for winter Qtrs and we have some nice huts going up. Let me hear from you soon with love to all.

Your affectionate Brother,

J. C. Anderson

[116] Franklin Leland Anderson to Mary Elizabeth and Nettie Anderson

Trenches Near Petersburg [*Va.*]

Dec. 28th, 1864

My Dear Neices,

I have been so pressed with my duties in camp as not to be able to write you sooner, my first most important work after I arrived was to provide quarters for myself and mess, whom I found sleeping from one hut to another first with one lazy soldier and then another, my little axe was just in place and with it we went to work and are now snugly stored in a snug shelter partly under, but as much as three logs above, the ground covered with an old fly and as poor an opinion as you may have of it from this description, I would not exchange it for the best quarters in the Regt. but until we got them up and into them I felt quite like an outcast and suffered from inconvenience as well as the cold nights, every place being so crowded that I could only find a place to lie down by taking someone's place who had gone on picket. The Regt occupies about the same ground as when I left some more comforts however are provided, and the duty not near so hard. I have been twice on picket but both nights were pleasant. I can't but sympathise with the poor fellows who are out tonight without shelter other than their blankets and it is raining in torrents and the wind is blowing cold. Mine is the 2nd watch tonight and will have to try a tour of forty minutes on post directly myself.

I congratulate you upon having Ino at home particularly at this time (during Christmas). He passed me somewhere on the road and was fortunate in getting off where he did; one day later and he most probably would have been detained a week on the road. The trains all being impressed for the transportation of troops to Wilmington. Lt. [Orr] Miller I met at Burkville, fifty miles on his way and when I left him thought he would not be able to get on for four days. I was nine days myself on the road. Tel Ino he will entail a job upon himself if he starts [back] with boxes. I heard when I got to the City that Ino was on furlough and therefore did not send the Christmas candy. His friend and mess-mate Col. Lester came on a visit to the Regt a few days since, I accidentally met him and having *quarters* invited him in. The candy had not been opened but in honor of the Col. I brought it out and he with my mess enjoyed it. I was somewhat surprised to find the nice share of bundle candles, but agreeably, for I found the one you gave me of great use, indeed to it you are indebted for a letter tonight. I gave the Col. half and kept the other of the one you sent Ino. In awhile upon that subject you will do me a great favor to send me one by Ino, on an extensive scale, for since using them, I don't see how soldiers do without. My Salad all came safe, loosing only the Vinegar. It is much prised by the mess. Tom Miller has been visiting the Brigade today electioneering called in a few minutes this evening. I fear his election is doubtful, in his own Brigade he got ninety to fifty, the elections will be held in this Brig. tomorrow. Tom is going up to the 13th tomorrow, he has leave of absence for only 48 hours.

I am anxious to hear from you all. Write soon. Affectionately, Your Uncle Frank

Letters, 1865

As 1865 arrived, troops were positioning themselves for perhaps a final fight for Richmond, the capital of the Confederacy. The unit Tom, Frank, and Sam belonged to was moved to Petersburg.

Food was scarce, and it wasn't getting through when sent to the soldiers from South Carolina. On March 31 Tom was appointed color bearer for Holcombe's Legion, a position considered officer rank. This made a significant difference in his treatment when he was captured the next day. He was a month shy of his twenty-second birthday.

John's letter of April 11 describes Lee's surrender and the Union's terms. It speculates on how he will return home. Tom was marched north to Washington and Baltimore and then further north to a prison camp on an island in Lake Erie. His later account of that experience and his return home completes the Civil War era.

A late 1865 letter from Frank's nephew describes the new postwar era Southern planters faced.

[117] Thomas John Moore to Thomas W. Hill

Trenches in front of Petersburg
Saturday 21st January, 1865

My Dear Sir:

I merely write this as a supplement to Sister's letter that is the one I wrote to her two or three days [brought] by Strange of this Company. I am sorry to say I am still complaining. My disease has changed its nature from Dysentery to a Diarrhoea which I hope is no bad sign. Last night I took a big dose of salts expecting it to give me a good scouring out but find it has not done so. I have therefore repeated the dose and hope when it has worn off that my bowels will be all right. I have never taken my bed though I have been very sick. I feel greatly better for the last day or two.

Today is extremely cold. A gentle rain has been falling since five o'clock this morning which freezes as soon as it strikes the ground. The ground now presents a beautiful sheet of ice. We are snugly ensconced in our little hut and bid defiance to cold. Alec has been out cutting down stumps and has consequently a good supply of fuel on hand. By the way I will explain the stumps question. We are encamped where once was a wooded tract which now however is nothing more than a few strips three or four feet high upon which we work and get the greater part of our fire wood. Frank and Charlie [Barry] have to go to picket tonight, also John Switzer. I am sorry for them.

I wrote you to gather up the surplus butter from all the houses of my mess and forward by the Central Association. If you have not already done so wait and send it by Bill Walker who takes this letter to Spartanburg. He goes home on a 21 days leave from tomorrow. You will doubtless see him about the village and fix your arrangements.

I would be glad to have a supply of sausage meat somehow or other. There are some men in my mess, Charles Barry for instance and others, who do very little to the support of the mess and I do not care to feed them. So long as you send boxes they will depend on you and I want now to let you know of it in order that you may carry out my intentions. We have made arrangements that each man has to have a box brought on at slated periods which shall contain certain things to be a box. My time comes last and I will then want [to] tell you what to send. I do not mean that you shall not send the sausage for you can send that with the butter. When you get ready, send for the butter not neglecting Mrs. Switzer. We want them to send to let you have all that they can spare. We put it upon you as you are the only man to attend to such things.

Butler's Cavalry has gone to So. Car. Bill Means is in Petersburg going to Richmond after the baggage. I am looking for him over this evening.

Orr Miller has not come yet. I hope you have sent the money. Whiskey is worth 150 dollars per gallon here. Don't you think you could have some made by the underground way?

Yours,
Thomas J. Moore

[118] John Crawford Anderson to Mary Elizabeth Anderson

[Transcribed by J. A. Winn]

Near Petersburg, Va.
March 9, 1865

Dear Sister,

On day before yesterday I was made to rejoice by receipt of yours of the 17 Feby. I am very glad to hear you all have come off so well as to loose [lose] only the gray mule and little Flora. You are indeed fortunate at this time of affairs. Of course your spirits were a little low after you wrote the letter, for you soon learned the fate of Columbia.[1] It was quite an alarm to the boys here, but we have pretty well recovered from it at present.

I am very anxious to hear from Jim [Anderson] know he is having a tough time of it now for [Horace?] is on the flank of Gen. Sherman toward the Coast and the report goes fought him some when near Cheraw and got the best of it. I am in hopes it may be true and at the same time that Jim came out all right.

Doctor [Thomas A.] Evans has not returned yet. He is certainly acting very strange. I am looking for Poole in soon, when I expect to get something late from home.

Some few letters have come through but still the mail is very irregular. I write in hope you may receive.

Four men were shot in the presence of the Brigade today for desertion. They were from Horry Dist. and belonged to the first S.C. Vols. It was by no means a pleasant sight, but the merited justice of a deserter. The ceremony is very effecting and enough to deter anyone from following in their footsteps.

The Senate has passed the bill to arm the slaves and there is little doubt the House will do the same. It comes in at a late hour, but still may be better late than never. They have been afraid to take hold of it and have doubtless given it mature deliberation.

The last fight we had here amounted to very little except the killing by Billie Mahone [Maj. Gen. William] of about five hundred Yankees all running, for everyone was shot in the back. Everybody has been looking for a battle here, and for the last campaign to open, but the weather is too bad and we will have to forego for the present. I see Uncle Frank pretty often. Desertion has "played out" and the men are in better spirits. [Gen.] A. P. Hill sent over word this morning that we had repulsed a Yankee column in N.C. and captured 1500 prisoners and some artillery on yesterday the 8th. I am in hopes we will have more good news from there in a few days. We keep pretty well posted although the Papers will not publish anything. With love to all the family I am your Affectionate Brother John C. Anderson

1. Columbia was partially burned on February 17, 1865, when General Sherman's forces came through the South Carolina capital.

[119] Franklin Leland Anderson to Mary and Nettie Anderson

Picket Position, Hatch's Run [Hatcher's Run]
Eight miles from Petersburg
March 15th, 1865

Dear Neices,

You will see by the caption that at last we have changed position and have been relieved from the trenches. At first it looked a little lame that we should be sent up in the Line, endure the mud and all the consequent inconveniences all the Winter and then as the Campaign opens, to be thrown round here to do the fighting, but we are not as we expected to remain on the right of the Army and everything considered have a desirable position; our camp is three miles back from where I write and in contrast with the trenches it is really inviting. We found comfortable houses and accommodations for the whole Brigade all laid off in regular military order. The prettiest camp I have seen since I have been in service. In passing Gen Wallace's quarters yesterday, I went out to get some poles to fix my tent. I noticed they were enclosed by a cedar brush fence made by driving stakes all around three feet apart and then the limbs woven into the top and so also the quarters of the surgeons . . . T.M. [Tom Moore] and others . . . I mention simply to show you what pains has been taken by our predacessors [Virginians] to beautify their camp [the rest of the letter is indecipherable]

[120] Franklin Leland Anderson to James Mason Anderson

Camp on Hatches Run [Hatcher's Run]
Near Petersburg, Va. March 27th, 1865

Dear Father,

Since the communication has been so interrupted and I get no letters scarcely from home I have been slow to write, far more negligent I confess than I should have been, but to get letters, I assure you, is a great stimulus to one's writing and I hope you will jog the memory of my correspondents. Mary, Nett, and Henry (if he has returned) and David might write me occasionally. Scarcely a member of my Mess but receives two letters to my one (I wont say they dont write two to one)

Our Brigade has again been engaged and suffered considerably. The casualties in the Hol. [Holcombe] Legion amt to three killed, fifteen wounded, and forty-three captured. Capt. Briant who was in command of the Regt was killed. We had been moved from the trenches to this quiet camp some ten days ago and were beginning to feel secure of our quietude when after dusk on the 24th without five minutes notice we were ordered to face in, and dark as the night was, marched nine miles back to Petersburg and through the City to the trenches a mile to the left of where we spent the winter. When the Brigade arrived there, a Division of our troops had charged and taken the enemy's lines and batteries/forts for a mile. This was before daylight. Our Brigade was ordered over to their support; it being after sunrise our men were subject to severe fire from each flank from the time they left ours until they reached the Yankee lines. Their lines were held until twelve o'clock and orders came to fall back. The whole being a feint to divert Grant's attention from our right. As it turned out I fear it will prove a costly diversion, but we have such unbounded confidence in Gen. Lee that we think what he does is for the best. For the first time in my experience as a Soldier I was not with my Regt when it was in a fight. A few days before our Quartermaster Sergt was taken sick and I was appointed to act in his stead. He died very unexpectedly, even to the Surgeon, only four days illness and I now have the appointment. Capt. [A. B.] Woodruff was in command, very kindly tendered the me the position and it being one of the most desirable in the Army of course I accepted it, indeed I know of no position for which I would exchange it and coming too after three years hard service in the ranks where I hope I have shown on more than one occasion that I was not a coward and coming too as it did upon me entirely unsolicited I can't but feel truly greatful as well as proud of the position. Tom Moore, Fielder, and Switzer of my mess were in the fight and all came through safe. Barry has been detailed some time as a Provost guard, Tom Fielder poor fellow has had a letter from his Sister Mrs. West saying she thought his wife would hardly live through the Spring. The affliction of a Soldier it would seem is enough without such sad news from dear ones left behind.

I was at the 18th Regt last week and Jno [John Crawford Anderson] was quite well. McGowan's Brigade was engaged the same day ours was but the 13th was not in the fight. We are expecting a genl engagement every day We have almost despaired of seeing our boy with boxes. David Bennett [Burnett?] is at home sick, if he has not left tell Mary and Nettie they can send the shirts by him as I suppose Mr. Hill will not send the boy until he is assured he can come through. Take the troubles that are upon you as patiently as you can, if we can gain our independence even at the sacrifice of all we have, we will have great wealth.

I recd yours written by Henrietta and hope you will get the girls to do you the favour oftener, Affectionately your Son Frank

[121] Franklin Leland Anderson to David Anderson

[Sent together with the previous letter]

Camp on Hatches Run
March 27th, 1865

Dear Brother,

I have just finished a letter to Father which you will no doubt read to him, and which contains all the news I have worth communicating. I received three hundred dollars from you by Dr. T. A. Evins and forget whether or not I have acknowledged its reception. I bought a watch from E. H. Bobo for which I am to pay him five hundred dollars.[1] You will please pay Mr. S. [Simpson] Bobo his father that amount and forward me his receipt for the same.

Tell the girls I am anxious to get the Shirts and they must not neglect an opportunity to send them and also not to be formal with me as a correspondent but write often notwithstanding. I have said to receive letters is a great stimulus; I will enquire often after John and perhaps in the position I have will be able to give him assistance if he is wounded.

Sandy Earle[2] very kindly stopped to see me. He is acting Col. but says he desires the Chaplaincy of a Regt. My love to Sister Harriet and the children. I remember with much gratitude your many kindnesses since the death of Poor Will Norris and you are the only one to whome I can look to be a father to my dear little ones in the event I am taken. Your Brother, Frank

1. Probably in inflated Confederate currency.
2. Earle later married Hettie Brockman. His first name was either Sandy or Tandy, depending on the source.

[122] Franklin Leland Anderson to David Anderson

Hatch's Run, Va. [*Hatcher's Run*]
March 31, 1865

Dear Brother

The fighting goes regularly on and on account of that reason Capt. Woodruff's boy will not leave for some days at least not until there is quiet. Lt.

Cofield who has been Ensign of the Legn [Legion] leaves tomorrow and I will send by him.

Yesterday and day before there was hard fighting in our front and our Brig. lost severely the first day [illegible] to the right but did no fighting except light skirmishing with Cavalry. Today there has been some fighting in that direction but I can't learn whether our Brigade has been engaged or not. They are reported to be twelve miles off. The enemy are trying our front near Bridges Mill with desperation. Charge after charge has been made the past two days but our men so far hold their position.

Gowan's Brigade I hear had their picket lines captured and had retaken it. I am sorry not to be able to give you further particulars but I have told Lt. Cofield as he has friends in the 13th to enquire after Jno [John] if he meets anyone of whome he can get any information. I hardly think the Brigade has been in hard fighting. we have heard about B's Mill, their position, in the line being some three miles to the left though I guess has been reinforced all along the line. I will write you again by Capt. Woodruff's boy when he leaves. The enemy seems to be massing on our right There will be hard fighting there perhaps for several days but I hope we are fully prepared for them.

Yesterday it rained hard and incessantly but it did not arrest the fighting, but this much is in our favour, since we are on the defensive and will be against the enemy in moving Artillery. It cleared off beautifully last night, the moon and stars were shining bright when I went to sleep but I was awoke at 3 this morning by the rain pouring down which continued until dawn. It seems Providential, this had been the cause for months of Grant's not trying another advance upon our [illegible] meant that Gen. Lee will be able to hold his position. Capt. Woodruff has appointed Tom Moore Colour Bearer and I hear many speaking of his gallantry in the fight the day before yesterday. He was only appointed too that morning. Jno Switzer was wounded in the shoulder severely. Fielder came through safe. Belton Miller, son of Mr. G. Miller was wounded in the arm [three last lines illegible]
Brother Frank

Chronology:
April 2, 1865—Grant captures Petersburg; Confederate government flees Richmond.
April 8, 1865—Lee's army is surrounded.
April 9, 1865—Lee surrenders to Grant at Appomattox.

[123] John Crawford Anderson to David Anderson

Addressed: "Politeness of Mr. Julius Earle
Co. B, 7th S.C.C."

Clover Hill, Va.
April 11th, 1865

Dear Father:

I am glad that I have an opportunity to relieve your anxiety. By the blessing of Heaven I am in full vigor of health. True since the 30th of March I have seen many a hardship and made many a narrow escape, but the hand of God has been between me and all harm. We all mourn for our country and every man's face wears a haggard, dejected, and troubled look; but we can only say it must be the will of God and is therefore right. We are now surrounded by more than one hundred thousand of our Enemy and are all prisoners of War. The entire Army will be paroled as soon as the arrangements can be effected. We have been here for two days now without anything scarcely to eat, but Mr. Grant is sending rations this morning. The terms of surrender were very liberal and as yet we have had none of the Yankee's bravado of triumph.

The way of transportation home has not been decided upon, but I am of the opinion that the Infantry will go round by water to Charleston and the Cavalry through the country. In the meantime I hope some of my friends may get home sooner than we expect. Tom Moore[1] was taken near Petersburg and in fact all the Legion except one Officer and a dozen men. Uncle Frank is here with us.[2] He has been a "harm-proof." Very few of our men have [been] killed but many taken prisoner. I have lost everything but the clothes I have on. Peter[3] still proves true and says he will never desert the cause, but is very much elated at the idea of getting home.

With love to all the family I remain
Your Obt Son
John C. Anderson

1. Thomas John Moore (1843–1919) was captured at the Battle of Five Forks, April 1, 1865, and was taken via Baltimore to the prison camp on Johnson's Island, on Lake Erie. He was released June 16, 1865.

2. In his role as quartermaster for Holcombe's Legion, he was apparently in a rear position and not captured. He then made his way to John's unit.

3. A slave and John Crawford Anderson's personal servant, who served as valet and cook.

Return from the War

On April 1, 1865, Thomas John Moore and many of the men in Holcombe's Legion were captured at the Battle of Five Forks, Dinwiddie County, Virginia, seventeen miles southwest of Petersburg. Gen. Robert E. Lee placed a force under Maj. Gen. George E. Pickett with instructions to "hold Five Forks at all hazards. Protect the road to Ford's Depot and prevent Union forces from striking the Southside Railroad."[1]

Union forces, numbering 21,000, under Gen. Philip H. Sheridan attacked Pickett's 10,600 men, who were lined up behind a mile-and-three-quarters-long breastwork made of pine logs and dirt. The Confederates were overwhelmed and scattered.

The Union secured the Southside Railroad, and the next day forces under Gen. Ulysses S. Grant successfully attacked the main Confederate line at Petersburg. Lee abandoned both Petersburg and Richmond on April 3.

By his own account years later in the *Carolina Spartan* newspaper, Tom Moore indicated he was transported by boat to Washington and imprisoned in the Old Capitol Building for one week. He was then sent to Johnson Island, in western Lake Erie, opposite Sandusky, Ohio, and kept there until early June, when he was paroled, returning home on July 3.

As he had been promoted from sergeant major to color bearer, which was considered officer rank, he was sent to officers' prison, along with Capt. A. B. Woodruff and Lts. John M. Daniel and Jim Tolleson of the legion. Rations were scarce, but Tom sold a silver watch he had managed to smuggle through numerous searches for ten dollars and was able to buy enough food to survive a few weeks until remittances of five and ten dollars began to be received from his "cousin" Eliza T. Ellicott of Baltimore.

On April 10, 1865, during his march north to prison from Washington, Tom had passed through Baltimore, where large numbers of rebel sympathizers lined the streets crying. He was loaded into a railroad car, and the sympathizers thronged outside. He had written his name and address on a piece of paper, balled it up, and thrown it out the window at a girl whose attention he had attracted.

A few days after arriving at the prison on Johnson Island, he received this letter from her:

Dear Cousin Tom: I saw you as you passed through Baltimore, and was very sorry I could not speak to you. If you are in need of anything let me know and I will supply your wants. Your cousin,

Miss Eliza T. Ellicott
No. 6 Franklin St.
Baltimore, Maryland

Tom immediately replied to "Cousin Eliza"—a necessary subterfuge as only relatives were allowed to correspond with prisoners, requesting money to buy food. Upon his release from prison, she invited him to visit; he called at her house when passing through Baltimore.

He was in his tattered uniform and worn-out shoes, and Eliza took him to a Baltimore clothier to be outfitted. He visited for three days and upon his departure on June 16, she gave him a little book, Macduff's *Words and Mind of Jesus,* inscribed "A Token of remembrance / To / Thomas J. Moore / From / A Sympathizing friend, / June 16, 1865."

On his way to the boat landing to travel to Charleston, he encountered another Southern sympathizer, a Mrs. Bowie, who, after talking with him and inquiring of his family history, offered to pay his board at a first-class hotel for a few days, but he declined, eager to return home.

On July 3 Tom returned to a closed and shuttered Fredonia. His mother and father were dead; his older brother Andrew was dead; and his one sister, Ann, maintained her own residence with her husband, Sam Means. Bales of cotton—unsold because of the blockade—were stored in the large downstairs rooms, and furniture was stored in the upstairs rooms. Mr. Hill, the overseer, had made certain Tom's interests were looked after, and the sale of this cotton at a good price enabled him to hold on to the land and make a fresh start farming.

Former slaves Stephen Moore and his wife, Rachel, and Elihu and his wife, Lou, continued to live in their small cabins located near Fredonia's kitchen and remained on the plantation the rest of their lives as sharecroppers. Tom devoted himself to inventorying his assets and determining how to deal with the former slaves who remained. And he renewed contact with an old friend and neighbor, Mary Elizabeth Anderson, whom he married on February 27, 1866.

Thomas John Moore was pardoned in 1866 by President Andrew Johnson, the pardon being signed by Secretary of State William H. Seward. In 1866 he was appointed a colonel in the Thirty-sixth Regiment of the South Carolina Militia by the governor of South Carolina.

John Crawford Anderson returned to Pleasant Falls in late May 1865 to the delight of his parents and siblings. He joined his father in agricultural pursuits and milling at Anderson's gristmill. John married Emma Buist on February 27, 1866, the same day his sister Mary Elizabeth married Thomas John Moore.

Franklin Leland Anderson returned to Holly Hill, which his father, Tyger Jim Anderson, had kept open, as well as keeping the farms operating during his absence. At age eighty-one his father had confronted a group of Pennsylvania cavalry in pursuit of Jefferson Davis on May 1, 1865. They stole his livestock and plundered Holly Hill. That same day three deserters came to the house and strung him over a beam in the barn with a rope, demanding to know where his gold was hidden. There being none, they beat him severely and left him to die. He crawled to a cave on the bank of the South Tyger River and was eventually aided by a neighbor. He survived the ordeal and died five years later.

Frank, a widower with three children, arrived home soon after the incident and once again resumed management of Holly Hill, where he farmed the rest of his life. He married Ada Eppes, whom he had met when stationed on the Nottoway River, Virginia, on November 28, 1866.

All three men had to adjust to the new reality of dealing with the freed slaves who remained on their land and of determining how to compensate them for their labor.

1. Douglas S. Freeman, *Lee's Lieutenants: A Study in Command* (New York: Charles Scribner's Sons, 1946), 3:661.

[124] John Cunningham[1] to Franklin Leland Anderson

Fair Oaks, An [derson] Dist., S.C.
24th Dec 1865

Dear Uncle

This being Christmas Eve and a day of incessant rain—for it has poured in torrents all day—rendering it impossible to attend church.

Maj. Franklin Leland Anderson. From Edward Lee Anderson, *A History of the Anderson Family, 1706–1955* (Columbia, S.C.: R. L. Bryan Company, 1955); used with permission

After reading until I am tired, I have determined to infringe upon Presbyterian rules and scruples[2] by writing you a letter. You will learn by this that my old friend and neighbor Col. Parks is no more he died yesterday. It makes me sad to think of it. Parks had his faults, and grievous ones, but on the contrary he had some of the most noble traits of character I ever knew in any man. Let us remember his best, passing over his faults in silence and sadness. Remember them only to profit by philosophizing upon them.

Your condition being similar to my own I presume you are at home this Christmas. In fact I have not been able to go anywhere by remaining constantly at home keeping up with my freedmen. I have been able to keep them from becoming thoroughly demoralized, kept my stock, provisions, etc from being stolen and have been able to get some work out of them. I called them all up [together] on yesterday evening read them my proposition to contract another year and told them to consider upon it and let me know what they intended doing. I propose giving them one fourth the surplus arising from the sale of the cotton crop—after all the plantation expenses are paid such as salt seed all agricultural implements and family medacines. I feed them, buy their clothes, and pay their own doctor bills. I am to give them my attention in sickness as I have ever done. They are to conform to certain rules and regulations I have laid down which is pretty much of the old line of discipline only a little more rigid I think. They are all anxious to remain but are undecided about more pay but I have made a close calculation of the matter and that is the only way I can make the thing profitable to me and at the same time remunerate them liberally. I pay according to gradation out of this one fourth ... no. 1, 2, 3, and 4th class hands—charge two dollars per month board for non-producers, deduct all lost time on account of sickness or any other cause. Some few are proposing to give the ½ [share] and furnish everything and the negro feed themselves. A man will break in my opinion who follow that for 3 years. This will only be a year of experimenting my way with them anyway. And the more experiments are made the more we wil ascertain by this time next year. I shall try it for one year, and if I don't succeed I shall sell out and try my hand at something else. One thing certain I shall not keep a lot of mules, horses, hogs, cattle etc with land for a passel of free negroes to support themselves upon.

Frank, I feel as if I was commencing the world over and I can assure you it is anything but an agreeable thought.

What are you doing for yourself in the way of getting a wife? I have heard some conjecture, surmises, reposts, etc. I think you ought to marry. You have a big plantation out of debt and prosperous kin. You can afford the luxury. As for myself I am too poor. I am doing nothing for myself in that line. I have seen but a few ladies since I have come home. Sometime the latter part of the summer the Misses Perrin paid a visit to Andersonville. I was on hand of course. Must confess my old flame looked very charming. I had an invitation to go down with Lewis P. [Perrin] Christmas but for this nigger business I should have gone ... Sometimes I am tempted to take a second jump for the apple.

I intend just as soon as these negroes determine what they will do and I get my matters in running order on the plantation I shall come over to pay you all a visit. We have no news of a general nature.

The Yankees are still with us and so long as they remain here we will have turmoil and trouble. A party of bushwhackers took 9 mules from Mr. Frankie

Garrison a few days since and horse stealing is almost a daily occurrence. If you have an opportunity drop me a few lines. Love to Grandfather and Uncle David and family.

Your affectionate nephew—
John Cunningham

What could you sell me 150 bushel of cotton seed at in $ or barter them at for corn?

1. John Cunningham (1836/37–1911) was the son of Nancy Miller Anderson Cunningham (Mrs. Thomas Cunningham, 1812–1838). "Uncle Frank" was Cunningham's mother's brother.

2. Strict Presbyterians of the time avoided doing frivolous things, such as writing letters, on the Sabbath.

APPENDIX 1

Rules of Thalian Academy (Slabtown School), 1858

Thalian Academy in Anderson County, South Carolina, was also known as Slabtown School. John Crawford Anderson was a student there prior to entering the South Carolina Military Academy in 1859. Thomas John Moore was a student there before entering South Carolina College in January 1859, at age fifteen.

Rev. John L. Kennedy
Feb. 14, 1858

To aid in the forming and establishing the habits of youth, for respectability through after life.

To watch and guard their morals. To inculcate those principles which constitute the true gentleman have been justly regarded by all the wise and good as duties incumbent on Teachers no less than training their minds in literature and science. Therefore, to [illegible] as far as possible evil; and to promote the best interests of those who may hereafter become Students of Thalian Academy, the following Rules must be observed:

Rule 1st—No student may use profane, vulgar, or unbecoming language at the Academy boarding house or elsewhere with impunity.

Rule 2nd—No student may provoke a quarrel or fight by giving the lie or by any insulting language.

Rule 3rd—No student may keep or use intoxicating drinks, any deadly weapons or cards with impunity.

Rule 4th—Punctual attendance to all the duties and exercises of the Academy is enjoined and excuse for absence or tardiness must be rendered when demanded.

Rule 5th—No student may absent himself from school, or leave the Academy until regularly dismissed, without permission from the Teacher.

Rule 6th—No student shall be allowed to leave his boarding house or be absent therefore at nights after certain hours to be maid [*sic*] known by the Teacher.

Rule 7th—Every student shall devote to study such hours both at the Academy and boarding house as the Teacher may announce from time to time, unless prevented by sickness or other justifiable cause; nor may any student disturb or annoy others by intrusion or noise.

Rule 8th—Politeness and gentlemanly deportment are expected of all and let each student bear in mind that application to study and correctness of deportment will promote his and our honor & interest no less than that of the Institution to which he is attached.

Rule 9th—Should any student prove himself so lost to all sense of honor and shame as to disregard the 8th rule and not conduct himself towards his landlord and landlady with due respect to their feelings; or not be conformed as a gentleman to rules and regulations of the family in regards to meals and repast, or report to Teachers such offences shall be liable to reprimand, censure, chastisement, or dismission as may in his judgement be adequate.

Rule 10th—Any student known willfully or carelessly to injure or destroy any furniture or property at the Academy or where he may board, shall be liable to fine as such penalty the Teacher may impose.

Rule 11th—All the students shall behave quietly and becomingly on the Lord's Day and attend Church regularly.

Rule 12th—The penalties for these Rules where none are annexed; or for offences not specified such as idleness, rudeness, lying, taletelling, or slander shall be punished as by reproof, confinement at noon or evening, by corporal punishment, dismission just as the Teacher may judge best for the interest of the offender and the honor of the School.

Rule 13th—As the laws of land vest the Teacher with Parental authority he will strive to act in all cases with due regard to his high trust for the best interest of those entrusted to him as father and to effect this purpose. He will from time to time enquire of the landlord and lady with whom sons and wards may be put and thereby report, he the better able to exercise his guardian care.

Source: "Thalian Academy," 14 February 1858, Thomas John Moore Papers, South Caroliniana Library, University of South Carolina.

APPENDIX 2

Labor and Commodity Inventory of the Lands of Thomas John Moore, 1866

The information below was compiled by Thomas Moore Craig Sr. (1905–1964) from various pages of a plantation ledger book and from conversations in the 1930s with Ben Moore, the son of Stephen Moore.

Field hands were those able to work in the field all day long. This list does not include those too old or young to work. The value after each name indicates their value in a day's work. For example a 3/4 or 1/2 valuation would indicate a child or young person. This information received from Ben Moore before his death, (son of Stephen Moore, who served as Col. Moore's servant during the war).

Hands at Upper Place [Northeast side of N. Tyger River, site of Dorman High School today]

Numa	1	Bet	1
Ransom	1	Frances	1
Steven	1	Violet	1
Rachel	1	Martha	3/4
Rose	1	Zinn	1/3
Margaret	1	Elias	1/2
Ann	1	Chonty	1
Ino	1	Louise	1/3
Louis	3/4	Melvinda	1/3
Elihu	1/2	Cato	1/3
Nelly	1		
Simpson	1		

Hands at Home Place * Fredonia [Northwest side of N. Tyger River]

Jerry	1/3	Fanny	1
Noah	1	Georgeanna	1
Eliza	1	Mariah	1
Jinny	1	Laura	1
Gus	1	Sarah	1
Melissa	1/2	Titus	1
Dinah	3/4	Miles	1
Isaac	1	Ralph	1
Malvinda	1/3	Cato	1/3
Louisa	1/3	Alec	1

Hands at Middle Place * Cragmoor [Northeast side of N. Tyger River, just south of Upper Place]

Bob	1	Please	1
Alen	1	Candy	1
Bill	1	Mondy	1/4
Amos	1	George	1/4
Mose	1	Sylla	1
Chany	1	Alfred	1
Henry	1	Fanny	1
Benny	1	Becky	1
Cynthia	1	Louisa	1/3
		Malvide	1/3

Total full field hands:

Home Place	15.58
Middle Place	16.17
Upper Place	17.50

This being the evaluation of 61 hands listed above.

Capt. Sam Means continued to retain interests of his wife on Lower Place [Walnut Grove Plantation] and no estimate of available hands identified.

Agricultural Products 1866 and Division according to place. Taken from Account Book of Thomas J. Moore.

Molasses on hand, Jan. 1st, 1866

Middle Place

5 bbls	171 gal.
4 bbls	165 gal.

2 bbls 79 gal.
2 bbls 77 gal.
Total 492 gal.
¼ or 120 gal. Negroes share

Home Place
6 bbls 223 gal.
3 bbls 116 gal.
2 bbls 87 gal.
1 bbls 40 gal.
Total 466 gal.
¼ or 120 gal. Negroes share adjusted.

Upper Place
4 bbls 157 gal.
3 bbls 110 gal.
1 bbls 40 gal.
Total 307 gal.
¼ or 80 gal. Negroes share.

Old Molasses on hand
114
115
Total 229 Gal.

Hogs killed at Middle Place (Cragmoor), December 19th, 1865.

39 Head @ 187 ½ 7,312½ lbs.

Upper Place
35 Head @ 147 5,145 lbs.

Home Place
12 Head @ 145 1,740 lbs.
Total 14,197½ lbs.

The record shows the above was done on one day[.]
T.J.M. came home from the Army, July 1865 and was 22 years old the past April.

Size of cribs (Corn measured by cribs reduced to bushels)

Middle Place (New crib at Middle Place)
23 feet long, 7 feet 1 in. wide, 10 feet high 673½ bu.
Middle Crib.
17 feet, 6 in. long, 11 feet 1 in. deep, 7-4 wide 571½ bu.

End Crib.	
17 feet, 7 in. long, 7-4 wide, 10 ft. 10 in deep	561 bu.
Crib.	
4-5 High, 7-4 wide, 7-3 long	93½ bu.

Middle Place

Total	**1,899½ bu.**

Upper Place

South Crib	673 Bu.
North Crib	529 bu.
Entrance Crib	120 bu.
Crib in yard	819 bu.
Total Upper Place	**2,141 bu.**

Cribs at Home Place

19-1 long, 6-8 deep, 7-8 wide	392 bu.

Crib next stable

19-1 long, 7-7 wide, 3 deep	172 bu.
Total Home Place	**564 bu.**
Plantation—Total corn in cribs	**4,604½ bu.**

[This was as of Jan. 1, 1866]*

Peas at Upper Place

52 bu. ÷ 2 = 26 bu. Negroes share.
17½ hands or 1½ bu. Each.

Peas at Home Place

62 bu. ÷ 2 = 31 bu. Negroes share

To Manul Gwinn, Dr.

S. C. Means

For three (3) prs. shoes (fine)	$3.00
For three (3) prs. shoes (corse)	1.20
For three (3) prs. shoes (Mended)	.80
	$5.00

Thomas J. Moore

1 pr. shoes (mended)	.40
1 pr. Shoes (made)	.40

Means and Moore

83 pr. Negro shoes @ .40 cts.	$33.20

[The above would indicate that they had some 83 people to care for.]*

*Material appeared in brackets in the original.

Borrowed from Mr. Hill in Gold	$200.00
Paid by $100.00 GB @ 45	71.42
	$128.58

Let Mr. Hill have 3 ¾ lbs. Tobacco at 70 cts. specie $2.62

Borrowed Mr. Hill G.B.	$25.00

Source: MS vol. bd., 1860–1861 and 1865–1866, Thomas John Moore Papers, South Caroliniana Library, University of South Carolina.

Appendix 3

Labor Contract with Former Slaves at Fredonia, 1866

After the Civil War the former slave owners found that many ex-slaves stayed on the land and wanted to continue doing what they knew best: farming. In order to formalize the new relationship, the tenant farming or sharecropping system arose in the South. The document below is part of such an agreement reached between Thomas John Moore and nine male freedmen in 1866. Thomas John Moore is the "party of the first part"; the freedmen "the party of the second part." The marks they have affixed as signatures suggest that this group of former slaves probably could not read and write. Note the many rights reserved to the landlord.

And the Party of the Second part agrees to replace "in kind," whatever provisions they may have received from the said Thomas J. Moore at the current rates of said articles at the time they were furnished or pay the market value for the same at the time they were furnished. the said Thos J. Moore electing which he shall have done and it shall be the privilege of said T. J. Moore to appropriate to himself enough of the share of the crops of the party of the second part at the time they are gathered to satisfy all demands he may have against them at a price to be regulated by the current rates respectively at the time the obligation occurs upon the one part and at the time the crops are gathered on the other and they further agree that said Thomas J. Moore shall have the disposal of all fruit grown on his lands.

And the Party of the second part further agrees that they will by no means keep liquior to sell or anything else that will induce assemblage of persons upon the premises of said T. J. Moore nor will they allow such an assemblage if it can possibly be done, but on the contrary will report promptly to said T. J. Moore all such persons so assembled, especially such as are known to be forbidden the place and to aid him in expelling them if necessity require it.

And the party of the second also agree that in case any of them become offensive to the party of the first part either by continued habits of idleness and neglect of duties hereinbefore mentioned, by dishonesty, disorderly conduct, unprofitableness (unless in sickness) or insolence, it shall be lawful for the party of the first part to dispossess them of his property in their hands and expel them summarily from the place without compensation for part labor the same being construed as a forfeiture for violation of contract.

And they further agree that said T. J. Moore shall have exclusive control of Horses and Mules. Shall have the privilege of inspecting their houses, crops, etc. advising as he may think proper and they will receive him on all occasions respectfully and politely.

And the Parties to this contract in order to prevent endless litigation, agree that the equity of its provisions shall never be questioned but that in differences between said parties the question only as to whether the contract has been violated shall be adjudicated by the authorities appointed to settle such difficulties and upon the settlement of the question in dispute the successful party shall have power to enforce the decissions promptly and summarily.

In witness whereof we have hereunto affixed our hands and seals in the year and day above written.

In presence of

G. W. Hill (overseer) Thomas J. Moore (L.S.)

B. W. Hill

Jefferson his x mark (L.S.)
David his x mark (L.S.)
Joseph his x mark (L.S.)
Allen his x mark (L.S.)
Ransom his x mark (L.S.)
Alexander his x mark (L.S.)
Simpson his x mark (L.S.)
Amos his x mark (L.S.)
Jim his x mark (L.S.)

The above contract is also the contract between Thos. J. Moore of the first part and Numa and his family of the second part, save in the distribution of his crop when Numa gets one half instead of one third and in this particular that Numa exercises a supervission of the stock of the party of the first part.

In witness whereof we have hereunto affixed our hands and seals the day and year above written.

In presence of

G. W. Hill (overseer)	Thomas J. Moore (L.S.)
B. W. Hill	Numa his x mark (L.S.)

Source: Labor Contract [ca. 1865], Thomas John Moore Papers, South Caroliniana Library, University of South Carolina.

BIBLIOGRAPHY

Anderson, Edward Lee. *A History of the Anderson Family, 1706–1955*. Columbia, S.C.: R. L. Bryan Company, 1955.

Anderson Memorial Association. *William Anderson and Rebecca Denny and Their Descendants, 1706–1914*. Columbia, S.C.: R. L. Bryan Company, 1914.

Brockman, William Everett. *The Brockman Scrapbook*. Minneapolis: William Everett, 1952.

Brockman, William Everett, comp. *Early American History*. 2 vols. Minneapolis: Poucher Printers, 1926.

Edgar, Walter, ed. *The South Carolina Encyclopedia*. Columbia: University of South Carolina Press, 2006.

Freeman, Douglas Southall. *Lee's Lieutenants: A Study in Command*. 3 vols. New York: Charles Scribner's Sons, 1946.

Geary, John White. *A Politician Goes to War: The Civil War Letters of John White Geary*. Edited by William Alan Blair. Selections and introduction by Bell Irwin Wiley. University Park: Pennsylvania State University Press, 1995.

Gilbert, Horace Elbert. *Some Descendants of Henry Martin Brockman, 1764–1835, and Susanna Patterson, 1765–1842, of Virginia, Spartanburg County, South Carolina, and Greenville County, South Carolina.* Cincinnati: [Gilbert & Dusterhoft], 1996.

Hollis, Daniel Walker. *University of South Carolina.* Vol. 1, *South Carolina College.* Columbia: University of South Carolina Press, 1951.

Howe, Rev. George. *History of the Presbyterian Church in South Carolina.* 2 vols. Columbia, S.C.: Duffie & Chapman, 1870–83.

Landrum, J. B. O. *History of Spartanburg County*. Atlanta: Franklin Printing and Publishing Company, 1900.

Leckie, Robert. *None Died in Vain: The Saga of the American Civil War*. New York: HarperCollins, 1990.

McPherson, James M. *Ordeal by Fire: The Civil War and Reconstruction*. 3rd ed. Boston: McGraw-Hill, 2001.

Moore, Andrew Charles, comp. *Roll of Students of South Carolina College, 1805–1905*. Columbia, S.C.: The State Company, 1905.

Moore, Thomas John. Papers. South Caroliniana Library, University of South Carolina.

———. *Reminiscences of Nazareth Church Cemetery and Family Burial Grounds: A Discourse Delivered at the Church on Thanksgiving Day, November 26th, 1908*. Spartanburg, S.C.: Band and White, 1909.

Morris, Richard B. *Encyclopedia of American History*. New York: Harper & Row, 1965.
Palmer, B. M. *An Address on the One Hundredth Anniversary of the Organization of the Nazareth Church and Congregation*. Richmond, Va.: Shepperson & Co., 1872.
Reid, R. H. *Funeral Services of Col. Samuel N. Evins, May 26th, 1868*. Columbia, S.C.: Southern Presbyterian Review, 1868.
Revill, Janie. *Abstract of Moore Records of South Carolina, 1694–1865*. Columbia, S.C.: The State Company, 1931.
Spartanburg (S.C.) Carolina Spartan, February–March 1866.
Stewart, John Craig. *The Governors of Alabama*. Gretna, La.: Pelican Publishing Company, 1975.
Writers' Program. South Carolina. *A History of Spartanburg County, Compiled by the Spartanburg Unit of the Writers' Program of the Work Projects Administration in the State of South Carolina.* Spartanburg, S.C.: Band and White, 1941.
Writers' Program. South Carolina. *Palmetto Place Names, Compiled by Workers of the Writers' Program of the Work Projects Administration in the State of South Carolina.* Columbia, S.C.: Sloane Printing Company, 1941.

Index

Page numbers in bold refer to illustrations.